Building Intelligent Systems for the Future

Mastering the Revolution in Cognitive Computing

nova science publishers

www.novapublishers.com

Computer Science, Technology and Applications Series

Artificial Intelligence: Policy Perspectives and Global Impacts
Sonja Buckley (Editor)
ISBN: 979-8-89530-859-2
eBook ISBN: 979-8-89530-960-5

Immersive Technologies: The Role of Augmented and Virtual Reality in Civilian and Military Use
Rosalie T. Bryant (Editor)
ISBN: 979-8-89530-796-0
eBook ISBN: 979-8-89530-910-0

Big Data, Big Impact: Navigating Competition, Privacy, and Reform
Jessica Andrews (Editor)
ISBN: 979-8-89530-538-6
eBook ISBN: 979-8-89530-565-2

Computational Arts and Creative Products: Languages, Spaces and Practices
Alessandra Micalizzi, PhD
ISBN: 979-8-89530-426-6
eBook ISBN: 979-8-89530-499-0

Blockchain Technology for Healthcare Applications: Challenges, Privacy, and Securing of Data
Ahmed J. Obaid, PhD, Vinod Kumar Shukla, PhD, Soumi Dutta, PhD, Abhishek Bhattacharya, PhD, and Satyajit Chakraborti, PhD
ISBN: 979-8-89530-132-6
eBook ISBN: 979-8-89530-359-7

Cognitive Connections: Unleashing the Potential of Interactive Technologies
Yogesh Kumar Rathore, PhD, Shweta Bansal, PhD, Suman Kumar Swarnkar, PhD, Vishal Sharma, PhD, and Saroj Pandey, PhD
ISBN: 979-8-89530-157-9
eBook ISBN: 979-8-89530-310-8

Thinking Machine
Ping Zhu
ISBN: 979-8-89530-203-3
eBook ISBN: 979-8-89530-274-3

More information about this series can be found at
https://novapublishers.com/product-category/series/computer-science-technology-and-applications/

Anamika Ahirwar, PhD
Neelesh Jain, PhD
Sumitha Elayaperumal, PhD
Editors

Building Intelligent Systems for the Future

Mastering the Revolution in Cognitive Computing

nova
science publishers
www.novapublishers.com

DOI: https://doi.org/10.52305/ILJU1110

Library of Congress Cataloging-in-Publication Data

ISBN: 979-8-90134-050-9 (Hardcover)
ISBN: 979-8-90134-094-3 (eBook)

Published by Nova Science Publishers, Inc. † New York

"Building Intelligent Systems for the Future: Mastering the Revolution in Cognitive Computing" presents an extensive and multidisciplinary exploration of cognitive technologies, spanning foundational theories, advanced algorithms, and applied domains such as healthcare, finance, education, and ethics. The volume integrates perspectives from neuroscience, machine learning, big data analytics, and human cognition to provide readers with a holistic understanding of how intelligent systems are transforming research, decision-making, and innovation. This book stands as a timely contribution for academics, engineers, and policymakers striving to master the cognitive computing revolution in a responsible and human-centered manner.

"An intellectually rich and pedagogically sound work. The authors present a balanced integration of theory and application, making this book a significant contribution to both academic and industrial perspectives on intelligent systems."

— Dr. Ushaa Eswaran
Principal and Professor, Department of ECE
Mahalakshmi Tech Campus, Chennai, Tamil Nadu, India

"A timely and authoritative exploration of AI's transformative role in reshaping global innovation and governance. This book bridges technical understanding with ethical responsibility — a rare and valuable accomplishment."

— Vivek Eswaran
Principal Software Engineer
Oracle, Austin, Texas, USA

"An insightful work that captures the convergence of cognitive computing and cybersecurity. It offers a thoughtful perspective on building resilient and secure intelligent systems for the future."

— Keerthna Murali
Site Reliability Engineer II (SRE)
Dell EMC, Austin, Texas, USA

"A forward-looking and well-structured examination of AI's real-world applications. The book combines analytical rigor with practical insight, making it indispensable for data scientists and innovators."

— Vishal Eswaran
Senior Data Engineer
CVS Health Centre, Dallas, Texas, USA

This book is dedicated to all researchers, educators,
and practitioners who strive to expand the boundaries
of knowledge in artificial intelligence and cognitive computing.
It is also dedicated to the students and future innovators whose
curiosity and dedication will continue to shape the development
of intelligent systems for the betterment of society.

Contents

Foreword xi

Preface xiii

Introduction xv

Acknowledgments xvii

Chapter 1 **Overview of Cognitive Computing: Historical, Current, and Prospective Views** 1
Binod Kumar, Saurabh Mukherjee and Sheetal B. Prasad

Chapter 2 **The Evolution of Cognitive Computing: Foundational Principles, Applications, and Future Directions** 37
Jagadeshwari Puttanapura, C. Kishor Kumar Reddy, T. Monika Singh and Srinath Doss

Chapter 3 **Automatic Image Segmentation in Medical Imaging Using Machine Learning and Cognitive Computing** 81
Anamika Ahirwar, Shital R. Shegokar and Naresh Marwal

Chapter 4 **Cognitive Computing's Theoretical Underpinnings: From Neuroscience to Artificial Intelligence** 105
Shubhra Dixit, Ajay Sharma and Surbhi Gupta

Chapter 5 **Financial Applications of Cognitive Computing: Improving Risk Assessment and Decision-Making**..........129
V. Umadevi

Chapter 6 **Cognitive Computing's Place in Decision-Making in Uncertain Environments**..........147
Anamika Ahirwar and Akash Saxena

Chapter 7 **Smart Learning and Flexible Frameworks in Cognitive Computing for Education**..........177
S. Chitra and N. Vasunthira Devi

Chapter 8 **Innovations, Difficulties, and Ethical Issues in the Prospects of Cognitive Computing in Human Psychology**..........205
Yogita Thareja and Sakshi Khullar

Chapter 9 **Big Data and Cognitive Computing: Scalability and Efficiency Issues**..........221
Lovkesh Singh Vermani, Anamika Ahirwar and T. Velmurugan

Chapter 10 **Harnessing Deep Learning and Cognitive Computing to Revolutionize Medical Image Diagnostics**..........245
Hafsa Ihteshamuddin Ahmed, T. Monika Singh, C. Kishor Kumar Reddy and Srinath Doss

Conclusion..........271

About the Editors..........273

Index..........277

Foreword

The ideas and goals of "Building Intelligent Systems for the Future: Mastering the Revolution in Cognitive Computing" are introduced contextually in the book's foreword. In the field of intelligent systems, it emphasizes the importance of cognitive computing as a revolutionary force that has the ability to completely disrupt a number of different industries. The introduction provides context for the reader by outlining the changing dynamics between cognitive science, artificial intelligence, and system design. By giving readers a thorough grasp of important ideas, techniques, and applications, it emphasizes the goal of the book, which is to close the knowledge gap between cognitive computing theory and practice.

Preface

Welcome to the cutting edge of cognitive computing, a field that will transform how we perceive, analyze, and use data by fusing human intelligence with machine power. In "Building Intelligent Systems for the Future: Mastering the Revolution in Cognitive Computing," we take readers on a tour through the complexities of this quickly developing field, examining its historical foundations, present developments, and future directions that seem bright.

A turning point in the history of technology has been reached with the emergence of cognitive computing, wherein robots can now perceive, learn, and adapt in ways that are similar to human cognition in addition to processing information. This book offers insights into the theoretical underpinnings, real-world applications, and ethical issues related to cognitive computing, making it an invaluable resource for both beginners and specialists alike.

We explore different aspects of cognitive computing in the upcoming chapters, starting with an introduction that shows how it developed from a theoretical idea to an actual application. From there, we investigate its uses in a variety of industries, including psychology, finance, education, medical imaging, and more, demonstrating the revolutionary potential of intelligent systems in solving pressing problems in the real world.

Every chapter is carefully designed to offer a combination of theoretical analysis, real-world applications, and stimulating debates on the direction of cognitive computing. This book provides insightful viewpoints and direction to navigate the challenging field of cognitive computing, whether you are a researcher hoping to push the limits of artificial intelligence or a practitioner hoping to use it for concrete results.

Introduction

Cognitive computing is transforming the boundaries of artificial intelligence, enabling systems to learn, reason, and adapt in ways that closely resemble human cognition. *Building Intelligent Systems for the Future: Mastering the Revolution in Cognitive Computing* provides a comprehensive overview of the theoretical foundations, practical applications, and future directions of this rapidly evolving field.

The book opens with Chapter 1, *Overview of Cognitive Computing: Historical, Current, and Prospective Views*, which traces cognitive computing's intellectual evolution—from early philosophical ideas to modern advances in artificial intelligence and neuroscience. It highlights both the immense potential and the ethical considerations in replicating human-like intelligence.

Chapter 2 examines the foundational principles of cognitive computing and its applications across medicine, education, and business analytics. Chapter 3 focuses on automatic image segmentation in medical imaging, particularly for Multiple Sclerosis, integrating machine learning models and cognitive computing techniques to provide robust and patient-centered diagnostic tools.

Chapter 4 explores the theoretical underpinnings of cognitive computing, bridging neuroscience and AI, while addressing ethical issues such as data privacy and algorithmic bias. In Chapter 5, cognitive computing applications in finance are discussed, demonstrating enhanced risk assessment and decision-making using deep learning and generative models. Chapter 6 extends these insights to decision-making in uncertain and dynamic environments.

Education and human development are covered in Chapter 7, which examines smart learning frameworks that support personalized and flexible education. Chapter 8 explores innovations in human psychology, showcasing IoT and machine learning applications for detecting and visualizing mental health conditions.

Technical and future-oriented challenges are addressed in Chapter 9, which focuses on processing and analyzing large-scale data efficiently, and Chapter 10, which highlights the transformative potential of deep learning and cognitive computing in medical diagnostics.

Together, these chapters provide a multidimensional perspective on cognitive computing, integrating theory, practical applications, and forward-looking insights. The volume emphasizes the synergy between human cognition and machine intelligence, demonstrating how this interaction drives innovation across industries.

By combining conceptual understanding, case studies, and ethical considerations, this book serves as an essential reference for researchers, practitioners, and policymakers seeking to master the revolution in cognitive computing.

Acknowledgments

The editors wish to acknowledge their profound appreciation for the effort of all the contributors whose contributions have made this volume, Building Intelligent Systems for the Future: Mastering the Revolution in Cognitive Computing, complete and of immense depth. This book has become a valuable contribution in the world of cognitive computing and artificial intelligence because of its research, insight, and commitment.

We also wish to thank to the reviewers and other academic colleagues who helped a lot in the development of this work. Their brilliant ideas and their critical views highly enhanced the quality and the clarity of the chapters.

The editorial and production staff of NOVA Science Publishers are the people we want to express our sincere appreciation to and whom we want to acknowledge as having given us professional guidance, patience and support in the process of publication. They were helped in making this the best academic and publishing work.

We also would like to thank our colleagues, students, and institutions who supported this project, as without them, we could not have done it.

Chapter 1

Overview of Cognitive Computing: Historical, Current, and Prospective Views

Binod Kumar[1,*], PhD
Saurabh Mukherjee[2,†], PhD
and Sheetal B. Prasad[3,‡]

[1]Department of Computer Applications, Rajarshi Shahu College of Engineering, Pune, India
[2]Department of Computer Science, Banasthali Vidyapith, Rajasthan, India
[3]Department of Computer Science, Tondon College of Engineering, New York University, NY, USA

Abstract

Cognitive computing, a multifaceted field, explores the complexities of human cognition. Drawing on psychology, neuroscience, artificial intelligence, philosophy, linguistics, anthropology, and education, it builds upon the foundational work of ancient thinkers like Plato and Aristotle, who first investigated knowledge and thought, thus initiating the ongoing study of the mind.

Enlightenment philosophers, such as René Descartes, highlighted introspection's importance in understanding consciousness, contrasting with John Locke's "blank slate" theory emphasizing experience. This transition from philosophical reflection to empirical investigation paved the way for modern cognitive computing. The 19th century saw psychology embrace empirical methods, spearheaded by Wilhelm

* Corresponding Author's Email: binod.istar.1970@gmail.com
† Corresponding Author's Email: saurabh.apply@gmail.com
‡ Corresponding Author's Email: prasadsheetal16@gmail.com

In: Building Intelligent Systems for the Future
Editors: Anamika Ahirwar, Neelesh Jain and Sumitha Elayaperumal
ISBN: 979-8-90134-050-9

Wundt, widely regarded as experimental psychology's founder. Wundt established the first psychology laboratory and conducted controlled experiments on mental processes. Nevertheless, the rise of behaviorism in the early 20th century shifted focus to observable behavior, significantly limiting the study of internal mental states for an extended period.

A significant transformation occurred in the mid-20th century: the cognitive revolution. This renewed interest in mental processes was fueled by advances in computer science and linguistics. Leading thinkers like Alan Turing and Noam Chomsky countered behaviorism, arguing that comprehending the mind necessitates focusing on information processing and innate language skills.

Cognitive computing has revolutionized education, artificial intelligence, and clinical psychology. Its influence extends to improved instructional design and more effective teaching methods, as well as enhanced therapeutic approaches to mental health. The establishment of the Cognitive Computing Society highlights the field's interdisciplinary nature, promoting groundbreaking research and collaborative partnerships.

Neurocomputing advancements, particularly fMRI and EEG technologies, have driven recent progress in cognitive computing. These technologies visualize brain activity during cognitive processes, providing insights into memory, perception, and decision-making, including the neural pathways involved in different memory types. This knowledge is vital for developing treatments for conditions like Alzheimer's disease.

Machine learning and deep learning have revolutionized our understanding of human behavior. Brain-inspired algorithms analyze massive datasets, uncovering behavioral patterns and raising questions about AI's potential to mimic human thought.

Cognitive abilities are increasingly understood to be deeply intertwined with physical interactions with the environment, reflecting the growing popularity of embodied cognition. This challenges the traditional view of cognition as purely abstract, emphasizing the crucial roles of sensory and motor processes. Furthermore, advances in social cognition research have improved our understanding of social information processing, especially in contexts like autism spectrum disorder (ASD).

The progress of cognitive computing enhances our understanding of intelligence and consciousness, opening doors to applications that benefit humanity. However, addressing the ethical implications of AI and neurotechnology is essential for responsible development and the successful integration of human and machine intelligence.

Keywords: psychology, neuroscience, artificial intelligence (AI), philosophy, functional magnetic resonance imaging (FMRI), electroencephalography (EEG)

1. Introduction to Cognitive Computing

1.1. Cognitive Computing: Bridging Mind, Brain, and Intelligence

Cognitive computing is a multidisciplinary field studying information acquisition, processing, storage, and retrieval in humans and animals. Drawing on psychology, neuroscience, linguistics, philosophy, computer science, and anthropology, it aims to link biological processes with abstract mental states.

The mid-20th century saw the rise of cognitive computing, coinciding with the development of computational models that likened the brain to an information processor. Pioneering figures like Marvin Minsky viewed mental processes as algorithms, and Herbert Simon's bounded rationality theory explored limitations in human decision-making, emphasizing the importance of heuristics [1, 2].

Humans possess an innate capacity for language, a concept revolutionized by Noam Chomsky's theory of universal grammar, which reshaped our understanding of language acquisition. Neuroimaging techniques in cognitive neuroscience correlate brain activity with specific cognitive functions, offering crucial understanding of disorders like Alzheimer's disease. Despite significant progress in AI research, driven by cognitive computing, creating artificial general intelligence remains a substantial hurdle [3].

Educational methods have been significantly influenced by Jean Piaget's cognitive development framework and Lev Vygotsky's sociocultural theory, both of which emphasize the impact of culture and learning on cognitive processes. Conversely, the computational theory of mind, which breaks down cognitive functions into simpler operations, has been criticized for oversimplifying the intricacies of human thought. Finally, newer theories, like embodied cognition, highlight the crucial role of sensory and motor experiences in shaping cognitive processes [4].

Culture's impact on thought is the focus of cognitive anthropology, a field that contrasts sharply with the considerable difficulty of understanding consciousness. Integrated Information Theory and Global Workspace Theory offer some explanations for consciousness. Meanwhile, cognitive computing's practical applications in education, artificial intelligence, and human-computer interaction continuously drive technological and societal advancements.

1.2. Exploring the Complexities of Neuroscience: Unveiling the Biological Foundations of Cognition

Cognitive computing benefits significantly from neuroscience's study of the nervous system and brain. Neuroscience offers crucial insights into the biological basis of thought, behavior, and emotion, using techniques like molecular biology and neuroimaging to link the brain's structure to mental processes. This improves our comprehension of cognitive functions such as perception, memory, and decision-making [5, 6].

Real-time observation of brain activity, facilitated by advanced neuroimaging techniques like fMRI and PET scans, reveals the functions of specific brain regions, including the prefrontal cortex and amygdala, in cognition and emotion. Research into neurotransmitters, such as dopamine and serotonin, has significantly advanced our understanding of mental health disorders and suggested new pharmacological treatments [7, 8].

Learning, memory, and injury recovery depend heavily on neuroplasticity—the brain's capacity to restructure itself based on experiences. This capacity suggests therapeutic interventions for brain-damaged individuals. Advances in rehabilitation and cognitive enhancement are emerging from the convergence of neuroscience and artificial intelligence, producing neuro-inspired algorithms and brain-computer interfaces (BCIs) [9, 10].

Evidence-based learning strategies and targeted treatments for neurological and psychiatric conditions are informed by neuroscience's impact on education and mental health. Further research promises to unlock new avenues for enhancing human cognitive development and well-being, driving innovation in healthcare and technology [11, 12].

1.3. Perception and Sensation: Connecting Human Experience with Artificial Intelligence

Cognitive computing hinges on sensation and perception, which are key to understanding environmental interpretation in both humans and machines. Sensation is the detection of stimuli by sensory organs, transforming them into neural signals via transduction. The brain then receives and processes these signals, creating meaningful experiences—a process called perception. Unlike the basic sensory contact of sensation, perception utilizes advanced cognitive processes such as attention, memory, and expectations to construct a cohesive worldview [13, 14].

Artificial intelligence (AI) mimicking human cognition hinges on understanding the sensation-perception relationship. Replicating sensory processes—vision, attention, and multimodal sensory integration—presents significant challenges. Computer vision, for instance, employs cameras and algorithms to process visual information, yet achieving human-like perception, particularly in dynamic and context-rich settings, remains a complex undertaking [15, 16].

Integrating diverse sensory data (like visual and auditory input) and modeling selective attention—the ability to filter distractions—poses a significant challenge in AI development. Furthermore, the context-dependent nature of human perception necessitates AI systems capable of adapting to considerable variability. Finally, replicating the human capacity for experiential learning remains a key objective, a goal pursued through machine learning and deep learning techniques [17, 18].

Neuroimaging techniques bolster the study of sensation and perception in cognitive computing, yielding insights into brain mechanisms. These insights are crucial for enhancing AI and understanding human-world interaction. Further research promises more sophisticated AI systems, potentially achieving human-like interaction and perception, thus closing the gap between human and artificial cognition [19].

1.4. Connecting Minds and Machines: Investigating Memory and Learning in Cognitive Computing and AI

Cognitive computing hinges on the crucial relationship between memory and learning, impacting both human cognition and AI development. Human and machine information acquisition and use depend fundamentally on memory (encoding, storing, and retrieving information) and learning (experience altering knowledge or behavior) [20].

Sensory, short-term (STM), and long-term (LTM) memory comprise the memory system. Sensory memory provides a fleeting impression of stimuli; STM temporarily processes information; and LTM stores vast amounts of information potentially indefinitely. Encoding, attention, consolidation, and retrieval are crucial steps in memory formation, enhanced by contextual or emotional factors. Decay and interference are causes of forgetting [21, 22].

Memory is fundamental to learning, a process encompassing classical and operant conditioning, as well as cognitive developmental theories like those of Piaget and Vygotsky. Mirroring human learning, AI's machine learning incorporates supervised, unsupervised, and reinforcement learning techniques. Deep learning AI systems, for instance, leverage neural networks to analyze intricate data patterns, much like the brain's neural networks encode information [23, 24].

Cognitive computing and AI's merger reveals how memory and learning function. Reinforcement learning in AI, for instance, reflects the brain's neural processes for decision-making and reward processing, especially those involving dopamine. This knowledge improves education through AI-powered personalized learning and intelligent tutoring systems. Furthermore, AI aids healthcare by providing personalized cognitive rehabilitation and mental health support via AI-enhanced therapies and virtual environments [25].

Developing AI requires addressing ethical challenges like privacy, bias, and accountability. Collaboration between cognitive scientists, ethicists, and technologists is essential to ensure AI systems are ethically sound. Memory and learning are fundamental to human cognition and AI, impacting education, technology, and healthcare significantly. The ongoing integration of cognitive computing and AI promises transformative progress, but ethical considerations must be prioritized.

1.5. Exploring the Connection between Language and Cognition: An In-Depth Analysis

Human intelligence fundamentally depends on the deep interplay between language and cognition. Cognitive computing investigates this bidirectional relationship—how language molds thought and vice versa—by integrating perspectives from psychology, linguistics, neuroscience, and AI. Our uniquely human capacity for language enables communication, thought, and cultural inheritance. The Sapir-Whorf hypothesis posits that this influence manifests in two ways: linguistic determinism (language dictates thought) and linguistic relativity (language impacts thought). Research across diverse cognitive domains, including spatial reasoning, color perception, and number processing, corroborates this, demonstrating language's power to reshape how we perceive and process information [26].

Research in neuroscience reveals that brain areas crucial for language also support other cognitive processes, demonstrating the strong link between language and broader cognition. The development of AI systems like NLP models illustrates the challenges of replicating human language capabilities, highlighting the intricate cognitive mechanisms involved in language comprehension. Furthermore, AI showcases language's capacity to augment cognitive skills, evident in applications such as translation and information retrieval [27].

The interplay between language and cognition is highlighted by infant language acquisition, bilingualism, and language disorders. Exposure to language influences infants' cognitive development, and bilingualism often improves executive function. Furthermore, conditions such as aphasia demonstrate the intricate connection between language and cognition by illustrating how localized brain damage can impair language abilities.

The complex interplay of language and cognition shapes perception, memory, executive function, and cognitive adaptability. Neuroscience and artificial intelligence research illuminate this connection, offering potential advancements in language education, cognitive improvement, and treating language disorders. Ultimately, comprehending this relationship is crucial for enhancing human intelligence and creating AI that mimics human cognitive processes.

2. History and Fundamental Theory of Cognitive Computing

2.1. Foundations and Advancements in Cognitive Computing: An Interdisciplinary Exploration

Cognitive computing draws upon psychology, neuroscience, artificial intelligence, philosophy, linguistics, anthropology, and education to understand human cognition. Its roots lie in ancient philosophical discussions, including Plato's theory of forms and Aristotle's empiricism, which initiated the exploration of knowledge and thought. Later, figures such as René Descartes and John Locke significantly advanced our understanding of consciousness and the mind.

Nineteenth-century experimental psychology, pioneered by Wilhelm Wundt and William James, initiated a move toward empirical research in mental processes. Early twentieth-century behaviorism, emphasizing observable actions, eventually gave way to the cognitive revolution. Fueled by progress in computer science and linguistics, this revolution reconceptualized the mind as an information processor. Alan Turing and Noam Chomsky were instrumental in this shift, especially within artificial intelligence and language acquisition [28].

Cognitive computing emerged as a formal discipline in the late 20th century, characterized by its interdisciplinary approach. This led to advancements in computational models and neuroimaging techniques. David Marr's vision science research exemplified the analysis of complex cognitive functions across multiple levels. Furthermore, connectionism, neural network models, and the growth of cognitive neuroscience have significantly enhanced our comprehension of the brain-cognition relationship.

Traditional views of cognition are challenged by emerging fields like embodied cognition, which emphasize the influence of physical actions. Concurrently, research into consciousness grapples with fundamental questions about subjective experience. Furthermore, cognitive computing has significantly impacted education, artificial intelligence, and clinical psychology, notably influencing instructional design, human-computer interaction, and mental health treatments [29].

Cognitive computing integrates historical, philosophical, and scientific perspectives to understand the human mind. Its interdisciplinary nature fosters innovations connecting human and artificial cognition, impacting both theoretical knowledge and practical applications across diverse fields.

2.2. Theoretical Foundations of Cognitive Computing and Their Influence on AI

The interdisciplinary field of cognitive computing draws on psychology, artificial intelligence, neuroscience, philosophy, linguistics, and anthropology to understand the intricacies of human thought. Fundamental theories within this field inform both our comprehension of the mind and the creation of AI.

The mind, according to the Computational Theory of Mind (CTM), functions like a computer, processing information via algorithms and data structures. This has led to AI models, including neural networks for natural language processing and decision-making that mimic human cognition.

Parallel Distributed Processing (PDP), also known as connectionism, proposes that cognitive functions arise from the interactions of numerous simple processing units, similar to neurons within a network. This framework supports many machine learning methods, particularly deep learning, where multi-layered neural networks leverage extensive datasets to identify patterns and make informed decisions, as exemplified by the capabilities of AI in image recognition.

Cognition is shaped by bodily interaction with the environment, a central tenet of Embodied Cognition theory. This theory's influence is evident in advanced, mobile, and adaptable robots like Boston Dynamics' Spot and Atlas.

Context significantly influences cognitive processes, a concept central to Situated Cognition. This theory's influence is evident in AI designs, such as Google Duplex, which demonstrate adaptability and natural conversational skills within dynamic environments.

Cognitive processes, according to Distributed Cognition, are not solely within individuals, but are spread across people, tools, and their surroundings, emphasizing collaboration in thought. This has led to the development of AI systems intended for human-machine collaboration, enhancing efficiency in fields such as healthcare and education.

Cognitive theories offer a comprehensive understanding of cognition, informing the development of AI systems that mimic and surpass human intelligence. This integration of cognitive principles has driven progress in deep learning, context-aware systems, and embodied AI, significantly impacting the creation of more intelligent and adaptable AI.

2.3. Bridging Minds and Machines: The Interdisciplinary Foundations of Cognitive Computing

Cognitive computing, a multidisciplinary field drawing on psychology, neuroscience, AI, linguistics, anthropology, and philosophy, seeks to enhance our comprehension of human cognition. Its origins lie in the mid-20th century, spurred by the demand for more holistic models of mental processes during the cognitive revolution's shift from behaviorism to internal cognitive mechanisms. Groundbreaking research, exemplified by George A. Miller's studies of information processing, established the groundwork for contemporary cognitive computing [30].

Experimental psychological insights illuminate perception, learning, and decision-making, while neuroscience uses fMRI and EEG to investigate the underlying neural mechanisms. Cognitive theories inspire AI models for tasks like language processing and image recognition. Linguistics contributes crucial insights into cognition through its study of language structure, and anthropology offers valuable cultural and evolutionary contexts.

Foundational questions about the mind, consciousness, and AI ethics are raised by philosophy, shaping the ethical framework for cognitive computing. Unified theories of cognition are offered by integrated models, such as ACT-R and the Bayesian brain hypothesis, which combine insights from multiple disciplines. Practical innovations in education, healthcare, and human-computer interaction have resulted from these interdisciplinary collaborations [31].

Cognitive computing's interdisciplinary nature provides a holistic understanding of the mind, driving advancements in artificial intelligence, cognitive health, and other fields. Its continued development promises further breakthroughs in the convergence of human cognition and machine intelligence.

2.4. Recent Advances in Cognitive Computing

To appreciate the intersection and synergy of artificial intelligence (AI) and cognitive computing, understanding their foundations is crucial. AI concentrates on developing algorithms and systems that mimic human intelligence, whereas cognitive computing is a multidisciplinary field investigating the mind's cognitive processes—including perception, memory, and learning. This combined approach facilitates the creation of intelligent systems that mirror or surpass human cognitive skills, effectively connecting human minds and machines.

The foundation of artificial intelligence (AI) rests on the development of algorithms and computational models that mimic human cognitive abilities. A pivotal moment in AI history was Alan Turing's 1950 invention of the Turing Test, a benchmark for evaluating a machine's capacity to display human-like intelligence. This test profoundly impacted AI research, driving significant advancements in machine learning, natural language processing (NLP), and robotics [32].

Artificial intelligence's subfield, machine learning, employs algorithms enabling computers to learn from data and predict outcomes. This technology has led to advancements in fields such as image and speech recognition. Convolutional neural networks (CNNs), modeled after the human visual cortex, exemplify this, revolutionizing image recognition through learned spatial hierarchies of visual features. Similarly, natural language processing (NLP) models, including BERT, leverage cognitive frameworks to enhance machine comprehension and generation of human language, improving applications like sentiment analysis and machine translation.

Cognitive computing models human cognition, drawing upon psychology, neuroscience, linguistics, anthropology, and computer science. The ACT-R cognitive architecture is a key example, simulating and predicting human performance in cognitive tasks. Furthermore, AI and cognitive computing have yielded hybrid models, combining symbolic AI's logical rules with the neural network-based approach of connectionist AI [33].

Cognitive robotics, exemplified by robots such as the iCub, demonstrates the power of this collaboration. These robots are designed for autonomous perception, reasoning, learning, and interaction. Researchers are creating systems capable of navigating and completing tasks in complex settings by integrating AI, cognitive computing, and robotics. Furthermore, in human-computer interaction (HCI), cognitive computing shapes user interface design by incorporating human cognitive processes. Predictive models, such as GOMS, estimate user performance, leading to the development of more intuitive systems [34, 35].

Intelligent tutoring systems (ITS), powered by AI and cognitive computing, personalize education by adapting to individual student learning styles. The Cognitive Tutor exemplifies this, employing cognitive models to deliver tailored math instruction, thereby improving student engagement and achievement [36, 37].

The increasing societal integration of AI and cognitive computing necessitates a critical examination of their ethical implications. Bias, fairness, transparency, and accountability are crucial concerns that must be tackled; moreover, cognitive computing offers potential solutions to ethical challenges, particularly those stemming from human biases affecting AI development and function [38].

The interdisciplinary collaboration between AI and cognitive computing is crucial for realizing their full potential. This partnership fuels progress in machine learning, NLP, cognitive robotics, HCI, and intelligent tutoring systems. Combining expertise from these fields enables the development of more intelligent, adaptive, and ethical AI. Ultimately, this approach enhances our understanding of human cognition, improves AI capabilities, and benefits society [39, 40].

3. Interdisciplinary collaboration in AI and Cognitive Computing

3.1. Understanding the Foundations of AI and Cognitive Computing

To understand the interplay and synergy between artificial intelligence (AI) and cognitive computing, it's crucial to grasp their fundamental principles. AI, a computer science discipline, focuses on creating algorithms and systems capable of tasks normally requiring human intelligence. In contrast, cognitive computing is an interdisciplinary field exploring the mind's processes—perception, memory, learning, and thought. Their convergence illuminates how machines can mimic or improve on human cognitive abilities, thereby connecting human minds and artificial systems. [41].

Artificial intelligence centers on developing algorithms and models that mimic human thought processes. A landmark event in AI's history was Alan Turing's 1950 creation of the Turing Test, a benchmark for machine intelligence that mirrors human capabilities. This test has profoundly shaped AI research, driving advancements in machine learning, natural language processing, and robotics. [42].

Machine learning, a crucial component of artificial intelligence, enables computers to learn from data and make predictions through specially designed algorithms. This has fueled advancements in technologies like image and speech recognition. Image recognition, in particular, has been revolutionized by convolutional neural networks (CNNs), which mimic the human visual cortex and allow machines to identify complex visual patterns. Natural language processing (NLP) similarly leverages cognitive models to improve machine comprehension, interpretation, and generation of human language. Transformer models such as BERT further enhance tasks such as sentiment analysis and machine translation by identifying sophisticated language structures [43].

Cognitive computing draws upon psychology, neuroscience, linguistics, anthropology, and computer science to build models of human thought. A key model in this field is the ACT-R cognitive architecture, which simulates and forecasts human cognitive abilities in diverse tasks. The convergence of AI and cognitive computing has yielded hybrid models blending symbolic AI (using logic and rules) and connectionist AI (employing brain-inspired neural networks).

Cognitive robotics, a prime example of interdisciplinary collaboration, integrates artificial intelligence, cognitive computing, and robotics to produce autonomous robots with perception, reasoning, learning, and environmental interaction capabilities. The iCub robot, for instance, is designed for autonomous interaction and the emulation of human cognitive functions. Furthermore, human-computer interaction (HCI) leverages cognitive models to create user interfaces that account for human cognitive strengths and weaknesses. Predictive models, such as GOMS, improve interface design, resulting in more intuitive and user-friendly systems. [44].

Intelligent tutoring systems (ITS), powered by AI and cognitive computing, personalize learning experiences in education. By adapting to each student's unique cognitive profile, these systems improve learning outcomes. The Cognitive Tutor, for instance, leverages cognitive models to customize math instruction, boosting both student engagement and learning effectiveness.

The integration of AI and cognitive computing necessitates a growing emphasis on ethical considerations. Because AI's societal integration deepens, it's vital to address bias, fairness, transparency, and accountability. Cognitive computing offers a means to tackle these issues, primarily by revealing how human biases impact AI and promoting fairer results.

Appreciating the collaborative power of AI and cognitive computing requires understanding their underlying principles. This synergy has driven significant progress in machine learning, natural language processing, cognitive robotics, human-computer interaction, and intelligent transportation systems. The integration of diverse disciplinary perspectives enables the development of more intelligent, adaptable, and ethical AI systems, bridging the human-machine divide. This interdisciplinary approach promises profound advancements in our understanding of human cognition and AI capabilities, benefiting society at large [45].

3.2. Exploring the Intersection of AI and Human Cognition

AI and human cognition are deeply intertwined, revolutionizing both and fostering new understandings of human intelligence while improving machine capabilities. This interdisciplinary collaboration, merging AI with the cognitive computing study of mental processes (thought, intelligence, and learning), promises transformative innovations in technology and cognitive computing itself. The resulting integration will significantly impact healthcare, education, and human-world interaction, yielding valuable new discoveries as research advances.

AI models, simulating cognitive functions such as perception, memory, and decision-making, enhance our comprehension of human cognition. Crucially, brain-inspired neural networks illuminate neural processes involved in learning and memory. By exploring the brain's neural architecture, these AI models provide valuable insights into human cognitive development. Furthermore, AI's capacity for massive data processing reveals patterns in brain activity undetectable through manual analysis. For instance, AI-driven fMRI data analysis has uncovered new knowledge about brain connectivity, potentially advancing both AI and our understanding of the brain [46,47].

AI development significantly benefits from cognitive computing. Cognitive theories of attention, learning, and problem-solving inform the design of AI models that emulate human cognitive functions. For instance, reinforcement learning, inspired by behavioral psychology and neuroscience, enables AI to learn via trial and error. This continuous interplay between AI and cognitive computing ensures AI systems are rooted in a strong understanding of human cognition, thereby improving their ability to replicate human capabilities [48].

Natural language processing (NLP) significantly benefits from the combined power of AI and cognitive computing, enabling AI systems to comprehend and produce human language. Cognitive linguistics informs the creation of more precise NLP algorithms by illuminating the relationship between language and thought. This collaboration promises advancements in machine translation, sentiment analysis, and conversational AI. Furthermore, AI and cognitive computing are integral to assistive technologies like brain-computer interfaces (BCIs), decoding neural signals to operate devices. These systems improve the lives of people with disabilities, demonstrating the innovative potential of interdisciplinary collaboration in enhancing human-world interaction [49, 50].

Ethical and philosophical concerns arise from the integration of AI and cognitive computing. The increasing sophistication of AI systems challenges our understanding of intelligence and consciousness, prompting concerns about the responsible development of human-like cognitive abilities in machines. This is crucial given AI's expanding role in society.

Practical applications of AI in education and healthcare stem from its interaction with human cognition, going beyond theoretical and ethical concerns. AI-powered educational tools personalize learning, boosting retention and comprehension through cognitive principles such as spaced repetition and active learning. Similarly, in mental healthcare, AI algorithms analyze data to identify early warning signs of mental illness, facilitating timely intervention and customized treatment strategies. [51].

Complex domains are experiencing a revolution in decision-making thanks to AI and cognitive computing. AI systems, for instance, aid medical diagnoses by analyzing clinical data and identifying patterns human experts might overlook. These AI systems, incorporating cognitive decision-making theories, enhance human judgment, leading to more accurate and efficient decisions [52].

AI and human cognition are dynamically intertwined, fostering advancement in both. Combining AI's computational strength with cognitive computing's theoretical basis yields improved human cognition models and more adaptable, human-like AI. This interdisciplinary work significantly impacts neuroscience, education, healthcare, and decision-making. Responsible AI development and societal benefit depend on cognitive computing insights as AI progresses, paving the way for new discoveries and innovation.

3.3. Methods and Tools for Cross Disciplinary Research

Cross-disciplinary research at the intersection of artificial intelligence (AI) and cognitive computing is producing significant breakthroughs. This combined approach, integrating varied methodologies and viewpoints, unites knowledge, data, and techniques to yield deeper understanding of human cognition and more advanced AI. Success, however, hinges on a thorough grasp of both fields and their respective research methodologies.

Artificial intelligence (AI) aims to build systems that mimic human intellectual capabilities such as learning, reasoning, and problem-solving. Cognitive computing, conversely, investigates the workings of the human mind, encompassing processes like perception, memory, and language. The convergence of these fields offers valuable insights into both human cognition and artificial systems. A key element of this interdisciplinary research is computational modeling, employing algorithms and neural networks to simulate cognitive processes and predict cognitive behaviors. Connectionist models, such as artificial neural networks, replicate the structure and function of the brain, thereby informing the development of more sophisticated AI [53, 54].

Data mining and machine learning, crucial for this research, extract patterns from large datasets relevant to both AI and cognitive computing. Decision trees and deep learning models, among other machine learning algorithms, significantly influence these fields. Deep learning, for instance, has revolutionized image and speech recognition, mirroring human cognitive processes. This modeling improves our comprehension of human complex task processing.

AI and cognitive computing rely heavily on Natural Language Processing (NLP). Transformer models such as BERT and GPT-3 have dramatically advanced AI's language comprehension capabilities. These models facilitate sophisticated language processing and offer valuable insights into the cognitive mechanisms of language understanding and generation [55].

Cross-disciplinary collaboration relies heavily on experimental research. Cognitive computing experiments manipulate variables to understand their impact on cognitive processes. AI enhances these studies by simulating environments and behaviors—for example, using virtual reality to model complex human interactions. This combined approach of experimental research and AI unveils new insights into cognition, generating valuable data for building similarly capable AI systems.

GitHub, Jupyter Notebooks, and the Open Science Framework are collaborative tools and platforms that promote transparency, reproducibility, and accessibility in research by facilitating data and methodology sharing. Their use enhances cross-disciplinary project efficiency and broadens accessibility, thereby driving future advancements.

Regression analysis and Bayesian inference are crucial statistical methods in both fields, enabling researchers to analyze relationships between variables and test hypotheses rigorously, thereby enhancing the reliability and generalizability of research. Bayesian inference, especially, has proven invaluable for modeling human decision-making, illuminating how beliefs are revised in light of new evidence.

AI and cognitive computing research must prioritize ethical considerations. Privacy, fairness, and accountability are key concerns arising from their integration. Researchers developing AI-assisted cognitive assessments, for example, must carefully address these ethical issues to prevent bias and guarantee fairness. Ethical research practices are crucial for societal well-being, protecting individual rights and mitigating harm.

Cross-disciplinary research holds significant potential, as evidenced by successful case studies. For instance, intelligent tutoring systems (ITS), leveraging AI and insights from cognitive computing on learning and information processing, personalize instruction and demonstrably improve educational outcomes. This success suggests that the underlying principles of ITS could benefit other AI-powered educational tools, leading to further enhancements in learning effectiveness [56].

AI significantly advances neuroimaging research. Machine learning and pattern recognition enhance fMRI and EEG techniques, revealing new insights into brain function and cognition. This integration promises a revolution in neurological and psychiatric care through more accurate and personalized diagnoses and treatments [57].

Cross-disciplinary research integrating AI and cognitive computing reveals novel insights into human cognition and facilitates the development of intelligent systems. This process relies critically on computational modeling, machine learning, natural language processing, experimental research, collaborative tools, statistical analysis, and ethical considerations. The adoption of these methods promises innovative solutions and groundbreaking discoveries, revolutionizing our comprehension of the mind and yielding AI systems beneficial to humankind.

3.4. Case Studies in AI and Cognitive Computing Collaboration

Cross-disciplinary collaboration between Artificial Intelligence (AI) and Cognitive Computing is driving significant progress, as demonstrated by numerous impactful case studies. These collaborations highlight the powerful synergy between AI and Cognitive Computing, resulting in groundbreaking innovations that expand the capabilities of both humans and machines.

Cognitive Architectures: Developed by John Laird, Allen Newell, and Paul Rosenbloom, the Soar cognitive architecture exemplifies the intersection of AI and cognitive psychology. Soar models human problem-solving and decision-making by integrating principles from cognitive psychology, creating a comprehensive model. The system's ability to mimic memory, learning, and perception showcases how AI can replicate complex human cognitive functions. This demonstrates the crucial influence of cognitive computing theories in building more adaptable and intelligent AI, emphasizing their importance for enhancing AI's flexibility and human-like cognitive abilities. [58].

The Human Brain Project (HBP): The Human Brain Project (HBP) is a large-scale initiative using computational models to understand the human brain. AI processes massive neurological datasets, enabling the project to simulate brain functions with high precision. Cognitive scientists collaborate to refine models of neural processes, potentially leading to improved treatments for neurological disorders and advancements in AI. This interdisciplinary approach demonstrates how brain research can significantly enhance AI, increasing both its accuracy and sophistication [59].

Natural Language Processing (NLP) and GPT-3: OpenAI's GPT-3 exemplifies the benefits of cognitive computing in AI. This language model leverages linguistic and psychological principles to produce human-quality text and interpret intricate language structures. By integrating cognitive computing principles, GPT-3 vastly improves AI's language comprehension and generation, significantly impacting fields such as human-computer interaction and automated translation. This successful application highlights cognitive computing's crucial role in enhancing AI's linguistic abilities, leading to improvements in tasks like comprehension, translation, and text generation [60].

Reinforcement Learning in Robotics: Robotics leverages reinforcement learning, a technique inspired by behavioral psychology, to integrate artificial intelligence (AI) with cognitive theories of human learning. This allows robots to learn through trial and error, mastering tasks such as autonomous navigation and manipulation. Consequently, robots become more adaptable and proficient. The synergy between AI and cognitive computing highlights the power of behavioral theories in improving the learning and adaptability of robotic systems [61].

AI in Mental Health Diagnosis: AI is transforming mental healthcare by diagnosing and treating conditions like depression and anxiety. Cognitive Computing enhances AI systems, enabling them to analyze speech, behavior, and physiological data to more accurately detect mental health issues. This leads to earlier diagnosis and personalized treatments [62].

Intelligent Tutoring Systems (ITS): Intelligent tutoring systems (ITS), personalized learning experiences powered by AI and cognitive computing, leverage memory and learning theories to adapt to individual student needs. These systems assess knowledge, predict learning trajectories, and, through cognitive computing insights, deliver more engaging and effective instruction, ultimately improving learning outcomes. The potential long-term impact on education is a substantial enhancement of student engagement and learning processes [63].

Brain-Computer Interfaces (BCIs): Brain-computer interfaces (BCIs) are a groundbreaking collaboration between artificial intelligence (AI) and cognitive computing. BCIs allow direct brain-to-device communication, providing new ways for people with disabilities to engage with their surroundings. AI systems, using cognitive computing to analyze motor control and sensory perception, more accurately interpret brain signals, making BCIs more effective and user-friendly. This technology promises to significantly improve the lives of people with disabilities and greatly enhance human potential [64].

Interdisciplinary collaboration between AI and cognitive computing is demonstrably crucial for advancing AI. This combined approach enables the development of superior AI systems that mimic human cognitive abilities and contribute to improvements in mental healthcare, education, and assistive technologies. Continued collaboration in these fields will significantly expand the capabilities of both AI and cognitive computing, ultimately fostering a deeper understanding of human cognition and closing the gap between humans and machines.

Cross-disciplinary AI and cognitive computing research offers immense potential for future advancements in both fields. Collaborative efforts are fueling innovation, leading to societal benefits and a deeper understanding of the human mind, while simultaneously creating more sophisticated, adaptable systems. This will revolutionize healthcare, education, robotics, and human-computer interaction, profoundly improving lives.

3.5. Future Directions in Interdisciplinary AI and Cognitive Computing

AI and cognitive computing are rapidly converging, creating more sophisticated, adaptive, and intelligent systems. Their combined computational power and understanding of human cognition promise groundbreaking advancements. This article explores this powerful fusion, examining emerging trends, key developments, and its transformative effects on both fields.

1. *Cognitive Models in AI:* Structured, often mathematical cognitive models, representing human thought processes, drive this convergence. These models encapsulate key cognitive functions—perception, memory, decision-making, and problem-solving. Researchers integrate these models into AI to create machines with human-like reasoning and understanding. This approach is crucial, particularly in natural language processing (NLP), which necessitates contextual and nuanced comprehension. The article emphasizes the need for further research to determine which cognitive functions should be prioritized for AI system enhancement [65].
2. *Hybrid AI Systems:* Hybrid AI systems, combining symbolic and connectionist AI, represent a highly promising development. Symbolic AI, with its reliance on explicit rules and logic, excels at structured reasoning, while connectionist AI, employing neural networks and data-driven learning, handles ambiguous, data-rich situations effectively. This hybrid approach aims to unify these strengths, resulting in more robust and adaptable AI. Consequently, researchers are investigating how this combination can yield more comprehensive AI systems capable of simulating complex human thought processes [66].
3. *Embodied Cognition:* The exploration of embodied cognition, the idea that cognitive processes are inextricably linked to bodily interaction with the environment, represents a thrilling new avenue of research. This contrasts sharply with the traditional, purely computational model of cognition. Consequently, AI researchers are creating robots and virtual agents that learn through physical environmental interaction. This approach is especially vital in robotics and autonomous systems, which demand contextual awareness and adaptability. The article highlights the crucial role embodied cognition plays in developing robots and AI systems capable of learning and adapting in real-world settings [67].
4. *Human-Computer Interaction (HCI):* AI and cognitive computing offer significant potential for enhancing human-computer interaction (HCI). Intuitive and user-friendly interfaces are possible because cognitive models enable AI systems to better understand and anticipate human needs. AI-driven personal assistants, for instance,

provide more personalized and seamless experiences by adapting to individual user preferences and behaviors. This is especially impactful in educational technology, where AI-powered systems personalize learning content and pace according to student cognitive profiles, thereby improving educational results [68].

5. *Affective Computing:* Affective computing, the creation of systems that understand and respond to human emotions, is propelled forward by the integration of artificial intelligence (AI) and cognitive computing. Cognitive emotion models embedded in AI systems enable a deeper understanding of user emotions, fostering empathetic and contextually relevant interactions. This has profound implications for mental healthcare, allowing AI-powered therapeutic tools to offer personalized support tailored to individual emotional needs. The article examines how these advancements may revolutionize mental healthcare through more effective and personalized treatments [69].
6. *Healthcare and Diagnostics:* Healthcare, especially mental health and neurological care, stands to be profoundly impacted by the combined power of artificial intelligence and cognitive computing. AI systems, leveraging cognitive models, will refine diagnostic tools and treatment methods, leading to more accurate early detection and personalized treatment plans. This understanding of the cognitive mechanisms behind mental illness will enable AI to create tailored interventions, ultimately improving patient outcomes. The article explores how these advancements will enhance healthcare and patient care through more precise and targeted strategies.
7. *Ethical Considerations:* Ethical considerations surrounding bias, privacy, and misuse are paramount as AI systems evolve to become more sophisticated and human-like. The article advocates for a multidisciplinary approach to creating ethical guidelines for AI development. Understanding human behavior, as provided by Cognitive Computing, can contribute to responsible and equitable AI design and implementation. Establishing ethical standards is vital for mitigating risks and ensuring AI benefits society.

AI and cognitive computing's future is bright, promising more adaptive, intuitive, and human-like intelligent systems through their integration. This interdisciplinary collaboration benefits both fields, advancing AI while providing cognitive computing with powerful tools and insights. Responsible innovation requires careful consideration of the ethical implications of AI advancements. Continued collaboration between AI and cognitive computing is crucial for breakthroughs, ultimately connecting human and machine intelligence.

The merging of AI's computational power and Cognitive Computing's theoretical understanding is poised to create systems exhibiting greater intelligence and more human-like adaptability, reasoning, and emotional understanding. This collaboration promises to revolutionize numerous industries, including healthcare and education, and simultaneously advance our comprehension of the human mind.

4. Emerging Trends and Future Direction in AI and Computing

4.1. Introduction to Emerging Trends in AI and Cognitive Computing

Artificial intelligence (AI) and cognitive computing are merging, revolutionizing technology and revealing profound insights into human cognition. This powerful combination promises significant advancements in both fields, enabling better simulations of human intelligence and enhancing our understanding of the mind. Numerous emerging trends are driving the development of both AI and cognitive computing, impacting numerous sectors.

1. *Neural Networks and Deep Learning*: Neural networks and deep learning represent a major advancement in artificial intelligence. Modeled on the human brain, these systems excel at image recognition, speech processing, natural language understanding, and games. Convolutional and recurrent neural networks, for example, are achieving near-human performance in specific areas. Furthermore, generative adversarial networks (GANs), featuring a generator and discriminator network working in competition, are producing remarkably realistic data, impacting creative industries, research, and entertainment.
2. *Explainable AI (XAI):* The increasing complexity of AI systems and their integration into crucial sectors like healthcare, finance, and autonomous vehicles necessitate explainable AI (XAI). XAI

enhances transparency, interpretability, and human understanding of AI, thereby building trust and accountability. This is especially crucial in high-stakes applications with significant consequences, such as medical diagnoses and financial transactions. This article investigates the feasibility of balancing AI's complexity with human interpretability.

3. *Cognitive Architectures*: ACT-R and SOAR, two prominent cognitive architectures, integrate psychological, neuroscientific, and computer science knowledge to simulate human cognition. Modeling key cognitive functions such as memory, problem-solving, and learning, these frameworks offer valuable insights into building cognitively flexible AI systems. Their development advances AI's capacity for human-like adaptability and intelligence, ultimately fostering the creation of truly cognitive AI.
4. *Ethical and Societal Implications*: Critical ethical issues arise from integrating AI and cognitive computing. Facial recognition, for example, highlights concern about bias and discrimination, particularly against racial and gender groups. Equitable and responsible AI use demands addressing these ethical concerns and establishing guidelines as AI becomes more prevalent. This article examines how multidisciplinary approaches can mitigate bias and develop ethical AI deployment standards.
5. *Decoding Human Cognition*: Neuroimaging, employing fMRI and EEG, is a converging point for AI and cognitive computing. Analysis of neural data by AI algorithms unveils patterns linked to cognitive functions including memory, attention, and decision-making. This interplay between AI and cognitive computing yields fresh understanding of both human cognition and AI itself, driving progress in both areas.
6. *Human-Computer Interaction (HCI):* AI and cognitive computing are significantly advancing human-computer interaction (HCI). Natural language processing (NLP), an AI technology, is improving human-machine communication. Sophisticated chatbots and virtual assistants now understand and generate human-like language, creating more natural and intuitive interactions. This NLP potential enhances user experience, particularly for those with disabilities or language barriers, increasing information access.
7. *Brain-Computer Interfaces (BCIs):* Brain-computer interfaces (BCIs), enabling direct brain-to-device communication, represent an

exciting area of development. Fueled by artificial intelligence, BCIs offer the potential to revolutionize neurorehabilitation, potentially enabling individuals with disabilities to control robotic limbs or regain some vision. Their promise in healthcare extends to more effective treatments and improved communication for those with severe disabilities.

8. *Interdisciplinary Collaboration:* Interdisciplinary collaboration is crucial for the continued advancement of AI and cognitive computing. The Human Brain Project and the BRAIN Initiative are prime examples of this collaboration, aiming to map the human brain and create neurobiologically-inspired AI. Such partnerships between AI researchers, neuroscientists, and psychologists accelerate progress in both cognitive science and AI development.
9. *Lifelong Learning in AI:* Lifelong learning offers a dynamic alternative to the traditional reliance of AI systems on static training data. Like humans, AI systems employing lifelong learning continuously acquire new knowledge. This adaptability is essential for applications such as autonomous vehicles and personalized education, demanding real-time learning. The article explores the implications of this approach for future AI applications and their capacity to navigate evolving environments.

Intelligence, cognition, and human-machine interaction are being redefined by the merging of AI and cognitive computing. This is just the initial phase, fueled by progress in neural networks, explainable AI, cognitive architectures, and brain-computer interfaces (BCIs). The intersection of these fields will have profound effects on technology, society, and human well-being, impacting areas as diverse as healthcare and education. Responsible technological development, guided by ethical considerations and interdisciplinary collaboration, will unlock innovation and discovery while enhancing human life. AI and cognitive computing's future holds transformative advancements that will revolutionize human-machine interaction, our understanding of human cognition, and our ability to address complex societal problems.

4.2. Integration of AI and Neuroscience

Artificial intelligence (AI) and neuroscience are converging to revolutionize our understanding of the brain and create machines that mimic human cognition. This interdisciplinary field is producing significant advancements with transformative potential for medicine, psychology, and technology. The following summarizes key findings.

1. *Neural Networks and AI:* Neural networks, models simulating brain structure and function, form the intersection of artificial intelligence and neuroscience. Machine learning relies heavily on artificial neural networks (ANNs), which mimic biological neurons and enable pattern recognition, decision-making, and learning from data. The ANN process of backpropagation reflects how biological neurons adjust synaptic weights through experience, mirroring the concept of synaptic plasticity—a key influence on AI development. Furthermore, deep learning architectures such as convolutional neural networks (CNNs) utilize a hierarchical processing structure, inspired by the brain's layered approach to visual stimuli. This has been instrumental in advancements across image recognition, speech processing, and complex game mastery, notably Go.
2. *Learning and Memory in AI*: Neuroscientific insights, especially Hebbian theory ("cells that fire together, wire together"), have significantly influenced AI algorithm development, particularly in unsupervised learning. AI systems in unsupervised learning derive patterns without explicit instruction. Similarly, reinforcement learning, mirroring the brain's reward system, has driven AI progress, enabling AI mastery of Atari games and victories over human champions in complex games. This success suggests the potential of applying reinforcement learning to create novel educational tools that improve human learning.
3. *AI in Neuroscience*: Conversely, artificial intelligence (AI) is proving invaluable in neuroscience, particularly for data analysis and modeling. The large datasets generated by techniques such as fMRI and EEG are efficiently analyzed by AI, revealing patterns imperceptible to humans. Furthermore, AI is driving innovation in brain-computer interfaces (BCIs), facilitating direct brain-device communication. This allows disabled individuals to recover lost functions, including prosthetic limb control and computer interaction.

By improving the accuracy and dependability of neural signal decoding, AI is significantly advancing human-computer interaction.

4. *Challenges in Replicating Human Cognition*: AI development faces a significant hurdle: the human brain's complexity. Limited understanding of brain processes, especially consciousness, hinders the replication of these processes in artificial systems. Furthermore, the brain's intricate neural architecture poses challenges to creating AI that fully mimics human cognition.
5. *Ethical Considerations*: The rapid progress of AI and neuroscience raises significant ethical questions. These include the potential for thought decoding to breach privacy and the societal impact of cognitive enhancement technologies. Therefore, ethical guidelines are crucial for the responsible development and application of AI and neurotechnology, minimizing risks while maximizing societal benefits.
6. *Interdisciplinary Collaboration*: Interdisciplinary collaboration is crucial for addressing the challenges in the intersection of AI and neuroscience. Scientists—including neuroscientists, AI researchers, ethicists, and policymakers—must collaborate to ensure that advancements are scientifically rigorous, ethically sound, and socially beneficial. The Human Brain Project and BRAIN Initiative exemplify the value of global cooperation, as their collaborative efforts to map the brain and develop brain disorder treatments demonstrate the importance of this interdisciplinary approach.
7. *Future Directions*: The convergence of artificial intelligence and neuroscience promises transformative advancements. Neuroimaging data analyzed by AI will significantly improve our understanding of brain function, potentially enabling the creation of AI systems capable of mimicking higher-level cognitive abilities like reasoning, creativity, and emotional intelligence. Furthermore, AI-driven personalized medicine offers the potential to revolutionize the treatment of neurological and psychiatric conditions by tailoring therapies to individual brain characteristics.
8. The Promise of Personalized AI-Driven Interventions: Personalized healthcare, powered by AI, may yield tailored treatments for brain disorders, resulting in more effective and individualized care. However, responsible use across diverse populations requires careful consideration of the ethical implications.

AI and neuroscience are revolutionizing our understanding of the brain and intelligent systems. AI's emulation of brain structure and learning has yielded significant advancements in diverse applications. Furthermore, AI's data analysis capabilities are driving progress in brain-computer interfaces and related technologies. However, ethical considerations and the brain's complexity present ongoing challenges to fully replicating human intelligence artificially. Responsible technological development requires interdisciplinary collaboration and robust ethical guidelines as both fields progress. Ultimately, the combined potential of AI and neuroscience promises groundbreaking scientific discoveries, technological innovation, and societal benefit.

4.3. Ethical Considerations and Societal Impacts of AI

Understanding the development and implications of cognitive computing's emerging technologies requires careful consideration of AI's ethical implications and societal impact. AI's increasing integration into our lives presents both opportunities and challenges demanding close examination. The integration of AI, especially in decision-making processes, creates complex ethical dilemmas and significant societal shifts. The following is a detailed summary of these challenges and their societal consequences:

1. *AI's Ethical Dilemmas*: AI systems are impacting individuals and communities through decisions ranging from personalized shopping to critical areas like credit and healthcare. Ethical concerns about AI center on fairness, accountability, transparency, and bias mitigation. For instance, facial recognition algorithms demonstrate bias, exhibiting higher error rates for certain demographic groups, such as darker-skinned individuals and women. Buolamwini and Gebru's 2018 research revealed these biases, showing how AI can reinforce prejudice unless carefully managed.
2. *Job Displacement and Economic Disruption*: Automation driven by AI poses a major societal challenge: widespread job displacement. The McKinsey Global Institute estimates that AI-driven automation may require 375 million workers globally to change professions by 2030. This necessitates urgent consideration of how to prepare for and lessen the resulting economic disruption. Although AI may generate new jobs and boost productivity, harmonizing technological advancement with economic adjustment remains difficult.

3. *Privacy Concerns and Data Ownership*: The use of AI systems necessitates extensive datasets, frequently including personal information, thus raising significant privacy and data ownership concerns. The Cambridge Analytica scandal, a prime example of unauthorized use of Facebook user data for political manipulation, highlights the potential for data misuse. Therefore, robust data protection protocols and transparent data handling are crucial to safeguarding personal data from exploitation.
4. *Power Structures and Access to AI*: Large corporations' control over AI development raises concerns about monopolies and unequal access to AI advancements, potentially limiting access to beneficial technologies. However, AI also offers the potential to democratize access to information and resources, especially through personalized learning offered by AI-driven educational tools, which could help alleviate educational inequalities.
5. *Accountability and the "Black Box" Problem*: The complexity and opacity of AI decision-making processes create a "black box" problem, obscuring how decisions are reached. Consequently, assigning accountability for AI system outcomes—to developers, users, or the AI itself—becomes challenging. Explainable AI (XAI) offers a potential solution by enhancing the transparency and understandability of AI decisions, thereby fostering greater accountability and trust.
6. *AI in Surveillance and Civil Liberties*: The use of AI in surveillance, exemplified by China's social credit system, presents significant ethical and human rights challenges. Increased security through AI comes at the potential cost of individual freedoms and civil liberties. Policymakers and developers must prioritize balancing AI's security advantages with the safeguarding of fundamental rights.
7. *Healthcare AI and Biases:* Healthcare stands to be revolutionized by AI, especially in diagnostics and treatment. Yet, biases in AI, stemming largely from datasets dominated by white populations, risk creating healthcare disparities for minority groups. This can manifest as lower accuracy in AI systems for non-white patients, worsening existing inequalities. To achieve equitable healthcare, AI development must actively address bias through diverse datasets and inclusive perspectives.
8. *Inclusivity in AI Development*: Diverse perspectives are crucial for equitable and just AI development. Participatory design, engaging

end-users—especially marginalized communities—in the design process, ensures AI serves diverse needs and values. Broad stakeholder involvement, encompassing ethicists, social scientists, and affected communities, is key to creating socially responsible and equitable AI systems.

9. *Long-term Societal Impacts and Ethical Reflection*: The continued evolution of AI necessitates ongoing ethical reflection on its long-term societal consequences. This requires safeguarding privacy, establishing accountability mechanisms, and mitigating biases within AI systems. Societies must vigilantly monitor AI's influence on economic, social, and political structures, ensuring its development benefits all of humankind and avoids exacerbating inequality or creating new harms.

Addressing the ethical and societal challenges posed by AI development and application demands a comprehensive strategy. This includes guaranteeing fairness, accountability, transparency, privacy, and inclusivity in all AI systems. Ongoing ethical reflection and strong regulatory frameworks are crucial as AI advances, enabling societies to harness its potential for increased productivity, better healthcare, and broader access to resources while mitigating risks and building a more equitable and just future.

4.4. Future Directions and Innovations in Cognitive Computing

Cognitive computing significantly advances artificial intelligence by enabling machines to mimic human thought. This transformative field will revolutionize technology, society, and the economy, with profound and wide-ranging consequences stemming from continuous innovation. The following is a detailed summary of cognitive computing's progress and its societal, ethical, and technological effects:

1. *Neural Networks and Deep Learning Models*: Advancements in neural networks, especially deep learning models, are a cornerstone of cognitive computing's progress. Modeling the human brain's structure and function, these systems enable machines to perform image and speech recognition, natural language processing, and complex problem-solving. Deep learning's potential is illustrated by Google's AlphaGo victory over a Go world champion. Further

advancements, such as Generative Adversarial Networks (GANs) and Transformer models, are expanding deep learning's capabilities, producing realistic images and improving language understanding. These breakthroughs redefine the possibilities of AI across various fields.

2. *Cognitive and Quantum Computing*: Exponentially greater computational power is promised by the convergence of cognitive and quantum computing. Unlike classical computers, quantum computers harness quantum mechanics for computation, potentially solving previously intractable problems. Consequently, fields such as cryptography, materials science, and complex system simulations could be revolutionized, enabling solutions to formerly insurmountable challenges. This transformative development could fundamentally alter our approach to problem-solving and technological advancement.
3. *Explainable AI (XAI):* Deep learning models, despite their impressive performance, are often criticized for their opacity; their decision-making processes remain unclear. This lack of transparency is particularly problematic in high-stakes fields like healthcare and finance, where understanding the reasoning behind decisions is paramount. Explainable AI (XAI) aims to address this by enhancing the transparency and interpretability of AI systems, thus building trust. Methods such as feature attribution, model distillation, and surrogate modeling are being investigated to improve the explainability of these systems, a critical need in applications with significant consequences, involving human lives or substantial financial risks.
4. *The Internet of Things (IoT) and Cognitive Computing:* Cognitive computing and the Internet of Things (IoT) are converging, poised to revolutionize human-data and human-device interaction. This convergence facilitates autonomous data analysis and decision-making, creating more intelligent systems. Smart cities, for example, leverage AI and IoT to optimize traffic, conserve energy, and improve public safety. Similarly, in healthcare, the cognitive IoT allows for real-time patient monitoring and intervention, potentially saving lives through prompt medical responses. This technological fusion promises a new era of interconnected and intelligent environments.
5. *Ethical and Societal Implications*: The advancement of cognitive computing necessitates addressing crucial ethical concerns

surrounding its autonomy and societal effects. Privacy, security, and automation-driven job displacement demand immediate attention to ensure responsible development. Balancing technological innovation with societal well-being requires strong ethical guidelines, regulations, and accountability. Effective collaboration between policymakers, researchers, and industry is vital for navigating the complexities of cognitive computing and guaranteeing equitable distribution of its benefits.

6. *Education and Workforce Development*: Cognitive computing's increasing integration highlights the urgent need for education and workforce development. The rising importance of AI, machine learning, and data science across industries fuels a growing demand for skilled professionals. Universities and colleges are adapting by revising their curricula and developing specialized programs. To remain competitive, continuous learning and upskilling are vital. Finally, collaboration among academia, industry, and government is crucial for building a robust talent pipeline to support the expanding cognitive computing sector.
7. *Human-Technology Interaction*: Human-computer interaction is becoming more intuitive thanks to natural user interfaces like voice assistants and gesture recognition. These interfaces are improving their ability to understand human emotions and intentions, thereby enriching user experiences in diverse sectors such as customer service, mental health, and entertainment. The increasing sophistication of these technologies is blurring the distinction between human and machine interaction, resulting in smoother, more natural experiences. Ultimately, this technological advancement promises to revolutionize how we engage with technology daily.
8. *Cognitive Computing in Scientific Research*: Scientific research benefits significantly from cognitive computing's capacity to analyze massive datasets, revealing patterns and insights otherwise missed by humans. This accelerates discoveries in genomics, climate science, and neuroscience. One example is drug discovery, where AI streamlines candidate identification, effectiveness prediction, and clinical trial optimization, resulting in reduced time and costs. The speed with which it uncovers complex insights makes cognitive computing crucial for addressing critical global issues.
9. *Human-Machine Collaboration*: Cognitive computing augments, not replaces, human intelligence. This human-machine partnership boosts

human potential and tackles complex global issues like climate change and health emergencies. The fusion of human creativity and intuition with machine accuracy and processing power enables innovative, effective, and sustainable solutions to previously intractable problems.

Conclusion

Intelligent systems that mimic human thought processes—learning, reasoning, and natural interaction—define cognitive computing. This third era of computing blends human and machine intelligence to tackle complex challenges. Core technologies include artificial intelligence (AI), machine learning, natural language processing (NLP), and neural networks. Applications span diverse sectors, from business analytics and healthcare to finance and personal assistants such as Alexa and Siri. Ultimately, cognitive computing aims to enhance human lives through smarter, more efficient technology interactions. Future development will be significantly influenced by its growing integration into public and private spheres.

Cognitive computing is revolutionizing numerous areas. Its advancements, encompassing neural networks, quantum computing, explainable AI, IoT integration, and scientific research, offer vast potential. However, ethical considerations, education, and effective human-machine collaboration are crucial for its responsible development. Addressing these issues will unlock cognitive computing's power to benefit humanity and tackle global problems.

Cognitive computing's future is thrilling, promising a revolutionary transformation in human technology and human-human interaction. Machines will achieve human-like understanding, reasoning, learning, and communication, moving beyond mere data processing to insightful analysis. Voice assistants, generative AI, and autonomous vehicles represent only initial applications. Future applications could tackle significant challenges in climate change, healthcare, and education while nurturing creativity, innovation, and empathy. AI agents will be crucial in complex system development and management, empowering autonomous AI to self-improve and accelerate decision-making.

References

[1] Campbell, M., Hoane, A. J., & Hsu, F. (2002). Deep Blue. *Artificial Intelligence, 134*(1-2), 57-83.

[2] Miller, E. K., & Cohen, J. D. (2001). An integrative theory of prefrontal cortex function. *Annual Review of Neuroscience, 24*, 167-202.

[3] Tononi, G. (2008). Consciousness as integrated information: a provisional manifesto. *Biological Bulletin, 215*(3), 216-242.

[4] Lebedev, M. A., & Nicolelis, M. A. L. (2006). Brain–machine interfaces: past, present and future. *Trends in Neurosciences, 29*(9), 536-546.

[5] Ochsner, K. N., Bunge, S. A., Gross, J. J., & Gabrieli, J. D. E. (2002). Rethinking feelings: an fMRI study of the cognitive regulation of emotion. *Journal of Cognitive Neuroscience, 14*(8), 1215-1229.

[6] Raichle, M. E., MacLeod, A. M., Snyder, A. Z., Powers, W. J., Gusnard, D. A., & Shulman, G. L. (2001). A default mode of brain function. *Proceedings of the National Academy of Sciences, 98*(2), 676-682.

[7] Azevedo, F. A., Carvalho, L. R. B., Grinberg, L. T., Farfel, J. M., Ferretti, R. E., Leite, R. E., & Herculano-Houzel, S. (2009). Equal numbers of neuronal and nonneuronal cells make the human brain an isometrically scaled-up primate brain. *Journal of Comparative Neurology, 513*(5), 532-541.

[8] Goldstein, E. B. (2013). *Sensation and perception* (9th ed.). Wadsworth.

[9] Kandel, E. R., Schwartz, J. H., & Jessell, T. M. (2013). *Principles of neural science* (5th ed.). McGraw-Hill.

[10] Lee, T. S., & Ishii, M. (2007). *Multisensory integration: Neural and computational perspectives. Nature Reviews Neuroscience*, 8, 123-132. https://doi.org/10.1038/nrn2049.

[11] Oliva, A., & Torralba, A. (2007). *The role of context in object recognition. Trends in Cognitive Sciences*, 11(12), 520-527. https://doi.org/10.1016/j.tics.2007.09.009.

[12] Szeliski, R. (2010). *Computer vision: Algorithms and applications*. Springer.

[13] Binns, R. (2018). Fairness *in machine learning: Lessons from political philosophy*. Proceedings of the 2018 Conference on Fairness, Accountability, and Transparency, 149-159. https://doi.org/10.1145/3287560.3287598.

[14] Riva, G., Baños, R. M., Botella, C., Wiederhold, B. K., & Gaggioli, A. (2012). *Positive technology: Using interactive technologies to promote positive functioning. Cyberpsychology, Behavior, and Social Networking*, 15(2), 69-77. https://doi.org/10.1089/cyber.2011.0298.

[15] Bialystok, E. (2009). Bilingualism: *The good, the bad, and the indifferent. Bilingualism: Language and Cognition*, 12(1), 3-11.

[16] Kaan, E., & Swaab, T. Y. (2002). *The brain circuitry of syntactic comprehension. Trends in Cognitive Sciences*, 6(8), 350-356. https://doi.org/10.1016/S1364-6613(02)01920-1.

[17] Kuhl, P. K. (2004). *Early language acquisition: Cracking the speech code. Nature Reviews Neuroscience*, 5(11), 831-843. https://doi.org/10.1038/nrn1533.

[18] Levinson, S. C. (2003). *Space in language and cognition: Explorations in cognitive diversity. Cambridge University Press.*

[19] Miller, G. A. (2003). *The cognitive revolution: A historical perspective. Trends in Cognitive Sciences*, 7(3), 141-144. https://doi.org/10.1016/S1364-6613(03)00029-9.

[20] Nisbett, R. E., Miyamoto, Y., & Masuda, T. (2012). *Culture and the physical environment. Current Directions in Psychological Science*, 21(3), 149-153. https://doi.org/10.1177/0963721412436801.

[21] Rumelhart, D. E., & McClelland, J. L. (1986). *Parallel distributed processing: Explorations in the microstructure of cognition*, Vol. 1: Foundations. MIT Press.

[22] Squire, L. R. (2004). *Memory systems of the brain: A brief history and current perspective. Neurobiology of Learning and Memory*, 82(3), 171-177. https://doi.org/10.1016/j.nlm.2004.06.005.

[23] Rizzolatti, G., & Craighero, L. (2004). *The mirror-neuron system. Annual Review of Neuroscience*, 27, 169-192. https://doi.org/10.1146/annurev.neuro.27.070203.144230.

[24] Wilson, M. (2002). Six views of embodied cognition. *Psychonomic Bulletin & Review, 9*(4), 625-636. https://doi.org/10.3758/BF03196322.

[25] Anderson, J. R., Bothell, D., Byrne, M. D., Douglass, S., Lebiere, C., & Qin, Y. (2004). *An integrated theory of the mind. Psychological Review*, 111(4), 1036-1060. https://doi.org/10.1037/0033-295X.111.4.1036.

[26] Baddeley, A. (2000). The episodic buffer: A new component of working memory? *Trends in Cognitive Sciences*, 4(11), 417-423. https://doi.org/10.1016/S1364-6613(00)01538-2.

[27] Knill, D. C., & Pouget, A. (2004). The Bayesian brain: The role of uncertainty in neural coding and computation. *Trends in Neurosciences*, 27(12), 712-719. https://doi.org/10.1016/j.tins.2004.10.007.

[28] Koedinger, K. R., & Corbett, A. T. (2006). *Cognitive tutors: Technology bringing learning sciences to the classroom. In The Cambridge Handbook of the Learning Sciences* (pp. 61-78). Cambridge University Press.

[29] Doshi-Velez, F., & Kim, B. (2017). Towards a rigorous science of interpretable machine learning. *arXiv preprint arXiv:1702.08608*. https://arxiv.org/abs/1702.08608.

[30] Frith, C. D., & Frith, U. (2006). *The neural basis of mentalizing. Neuron, 50*(4), 531-534. https://doi.org/10.1016/j.neuron.2006.05.001.

[31] Goldin-Meadow, S., & Beilock, S. L. (2010). Action's influence on thought: The case of gesture. *Perspectives on Psychological Science, 5*(6), 664-674. https://doi.org/10.1177/1745691610388764.

[32] Park, D. C., & Bischof, G. N. (2013). *The aging mind: Neuroplasticity in response to cognitive training. Dialogues in Clinical Neuroscience, 15*(1), 109-119.

[33] Squire, L. R., & Wixted, J. T. (2011). The cognitive neuroscience of human memory since H. M. *Annual Review of Neuroscience, 34*, 259-288. https://doi.org/10.1146/annurev-neuro-061010-113720.

[34] Winawer, J., Witthoft, N., Frank, M. C., Wu, L., Wade, A. R., & Boroditsky, L. (2007). Russian blues reveal effects of language on color discrimination. *Proceedings of the National Academy of Sciences, 104*(19), 7780-7785. https://doi.org/10.1073/pnas.0701644104.

[35] Metta, G., Sandini, G., Vernon, D., & Natale, L. (2008). The iCub humanoid robot: An open-systems platform for research in cognitive development. *Neural Networks, 21*(10), 1196-1211. https://doi.org/10.1016/j.neunet.2008.03.014.

[36] O'Neil, C. (2016). *Weapons of math destruction: How big data increases inequality and threatens democracy*. Crown Publishing Group.

[37] Bostrom, N. (2014). *Superintelligence: Paths, dangers, strategies*. Oxford University Press.

[38] Jurafsky, D., & Martin, J. H. (2020). *Speech and language processing: An introduction to natural language processing, computational linguistics, and speech recognition* (3rd ed.). Pearson.

[39] Devlin, J., Chang, M. W., Lee, K., & Toutanova, K. (2019). BERT: Pre-training of deep bidirectional transformers for language understanding. *arXiv preprint arXiv:1810.04805*. https://doi.org/10.48550/arXiv.1810.04805.

[40] Poldrack, R. A., Huckins, G., & Varoquaux, G. (2015). Establishment of best practices for evidence for prediction: A review. *JAMA Psychiatry, 75*(4), 387-394. https://doi.org/10.1001/jamapsychiatry.2017.3678.

[41] VanLehn, K. (2011). The relative effectiveness of human tutoring, intelligent tutoring systems, and other tutoring environments. *Educational Psychologist, 46*(4), 197-221. https://doi.org/10.1080/00461520.2011.611369.

[42] Brown, T. B., et al. (2020). Language models are few-shot learners. In *Advances in Neural Information Processing Systems* (pp. 1877-1901).

[43] Markram, H. (2012). The Human Brain Project. *Scientific American, 306*(6), 50-55.

[44] Shatte, A. B., Hutchinson, D. M., & Teague, S. J. (2019). Machine learning in mental health: A scoping review of methods and applications. *Psychological Medicine, 49*(9), 1426-1448.

[45] Sutton, R. S., & Barto, A. G. (2018). *Reinforcement learning: An introduction.* MIT Press.

[46] Bostrom, N., & Yudkowsky, E. (2014). The ethics of artificial intelligence. In *The Cambridge Handbook of Artificial Intelligence* (pp. 316-334). Cambridge University Press.

[47] Picard, R. W. (1997). *Affective computing*. MIT Press.

[48] Russell, S. J., & Norvig, P. (2020). *Artificial Intelligence: A Modern Approach* (4th ed.). Pearson.

[49] Sun, R. (2016). *Anatomy of the mind: Exploring psychological mechanisms and processes with the CLARION cognitive architecture.* Oxford University Press.

[50] Buolamwini, J., & Gebru, T. (2018). Gender shades: Intersectional accuracy disparities in commercial gender classification. *Proceedings of the 1st Conference on Fairness, Accountability, and Transparency.*

[51] Goodfellow, I., Pouget-Abadie, J., Mirza, M., Xu, B., Warde-Farley, D., Ozair, S., Courville, A., & Bengio, Y. (2014). Generative adversarial nets. *Advances in Neural Information Processing Systems, 27.*

[52] Gunning, D. (2017). Explainable artificial intelligence (XAI). *Defense Advanced Research Projects Agency (DARPA).*

[53] Parisi, G. I., Kemker, R., Part, J. L., Kanan, C., & Wermter, S. (2019). Continual lifelong learning with neural networks: A review. *Neural Networks, 113*, 54-71.

[54] Vinyals, O., & Le, Q. V. (2015). *A neural conversational model.* arXiv preprint arXiv:*1506.05869.*
[55] Wolpaw, J. R., & Wolpaw, E. W. (Eds.). (2012). *Brain-computer interfaces: Principles and practice.* Oxford University Press.
[56] Krizhevsky, A., Sutskever, I., & Hinton, G. E. (2012). ImageNet classification with deep convolutional neural networks. *Advances in Neural Information Processing Systems, 25.*
[57] Mnih, V., Kavukcuoglu, K., Silver, D., Graves, A., Antonoglou, I., Wierstra, D., & Riedmiller, M. (2015). Human-level control through deep reinforcement learning. *Nature, 518*(7540), 529-533.
[58] Stober, S., Sternin, A., Owen, A. M., & Grahn, J. A. (2014). Deep feature learning for EEG recordings. *2014 22nd International Conference on Pattern Recognition,* 1750-1755.
[59] Cadwalladr, C., & Graham-Harrison, E. (2018). Revealed: 50 million Facebook profiles harvested for Cambridge Analytica in major data breach. *The Guardian.* Retrieved from https://www.theguardian.com/news/2018/mar/17/cambridge-analytica-facebook-influence-us-election.
[60] Creemers, R. (2018). China's social credit system: An evolving practice of control. *SSRN Electronic Journal.* https://doi.org/10.2139/ssrn.3175792.
[61] Manyika, J., Lund, S., Chui, M., Bughin, J., Woetzel, J., Batra, P. Sanghvi, S. (2017). *Jobs lost, jobs gained: Workforce transitions in a time of automation.*
[62] Schiff, D., Borenstein, J., Biddle, J., & Laas, K. (2020). AI ethics in the public, private, and NGO sectors: A review of a global document collection. *Science and Engineering Ethics, 26*, 2073-2098.
[63] Atzori, L., Iera, A., & Morabito, G. (2010). The Internet of Things: A survey. *Computer Networks, 54*(15), 2787–2805.
[64] Biamonte, J., Wittek, P., Pancotti, N., Rebentrost, P., Wiebe, N., & Lloyd, S. (2017). Quantum machine learning. *Nature, 549*(7671), 195–202.
[65] Brynjolfsson, E., & McAfee, A. (2014). *The second machine age: Work, progress, and prosperity in a time of brilliant technologies.* W. W. Norton & Company.
[66] Calvo, R. A., D'Mello, S., Gratch, J., & Kappas, A. (2019). *The Oxford handbook of affective computing.* Oxford University Press.
[67] Floridi, L., & Cowls, J. (2019). A unified framework of five principles for AI in society. *Harvard Data Science Review, 1*(1).
[68] Mak, K. K., & Pichika, M. R. (2019). Artificial intelligence in drug development: Present status and future prospects. *Drug Discovery Today, 24*(3), 773–780.
[69] Silver, D., Huang, A., Maddison, C. J., Guez, A., Sifre, L., Van Den Driessche, G., & Hassabis, D. (2016). Mastering the game of Go with deep neural networks and tree search. *Nature, 529*(7587), 484–489.

Chapter 2

The Evolution of Cognitive Computing: Foundational Principles, Applications, and Future Directions

Jagadeshwari Puttanapura[1]
C. Kishor Kumar Reddy[1]
T. Monika Singh[1,*]
and Srinath Doss[2]
[1]Department of Computer Science and Engineering,
Stanley College of Engineering and Technology for Women, India
[2]Faculty of Engineering and Technology, Botho University, Botswana

Abstract

Cognitive computing is a new framework for the development and implementation of intelligent systems; it advances artificial intelligence and attempts to replicate human cognition. This chapter examines cognitive computing from its foundational aspects such as natural language processing, machine learning, and human-computer interaction through the ways all these technologies work together to enhance decision-making processes. This chapter has been able to demonstrate the transformative impact of cognitive computing on critical industries through analyses of applications in healthcare, finance, education, and autonomous systems. The discussion thus addresses both the ethical and scalability challenges and technical limitations that need to be overcome for cognitive systems to unravel their full potential. In conclusion, a series of conclusions points to future research directions while

---

* Corresponding Author's Email: thakursinghmonika@gmail.com

In: Building Intelligent Systems for the Future
Editors: Anamika Ahirwar, Neelesh Jain and Sumitha Elayaperumal
ISBN: 979-8-90134-050-9

underlining the highly promising role cognitive systems will take in driving innovation while adhering to ethics. This overview will give readers the body of knowledge to come aboard the rapidly advancing field of cognitive computing.

Keywords: cognitive computing, natural language processing, machine learning, decision-making, cognitive architectures, deep learning, ethical considerations, data privacy

1. Introduction to Cognitive Computing

Cognitive computing is the next-level advancement paradigm that tries to mimic the human thinking process in a computer model. In this end, the prime objective is to design a system that interacts, reasons, and understands data, just like a human. Cognitive computing systems do not function according to rules and logic like typical computing systems; they further understand data through learning and constant improvement techniques, involving complex algorithms and data processing. The approach is applied in health, finance, and educational institutions for tasks that call for adaptive decision-making, pattern recognition, and predictive analytics [1].

Cognitive computing systems consist of a group of core elements, such as machine learning, natural language processing, and deep learning algorithms, all integrating to process and interpret tremendous volumes of unstructured data. It is intended to understand and interact with human beings naturally, which may be done more intuitively between human and computer systems. They work through constructing "knowledge graphs" that link concepts and information from a wide variety of sources, which allows the system to make informed decisions or predictions [2] Cognitive computing marks an important advance in artificial intelligence: the systems can think, reason, and understand in ways very similar to humans.

This can be seen in the following Figure 2.1, which displays the hierarchy that exists between the fields of artificial intelligence and cognitive computing. The outermost layer is Cognitive Computing. This includes AI technologies. Artificial Intelligence is situated within it since human behavior is mimicked, and broad applications are covered through it. Machine Learning is situated inside AI; algorithms are enabled with dynamic learning without any human guide. Deep learning is just the name for an extendable subset: the Neural Network with deeply nested learning, a concept borrowed from the architecture of the human brain as the basis for advanced techniques of learning. Deep Learning is a special subset that trains large models to operate with complicated patterns independently. Each layer shows a progression from broad cognitive tasks to highly specific and self-learning systems.

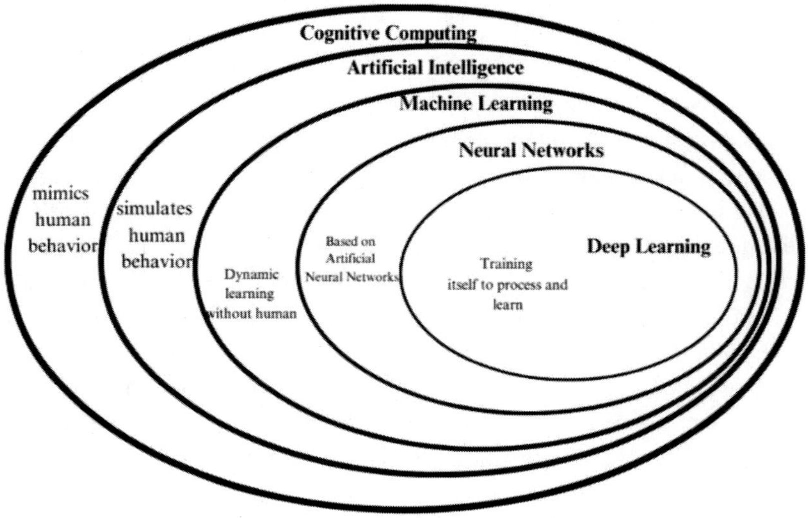

Figure 2.1. Hierarchy of Cognitive Computing.

Cognitive computing, in essence, is an interdisciplinary approach combining AI, cognitive science, and machine learning for building systems that model human intelligence and decision making. Cognitive systems differ fundamentally from the traditional approach of computers in applying strictly programmed logic; they learn from interactions with input and process information in a layered, hierarchical form by using neural networks and high-level machine learning models. With this change of strategy from rule-based to learning-based, such systems would be performing complex tasks much more like humans do-natural language understanding, decision-making under uncertainty, emotional perception, and many more. These systems not only analyse huge volumes of data but also prioritize, process, and organize it in a way that enables them to make sophisticated predictions and recommendations. For example, a cognitive computing system in the healthcare domain might analyse patient records, medical literature, and genetic data to make a diagnosis or suggest a treatment plan. Cognitive systems often employ what is known as "contextual awareness"; they take into account the specifics of a given scenario to provide meaningful insights, which is highly valued in areas such as customer service wherein understanding context is crucial for proper aid.

1.1. Difference Between Traditional Computing and Cognitive Computing

Traditional computing systems are primarily deterministic, based on pre-defined rules, algorithms, and explicit logic a human has programmed. They work linearly and predictably; therefore, they are excellent for routine tasks where parameters are well defined but fall short in situations that call for context interpretation and flexibility. A traditional computer, for instance, can calculate and remember data but cannot read the context or "learn" from new data. Contrasted to this, cognitive computing systems are designed to interpret data with a high degree of flexibility. They tend to adjust their responses with knowledge accumulated and environmental factors [3]. Another key difference is in how the system processes unstructured data, for example, text, images, and sounds. Traditional systems are structured around relational databases and clear hierarchies of data; they do not handle well inputs that are not standardized. Cognitive systems, by contrast, use machine learning and neural networks to interpret unstructured data, which are learned from large, heterogeneous datasets. This is what makes such systems able of execute more challenging tasks, such as processing natural language and images, which cannot be approached with traditional computing architectures [4].

Table 2.1 summarizes the differences between cognitive and traditional computing, like cognitive computing being adaptive as well as learning, taking care of unstructured data, and making smarter decisions. Unlike traditional systems based on rules, cognitive computing is capable of dynamic interactions, context-dependent, that are important for complex applications such as diagnostics and personal recommendations.

Table 2.1. Comparison of traditional computing vs. cognitive computing

Aspect	Traditional Computing	Cognitive Computing
Processing Approach	Deterministic; follows predefined rules and logic	Adaptive; learns from data and adapts based on new inputs
Learning Capability	Static; requires manual updates for new rules or changes	Dynamic; uses machine learning to improve and update autonomously
Data Type Compatibility	Primarily structured data in predefined formats	Handles both structured and unstructured data (text, images, audio)
Interaction with Users	Limited to command-based interaction; lacks natural communication capabilities	Natural interactions using NLP, enabling human-like communication
Decision-Making	Rule-based and predictable, with minimal contextual awareness	Context-aware; can make decisions based on environment and situation
Adaptability	Low adaptability; cannot adjust responses based on real-time data	Highly adaptable; learns and evolves over time based on data exposure
Core Technologies	Relational databases, algorithmic logic, fixed programming structures	Neural networks, deep learning, natural language processing
Examples of Use	Standard calculations, data storage, automation of repetitive tasks	Advanced tasks like diagnostics, risk assessment, personalized recommendations

1.2. Historical Evolution and Current Landscape

The idea of cognitive computing traces its roots back to the early days of the development of artificial intelligence and cognitive science, which tried to make machines think like a human being. Early models of cognition were influenced by the organization of brain and neural pathways but were limited by the computing power and data available at the time. This last decade, breakthroughs in the domain of machine learning and big data, alongside significant advances in cloud computing, finally have accelerated the maturation curve of cognitive computing. Well-known systems such as IBM's Watson, that went on to compete successfully with human players on the well-known quiz show Jeopardy!, demonstrate cognitive abilities that allow them to operate and converse in natural, human language, highlighting quite the amount of ground travelled from rule-based AI backends [5].

Today, cognitive computing pervades different sectors; they help develop fields, which include health and serve it by making diagnostic prescriptions to diseases and financial aspects wherein it increases risk appraisal for better decision-making. Also, the innovation brought with deep learning and neural network has improved cognitive systems towards complex activities, especially about image and speech recognition capabilities [6]. This evolution represents a complete phase shift from merely programming into enabling the computer machine learning from data, making this sector of cognitive computing really integral to the rapidly progressive scope of artificial intelligence.

By the 1990s and early 2000s, cognitive computing gained pace as scientists came up with new techniques in order to mimic the workings of human thought. As the computing power was at a very low level, along with a dearth of comprehensive datasets, these applications could only go on to work on extremely primitive tasks, such as speech recognition and simple language processing. Nevertheless, improvements in data storage, computing ability, and internet connectivity had a boom effect, creating a transition. It transformed the field, especially due to the development of cloud computing and the accessibility of big data resources, since it allowed cognitive systems to process and learn from much bigger, more diverse datasets than ever before. The same era of interdisciplinary research brought together insights from neuroscience, psychology, and computer science to build systems that better emulate human reasoning and perception.

Today, cognitive computing serves as an anchor to the modern definition of AI: healthcare diagnostics, financial modeling, smart cities, and autonomous systems. All these are continuously updated, and so there is continuous enhancement in addressing practical issues-like real-time decision-making improvement and improving personal user experience. Cognitive computing research by major tech firms and institutions is pouring heavily into advancing what the system can achieve. The current landscape also emphasizes ethical considerations, such as privacy and fairness, as cognitive computing systems increasingly influence everyday life. Thus, when driving continuous innovation, cognitive computing is all set to bring new, intelligent solutions in various sectors, making it an indispensable component of AI's future trajectory.

2. Core Components of Cognitive Computing Systems

Cognitive computing systems integrate the several advanced components that compose them into an engineering endeavor designed to simulate a model of human thought, but this model simulates both processing and analysis patterns within massive data quantities with cognitive abilities in elements that could be part of its model, such as Natural Language Processing (NLP), Machine Learning (ML) models, Knowledge Representation and Reasoning (KR&R), and Human-Computer Interaction (HCI). All components contribute to a harmonious system where data can be understood, analysed, reasoned upon, and presented in human-compatible ways. Using these technologies, cognitive systems can provide insights, make informed predictions, and continually learn from new data with minimal human intervention. Its key parts work together in tandem to develop powerful cognitive models. NLP allows a system to understand human language as an essential tool in enabling interaction with users in the natural way. The use of Machine Learning algorithms helps improve the ability to make decisions by allowing such systems to learn from experience, enabling these systems to build expertise through time. KR&R stores and processes information logically and enables reasoning and inferential capabilities that allow one to mimic human problem solving. Finally, HCI provides access, intuitive, and responsive systems to support effective, real-time interactions. Taken together, these elements form a foundation for developing cognitive systems that can be applied in healthcare, finance, education, and more - transforming the industrial practice and enabling smarter, more adaptive computing.

2.1. Natural Language Processing (NLP)

Natural Language Processing refers to a field in cognitive computing that aims to endow machines with the capabilities of Comprehending, analysing, and producing human language. It acts as a means to bridge human and machine interaction by allowing systems to analyse texts, spoken words, and context. NLP empowers systems to perform jobs like language translation, sentiment analysis, text summarization, and conversational interfaces [7]. Main NLP methods: Tokenization, or text broken down into words or phrases; syntax and grammar analysis; and semantic understanding to allow machines to extract insights from human language.

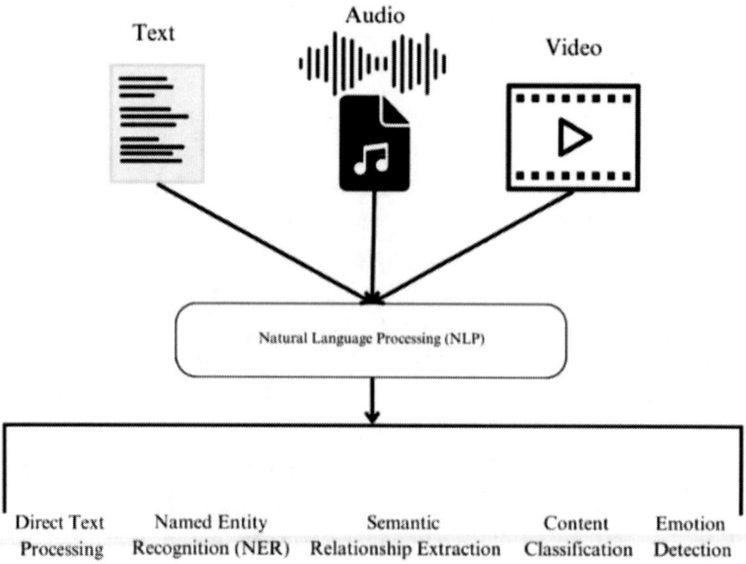

Figure 2.2. Multi-Modal Natural Language Processing Workflow.

Flowchart shown in Figure 2.2 illustrates NLP and how it addresses all these media types: Text, Audio, Video. All of these media types feed into the NLP system and then process data for those different analytical tasks. The core functions of NLP shown are Direct Text Processing, Named Entity Recognition (NER), Semantic Relationship Extraction, Content Classification, and Emotion Detection. Every function of NLP constitutes a module that takes information from data and provides valuable insights that applications like information retrieval take and bring us onto larger platforms for applications such as sentiment analysis and personalized content recommendations.

- *Applications:* NLP applications are virtual assistants like Siri and Alexa, customer service chatbots, and recommendation systems that analyse text reviews.
- *Major challenges*: Ambiguity management in language, dealing with context and tone, and differences in regional or cultural use of language.
- *Machine Translation and Language Models*: NLP relies on machine learning models, such as the Transformer-based models BERT and GPT, for text prediction, machine translation, and summarization tasks.

2.2. Machine Learning Models and Algorithms

Machine learning algorithms are one of the main components for cognitive computing as they can be programmed to learn about the data and improve accordingly without being explicitly programmed. Huge sets of data are subjected to machine learning processes, so that patterns can be established to make decisions and predict emerging trends in cognitive systems [8]. The three major categories of learning methodologies are Supervised learning, unsupervised learning, and Reinforcement learning. In the case of supervised learning, the model is trained on labeled data, while unsupervised learning is applied when no labels are there, but hidden patterns are discovered. In the case of reinforcement learning, agents learn by using rewards or penalties.

- *Supervised and Unsupervised Learning*: In supervised learning, the algorithm predicts the output with the help of labeled datasets. In the case of unsupervised learning, work is done with unlabeled data, which helps in discovering inherent patterns.
- *Reinforcement Learning*: It applies to applications such as self-driving, robotics, wherein the models learn the sequence of decisions that is needed in maximizing cumulative rewards.
- *Deep Learning*: It represents a subset of ML whereby systems use neural networks involving multiple layers to enable complex processes like image and speech recognition.

2.3. Knowledge Representation and Reasoning

Knowledge Representation and Reasoning (KR&R) are the ways in which information is structured for a computer to interpret and apply it in making logical inferences [9]. KR&R is the basis of decisions within cognitive computing systems because they enable machines to solve difficult problems by simulating human-like reasoning processes. Ontology is the relationship between concepts, logic represents rules and inference, and semantic networks-all help represent human knowledge in structured forms.

- *Ontology and Taxonomy:* Ontologies are structured knowledge representations, and taxonomies help in categorizing the information in a hierarchical structure, like that of a knowledge graph.
- *Logic-Based Reasoning*: Cognitive systems infer logically, which involves either deductive, inductive, or abductive logic used in reaching conclusions or decisions.
- *Case-Based Reasoning:* Using previous cases or instances to invoke them, it becomes possible for cognitive systems to generate solutions for new and novel, similar situations: a system that learns through experience.

2.4. Human-Computer Interaction in Cognitive Systems

This would be within the concept of Human-Computer Interaction (HCI) for cognitive computing, involving making the interfaces intuitive and responsive for natural humanmachine interaction to ensure users correctly interact with machines. Under this part, it should include a user-centered approach, including natural language understanding and adaptive interfaces to permit the machine to comprehend emotions, gestures, and facial expressions toward appropriate reactions. HCI permits improved decision-making through personalized experiences enhanced by users.

- *User-Centered Design*: It relies on the needs of the user and usability. It simplifies the interaction of cognitive systems and adaptability to personalized features.

- *Adaptive Interfaces*: interfaces adjust in real-time to the users, learning through interactions to suggest, automate routine work, and increase involvement.
- *Multimodal interaction:* Cognitive systems are combining modes of input -voice, gesture, touch-to make for richer, more immersive experiences. Applications here would be things like virtual and augmented reality.

3. Architectures and Frameworks for Cognitive Systems

The Architectures and frameworks for Cognitive Systems are structured designs intended to facilitate the development of intelligent, human-like processing in machines. Such a framework provides an organizational structure to cognitive processes such as perception, learning, or decision-making in inter-linked modules. While ACT-R as well as SOAR-based cognitive architectures rely on symbolic processing and logic, connectionist architectures such as neural networks actually function like the brain-a pattern recognizer. Hybrid frameworks combine aspects of the above approaches to allow high-level reasoning as well as adaptive learning. For the cognitive systems, specialized hardware, such as GPUs, TPUs; and also, software frameworks that can be used for extensive data processing and model training, for example, TensorFlow and PyTorch must be utilized. This design and technology combination allows natural learning, adaptation, and interaction of cognitive systems with complex environments.

3.1. Cognitive Architectures Overview

Cognitive architectures are the fundamental models that describe the structure and processing mechanisms of intelligent systems, inspired by the cognitive processes of the human mind. These architectures are a framework for building perception, reasoning, learning, and decision-making systems. Cognitive architectures can be symbolic, like ACT-R (Adaptive Control of Thought-Rational), or connectionist, as in neural network-based approaches. These frameworks are to engineer systems that do not merely perform tasks but understand them and learn new challenges to be tackled in a very human-like manner [10].

- *Symbolic Architectures:* In this, the best known is ACT-R, built upon rules and a logic-based structure that does tasks by a matched pattern with the stored rules.
- *Connectionist Architectures*: Connectionist architectures are like neural networks that propose weighted connections to simulate the learning processes. Most of the machine learning models are based on these.
- *Emergent Architectures:* These are architectures that combine both symbolic and neural elements, so they are designed to change dynamically as they process information, making them suitable for complex environments.

Cognitive architectures are typically developed with modules representing perception, motor functions, memory, and reasoning, and usually along with algorithms for memory encoding and retrieval, problem-solving, or adaptive learning in such a way that the system can evolve as it experiences.

3.2. Hybrid Systems Combining AI and Cognitive Approaches

Hybrid systems are cognitive frameworks that integrate AI and cognitive science methodologies to take advantage of the strengths of both. These hybrid systems can be symbolic AI's logic-based rules combined with machine learning's adaptive models to provide robust, flexible architectures. Hybrid systems find their utility in places where reasoning is combined with pattern recognition, such as in autonomous driving and personalized healthcare. They balance accuracy with flexibility and the decision-making frameworks of traditional AI along with the adaptability of neural networks in dynamic environments.

- A typical *Dual-processing model* is most clearly demonstrated in hybrid models where one module processes some form of structured knowledge; in the symbolic case, it might be a body of abstract concepts, the connectionist, a matrix of associative links between simple units.
- *Algorithmic Integration*: Some use rule-based reasoning for strategic decisions and machine learning algorithms to adjust in real-time.

Thus, this integration will give a multi-layered problem-solving approach.

Applications include Hybrid systems in applications where high adaptability may be required, such as virtual assistants, healthcare diagnostics, and predictive maintenance applications in industrial settings.

An example of a hybrid approach is symbolic reasoning to enforce high-level policy adherence in a self-driving car and deep learning for object recognition and environment perception. This arrangement allows the system to make both long-term and real-time decisions efficiently.

3.3. Software and Hardware Requirements

Systems are very dependent on a specific configuration in software and hardware to provide complex computation, and fast real-time data processing with a large handle of enormous amounts of data. Even cognitive systems use HPC support to manage the large demands produced by cognitive models, usually, for highly demanding jobs such as a natural-language-processing algorithm or one recognizing image in a snap. Examples include specific AI libraries for NLP and machine learning together with frameworks like TensorFlow or PyTorch, the basic tools for development and later deployment of cognitive applications.

- *Software:* Development frameworks. Examples include TensorFlow or PyTorch, containing such vital libraries as building models on neural networks, in addition to various types of machine learning models. Likewise, NLP support relates to language tasks of that kind, while supported with cognitive modeling are, in addition, rules-based architectures for, e.g. SOAR.
- *Hardware:* To train deep learning models, high-performance GPUs or dedicated TPUs are required. Specialized processors may be used for real-time data processing within cognitive systems that are deployed in robotics or IoT devices.

For this reason, cognitive systems would also need to have large memory and storage capacity to process big data and fast data retrieval. The hardware and software components selected should align with the applications intended for the system, balancing processing power with energy efficiency and scalability.

Table 2.2 captures the main ingredients of architectures that comprise the cognitive systems, including the cognitive frameworks, hybrid approaches to AI, and the most pertinent software and hardware requirements for efficient development as well as effective operation of cognitive computing applications.

Table 2.2. Comprehensive overview of cognitive system architectures and frameworks

Subtopic	Description	Key Components/Technologies
Cognitive Architectures Overview	Models simulating human cognitive processes, allowing machines to mimic reasoning, learning, and problem-solving.	Memory systems, learning mechanisms, inference engines
Hybrid Systems Combining AI and Cognitive Approaches	Blending traditional AI techniques with cognitive computing principles for improved performance and adaptability.	Rule-based systems, neural networks, symbolic reasoning
Software Requirements	Advanced programming languages and frameworks needed to build cognitive systems.	Python, TensorFlow, Keras
Hardware Requirements	Computational resources required for efficient cognitive system operation, including CPUs, GPUs, and specialized hardware.	High-performance CPUs/GPUs, FPGAs, TPUs
System Integration	Ensuring software and hardware work together effectively to achieve optimal performance in cognitive tasks.	Cloud computing, data storage solutions, integration frameworks

4. Key Techniques and Algorithms

The Key Techniques and Algorithms lay the basis for creating an intelligent system that is perceptive, learns, and interacts with the world in pretty much the same way that a human's mind would. Cognitive computing systems process massive data sets, recognize complicated patterns, and make experience-based or contextual decisions with machine learning models, natural language processing, deep learning, and other specialized techniques incorporated. These techniques enable systems to work dynamically with their users and environments as they influence entire industries like healthcare, finance, education, and customer services. Cognitive computing has learning approaches: supervised, unsupervised, and reinforcement learning, which enable machines to learn without human interference and optimize their performance. Neural networks and deep learning architectures enable systems to solve complex tasks like image recognition and language comprehension. NLP techniques help systems interpret human language; case-based reasoning and decision-making models offer structured approaches to dealing with complex real-world problems. Together, these constitute the core of state-of-the-art AI applications in realizing the potential of cognitive computing to analyse data, develop insights, and arrive at informed decisions.

4.1. Machine Learning Techniques in Cognitive Computing

Machine learning is the backbone of cognitive computing because it enables a system to improve automatically through experience gained by itself over time, with no task or intervention of a human in sight. The process of ML allows complex tasks such as visual data analysis, natural language understanding, and future trend prediction among others to be carried out by cognitive systems. All these are learned from extensive datasets using statistical methods and algorithms with minimal human input. Enhancing the capability of a machine to process information, to identify patterns, and then decide in the same way that a human would but far more rapidly and accurately is the core aim. Methods used in ML in cognitive computing include classification, regression, clustering, and association [11].

Each method provides advantages in its application; for instance, it can group data without known labels based on similarities so that hidden patterns are easier to discover. The method of dimensionality reduction takes data and simplifies the complexity while keeping key features of the information; as a result, data may be processed much more efficiently, and better results might be achieved in dealing with complex datasets. Collectively, these techniques lay down the foundation for the specialization of applications ranging from speech recognition to fraud detection.

4.2. Supervised, Unsupervised, and Reinforcement Learning

Supervised learning forms the base of predictive modeling, in which algorithms examine the historical labeled data and will predict the future. In this method, a model can be trained on data by associating each input with some correct output so it could learn the mapping from the input to the output. Some of the applications that one can use in predictive models include stock price forecasts and weather prediction, down to demand forecasting in supply chains. It would significantly help organizations predict trends or make data-driven decisions using the model's ability to generalize from the historical patterns, thus improving efficiency besides cutting costs.

Supervised learning is most effective when the task at hand needs to be highly accurate. That is, for quality control in manufacturing or assessing the risk in finance, a situation where accuracy is most essential. With labeled examples of past outcomes, it can predict outcomes for new data that have not yet been seen with high reliability. Although the dependence on labeled data in supervised learning is resource-intensive, its requirement is essential for those applications where accuracy and dependability are paramount.

Figure 2.3 is a diagrammatic comparison of Supervised Learning and Unsupervised Learning. The model of supervised learning is seen with its input and output carrying an example of the mechanism of supervised learning by training the model using labeled data then learns to associate specific features and learning those to do given labels. Training enables it to predict the labels for new data that has not been labeled; this is the output that categorizes data into the training labels as shown in the output. On the contrary, unsupervised learning learns from unlabeled data that aims to discover patterns or clusters in that data. The model groups similar data points based on their intrinsic features; no predefined labels are used for classification. This comparison illustrates the difference between how supervised learning is crafted towards point-specific, label-based prediction and the way unsupervised learning tries to capture structure in basically unlabeled data.

Unsupervised learning deals with unlabeled data, enabling systems to discover hidden structures and patterns in datasets without predefined labels. This kind of learning is particularly valuable for discovering inherent groupings or similarities in data and, therefore, is suited to applications like customer segmentation, where users with similar behaviors or characteristics are grouped. Clustering and dimensionality reduction are some of the common techniques in unsupervised learning because they can reduce complexity and reveal relationships between data, which otherwise would remain hidden, thereby providing insight that can support tasks like recommendation systems and exploratory data analysis.

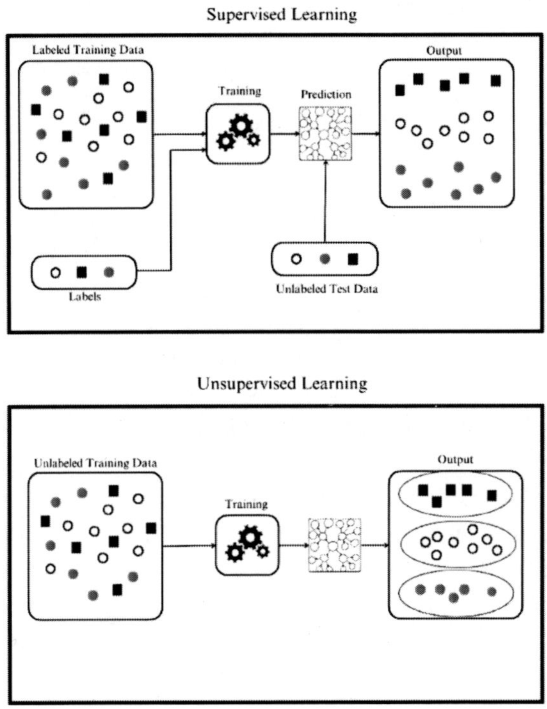

Figure 2.3. Comparison of Supervised and Unsupervised Learning Processes.

Another important application area is anomaly detection through unsupervised learning that seeks to find unusual patterns and outliers that may indicate the existence of a fault like fraud in financial transactions or defects in manufacturing processes. The field where unsupervised learning works well for business insight into trends and customer preferences is market analysis. Such learning does not predict with the same kind of accuracy that supervised learning might predict. However, such a discovery is invaluable to what could lead to the best possible decision in situations that are uncertain or exploratory [12].

Reinforcement learning (RL) forms quite an exceptional paradigm, which allows an agent to learn with real-life examples by communicating with the surroundings and receiving either reinforcements or consequences for what it has done. In contrast to supervised and unsupervised learning, RL is geared toward sequential decision-making for long-term objectives. The system continuously learns optimal strategies over time for maximum cumulative rewards, so RL is particularly useful in complex, dynamic environments like autonomous driving, robotics, and gaming.

In reinforcement learning, the agent tries out different actions and receives feedback, allowing it to adjust its strategy based on outcomes. For example, in a game, the agent may learn to avoid certain actions that result in penalties and concentrate on moves that increase its score. The ability of RL to handle long-term planning and dynamic adaptation allows cognitive systems to excel in applications where flexible, real-time decision-making is required. This makes RL well suited for systems that must perform well in changing environments while continually improving their strategy.

4.3. Neural Networks and Deep Learning

Neural networks function on the design of the human brain and thus, made up of so many nodes interconnected with each other, also called as neurons, whose whole processing relies on connection weight. These systems confer the ability on cognitive systems to perform functions ranging from image recognition through language translation to complex patterns of recognition. Deep Learning is a branch of machine learning that uses extremely deep multilayer networks in processing data of huge size to discover complex patterns, or simple insights that are not coded explicitly. Recurrent Neural Networks (RNNs) and Convolutional Neural Networks (CNNs) are perhaps two of the most celebrated models in the deep learning technique [13].

CNNs are especially appropriate for image and video processing since they can capture spatial hierarchies in data. They are, therefore, very critical in facial recognition, medical imaging, and object detection. RNNs are designed for sequential data. They are widely used in NLP applications, including speech recognition and language translation. Scalability will thus open the scope for complex representations in cognitive systems, pushing boundaries even further beyond what is possible with AI today-from autonomous vehicles to personalized recommendations.

4.4. NLP Techniques for Cognitive Systems

NLP techniques are at the core of enabling cognitive systems to interpret and generate human language, thus allowing machines to interact with users seamlessly. Common techniques include tokenization, stemming and lemmatization, and part-of-speech tagging. These steps enable systems to understand and process language more accurately in applications such as chatbots, sentiment analysis, and translation tools [14].

Some new approaches in NLP used sophisticated transformer-based models, which utilize attentions to capture the essence of relationships between words of a sequence. BERT, GPT, and its variants are some of these models that have achieved amazing results in question answering and text summarization, thereby being used for content creation. NLP has seen enormous maturity lately, allowing cognitive systems to understand context, nuance, and tone in humans' language, which benefits applications in customer service and even healthcare diagnostics and virtual assistance applications.

4.5. Case-Based Reasoning and Decision-Making

Case-based reasoning (CBR) is a technique for solving problems where cognitive systems refer to solutions for past similar cases to solve new problems. It simulates human decision-making, where the decisions today are informed by yesterday's experiences. CBR systems have a case library of past examples retrieved and adapted when a similar new problem arises. For instance, a customer service bot that uses CBR can be able to give solutions that are based on historical interactions to enhance the accuracy of the response.

The second dimension of decision-making is predictive modeling, where the algorithms will predict the outcome based on what they could learn from these data patterns. [15] Algorithms used in this area include the decision tree, Bayesian network, and the rule-based system. Where very complex domains involve choices under uncertainty such as in finance or healthcare, where there must be a decision, then the cognitive system does weigh in on a number of different perspectives and then makes a best recommendation to the individual. The combination of CBR and decision-making algorithms facilitates the dynamic change of cognitive computing systems in response to new situations, hence making them very effective for environments where timely, data-driven decisions are crucial.

5. Applications Across Industries

Cognitive computing is transforming various sectors with intelligent and data-driven solutions designed for particular needs within each domain. By imitating human thinking and learning from massive data, cognitive systems improve decision-making, simplify complex tasks, and provide personal experiences. The applications of cognitive computing are intended to meet very critical challenges such as diagnostic improvement and personalized treatment in healthcare and fraud detection with the best risk management processes in finance. On top of this, cognitive systems revolutionize education with adaptive learning environments, improve transportation through self-driving vehicles, and foster productivity across various disciplines. Flexibility and scalability make it an essential tool for innovation in the digital age.

Table 2.3. Applications of cognitive computing across industries

Industry	Cognitive Computing Application	Benefits	Challenges
Healthcare	Medical diagnostics, personalized treatment, predictive analytics	Enhanced diagnostic accuracy, personalized patient care, early detection of health risks	Privacy concerns, data quality and availability, regulatory compliance
Finance	Risk assessment, fraud detection, automated trading	Improved risk management, reduced fraud, optimized trading strategies	Data security, model interpretability, ethical concerns in decision-making
Education	Adaptive learning systems, virtual tutoring, administrative automation	Personalized learning experiences, increased accessibility, reduced administrative workload	High cost of implementation, data privacy issues, integration with existing systems
Transportation	Autonomous vehicles, traffic management, predictive maintenance	Reduced accidents, efficient traffic flow, cost savings in maintenance	Safety concerns, regulatory challenges, high initial investment

Table 2.3 indicates some key applications of cognitive computing in those industries where healthcare, finance, education, and transportation stand. It then lists specific applications, which bring benefits, and the challenges each industry has in adopting cognitive computing technologies.

5.1. Cognitive Computing in Healthcare

In health care, cognitive computing will be that which changes diagnostic procedures and treatment as well as in personalized medicine. In other words, analyses are given to patient data, literature, and records. Accurate assessments, henceforth, are developed when healthcare professionals use machine learning algorithms or NLP algorithms and, in some instances, even image recognition algorithms. A notable example of the operation of cognitive computing in the way it scans the images produced in radiology for anomalous features suggesting early conditions of diseases, such as cancer or cardiac problems [16]. This capability improves speed to diagnosis and accuracy with minimal risk of human errors in diagnosing and can actually provide interventions sooner and in more effective ways. In personalized medicine, cognitive systems evaluate large sets of data to work out treatment plans uniquely tailored to an individual's genetic information, lifestyle, and medical history. This means analysing their genetic profiles to predict ways in which patients would be likely to respond to particular drugs, thus minimizing trial and error with treatments and leading to better patient outcomes.

Besides, cognitive systems support predictive healthcare. Patterns in a patient's data can help identify potential health risks so that proactive care can be implemented. For example, IBM Watson has shown the potential of cognitive computing in recommending cancer treatment plans based on a patient's unique profile. Clinical decision support also advances with cognitive computing to aggregate data from a large number of sources, electronic health records, and devices that monitor patients in real-time. Doctors can then review the entire history of their patients in one glance to make more informed decisions. The integration with wearable health devices allows for the tracking of vital signs, sending alerts when readings deviate from the norm, and remote patient care through cognitive systems. These inventions make healthcare more accessible, efficient, and personalized.

In diagnostics and personalized medicine, [17] cognitive computing has taken center stage because the end result is not only to make accurate diagnoses but also to treat a patient differently. Cognitive systems analyse data from diagnostic tools like CT scans, MRIs, and blood tests in order to diagnose diseases at an early stage. These systems can identify patterns that are hard for a human doctor to spot, thereby improving diagnostic accuracy. For instance, the image recognition models trained on large datasets could identify anomalies in X-rays, contributing to improvements in disease diagnosis accuracy. Cognitive computing tailors treatment according to the specific genetic and lifestyle characteristics of an individual patient. The potential reaction of a patient toward several drugs can be well predicted by assessing the patient's genetic data through these cognitive systems. The effective medication and dosage could, therefore, be chosen as per the patient's response prediction. Cognitive computing systems are highly advanced and can follow through on rapidly evolving medical research. New or experimental treatments suited to specific patient profiles are, therefore, suggested to patients. This is actually an approach that reduces additional medical costs while helping avoid ineffective treatments to improve patient outcomes.

5.2. Financial Sector Applications

The cognitive systems in the financial sector allow better efficiency and accuracy and enable customer support. These are automated by cognitive systems such as support for customers, loan processing, and investment analysis in finance. Customers can find answers to any query via natural language processing that may be employed by the cognitive system of finance, resulting in improvement in the overall user experience and waiting times. This is further helped by sophisticated data analysis offered by these systems in regard to trending and predictive insight, ensuring that the firms can well manage their investments, rates of interest, and even market fluctuations.

Some of the major applications in the financial sector include risk assessment and fraud detection. These systems process millions of sets of transactional data; thereby making it easier to identify an anomaly that can signify possible fraud. For example, with the system equipped through machine learning capabilities, the abnormal spending done using the credit card can be highlighted. This triggers an instant alert system which aids fraud prevention. Other data based on historical cases help ensure accurate lending decisions, considering reduced defaults, as their credibility is assessed beforehand when assessing the creditworthiness of potential loan applicants [18]. Regulatory compliance is one of the most significant issues for financial institutions. Cognitive computing helps firms stay updated on changing regulations by automating data collection and analysis. It, therefore, minimizes the risk of non-compliance. It can also analyse the sentiment in news articles, social media, and financial reports, which helps portfolio managers plan strategically by determining market sentiments and making informed investment recommendations.

Historical financial data are considered in the performance of risk assessments by cognitive systems about a certain individual or company and their creditworthiness. Based on factors, including the history of payments and the amount in use within their credit facility, credit market conditions also help in computing the risk of loan or mortgage default. The potential financial risks that may occur are minimal since credit is issued responsibly by institutions. It incorporates advanced cognitive models, even with sentiment analysis from news and social media, so the risk manager can measure the market sentiment and take proactive financial decisions [19].

5.3. Education and Smart Learning Environments

Cognitive computing has introduced smart learning environments, where systems personalize the educational experience based on student's needs, learning styles, and progress. [20] Adaptive learning platforms leverage machine learning algorithms to evaluate student performance data and adjust content delivery in real-time. These systems recommend learning materials, exercises, and assessments tailored to each student, promoting better engagement and retention. For example, a cognitive system might adjust a math lesson's difficulty based on the student's quiz scores, ensuring the material is challenging yet manageable. Next application is language learning. NLP-based cognitive systems provide learners with instant pronunciation, grammar, and vocabulary feedback. Virtual tutors can utilize such systems by simulating conversational practice so that language skills would be developed naturally by students. Cognitive computing also helps in analysing the data of classrooms and identifies struggling students and proposes interventions for such students, so they are given the proper support needed, and the environment of learning is made to be more inclusive.

Administrative tasks such as grading, enrolment, and scheduling are streamlined through cognitive computing. Automated grading systems will efficiently and thoroughly assess assignments and exams while freeing educators to focus more on the interactive aspects of teaching. In addition, attendance can be analysed, and trends in performance or behavior found to enhance an educational institution's planning and students' outcomes. Because it personalizes learning and empowers the educator, cognitive computing better allows for a more adaptive and effective education system [21].

5.4. Cognitive Computing in Autonomous Vehicles and Transportation

Autonomous vehicle and improved traffic management are in transportation, where the development of cognitive computing occurs. These vehicles operate through the use of cognitive systems which enable them to understand events happening on the roads through sensor data, recognize potential obstacles, and make time-sensitivities decisions about them [22]. Machine learning algorithms have been taking input from cameras, radar, and LiDAR sensors; therefore, they can distinguish pedestrians, traffic lights, and hazards. Computer vision helps decide better on the roads along with predictive models of the autonomous vehicle to assure safety.

In cognitive computing, the systems analyse real-time data from sources such as GPS, road sensors, and weather forecasts in traffic management to predict traffic patterns and advise on optimal routes and congestion management. Such systems improve travel efficiency, reduce emissions, and enhance urban mobility through traffic signal adjustments and route recommendations.

Cognitive systems in fleet management optimize logistics by considering the route, fuel consumption, and maintenance needs for the vehicle. Predictive maintenance through machine learning continuously monitors vehicle performance and alerts the operator about impending issues that can turn into critical failures before that, thus avoiding time wastage and reduction of costs incurred in maintaining them. In general, cognitive computing in transportation will be used to improve safety, reduce costs, and make mobility solutions more efficient [23].

These industrial applications show how cognitive computing adds efficiency, personalizes services, and innovates across various industries, thus becoming a part of modern technological advancement.

6. Challenges and Limitations

With cognitive computing in place, there are lots of challenges and constraints that must be overcome for full utilization. This ranges from the ethical dimension to technical aspects and applications, thus raising a complexity point in developing effective systems in mimicking human cognition. It is hence important that researchers and practitioners understand such challenges in the development of strong, reliable, and ethically sound cognitive computing solutions. Such challenges require multidisciplinary efforts from technologists, ethicists, policymakers, and the public to design and deploy responsible cognitive computing systems.

6.1. Ethical and Privacy Concerns

Issues relating to cognitive computing from the aspects of ethics and privacy rise with the systems since many forms of data most of the cognitive computation devices operate on is considered as being sensitive. There arise big questions relating to how personal information handled in bulks is founded on what constitutes consent, ownership, or even exploitation [24]. For instance, a cognitive system used health may expose patient information or compromise the confidentiality of a particular relationship. Such a call therefore calls for a fortified protocol on protecting data. Another implication is that the algorithms driving cognitive computing systems inherit bias from the data used for training. This raises issues with respect to fairness, accountability, and transparency, because discriminatory outcomes in hiring, lending, and law enforcement could result from biased models. Ethical considerations should thus be integrated into the design, development, and deployment of cognitive systems to minimize these risks and promote equal access to technology.

These ethical dilemmas are further complicated by the lack of regulatory frameworks on the use of cognitive computing technologies. In the absence of clear guidelines, organizations may emphasize performance and innovation over ethical considerations, which may lead to practices that are harmful to individuals and society. There is a need for collaboration among stakeholders in establishing ethical standards and best practices guiding the responsible use of cognitive computing technologies [25].

6.2. Scalability and Computational Efficiency

The volume of data continues to exponentially increase, and scalability and computational efficiency become the major issues for cognitive computing systems. Cognitive algorithms in particular and most deep learning-based ones require considerably large amounts of computational resources and time for training and refinement; hence, as organizations scale up their cognitive solutions, the processing power, memory, and data storage in real-life deployment become severe bottlenecks for effective models.

In addition, as these cognitive systems ingest more and more sources of data to process in real-time, it becomes difficult to ensure that their computing efficiency does not degrade. High demands on processing lead to latency and slower response times from applications, which means degradation in the user experience [26]. As researchers have started looking at ways to optimize the algorithms and improve the hardware to reduce the effects, balancing scalability with efficiency remains a problem. Scalability also pertains to the adaptability requirement of cognitive systems to different environments and use cases. In this regard, such systems need to accommodate flexible processing of data types, sources, and requirements without compromising performance. Due to this reason, the scalable solutions in cognitive computing are highly dependent on developing modular architectures that could adequately manage resource allocation and the distribution of workload.

6.3. Data Requirements and Quality Issues

Data is the oxygen of cognitive computing, and high-quality data directly impacts the efficiency of a system. Cognitive computing models require big volumes of good data to be able to learn patterns to make intelligent decisions. The large quantities of relevant data are often difficult to obtain, especially for niche domains, with data being proprietary or simply arduous to source. Further, the data should be diversified and representative to avoid biased and incorrect outputs from the model. Data quality issues further complicate the development and deployment of cognitive systems: inaccurate, incomplete, outdated, or inconsistent information used might cause flawed predictions and decisions. Therefore, data governance and management best practices should be implemented to ensure quality, up-to-date, and representative information fed into cognitive systems. [27] Data integration is another challenge that cognitive systems face. In most cases, cognitive systems collect information from various sources and formats. Advanced techniques for cleansing, transforming, and harmonizing data are needed to make seamless data integration, which may be resource-intensive and complex. Strategies in developing methods for the efficient management and processing of data will bring solutions to these challenges and unlock the full potential of cognitive computing.

Table 2.4. Challenges in cognitive computing and mitigation strategies

Challenge	Description	Example Impact	Potential Solutions
Data Quality	Variability and inaccuracies in data can lead to unreliable insights and predictions	Reduced model accuracy in sensitive areas like healthcare or finance	Implement data validation protocols, use high-quality training datasets, and continuously monitor data inputs for accuracy
Scalability	Increasing data volumes and complex models can strain computational resources	Slower processing times in high-demand applications like real-time analytics	Use cloud-based solutions, optimize algorithms, and employ distributed computing
Ethical Concerns	Biases and unintended consequences in AI decisions can lead to ethical issues	Discriminatory outcomes in hiring processes or credit scoring	Integrate fairness audits, implement transparent AI models, and develop ethical guidelines for AI
Privacy Issues	Handling sensitive data raises privacy risks and compliance challenges	Potential breaches in applications handling personal data like medical records	Use data anonymization, comply with regulations (e.g., GDPR), and implement secure data storage and access controls
Ambiguity Handling	Cognitive systems may struggle with ambiguous or incomplete data	Misinterpretations in NLP-based customer service or healthcare diagnostics	Employ context-aware models, use fuzzy logic techniques, and implement human-in-the-loop strategies for complex decisions

6.4. Handling Ambiguity and Uncertainty

Real-world data and situations are ambiguous and uncertain, and therefore, cognitive computing systems have to confront these. A structured environment is not typical always, as real-world contexts are often incomplete, contradictory, or noisy, and the systems may not draw proper conclusions. For example, a natural language processing system might fail to understand sarcasm or ambiguous phrasing, which might lead to miscommunication and errors. Ambiguity and uncertainty have to be treated properly by the advanced capabilities of reasoning and inference found in cognitive systems. Models of that type must provide estimations of the levels of confidence, weight the evidence appropriately, and reflect the levels of uncertainty associated with those predictions. Techniques for probabilistic reasoning and uncertainty quantification improve the robustness of such cognitive systems when handling challenging scenarios.

Ambiguity and uncertainty have to be treated properly by the advanced capabilities of reasoning and inference found in cognitive systems. Models of that type must provide estimations of the levels of confidence, weight the evidence appropriately, and reflect the levels of uncertainty associated with those predictions. Techniques for probabilistic reasoning and uncertainty quantification improve the robustness of such cognitive systems when handling challenging scenarios.

Table 2.4 sums up some of the key issues in the adoption of cognitive computing systems, like data quality, scalability, ethical, privacy, and ambiguity issues. The issue is described along with an example impact that could happen in practice applications. Then, there could be some possible solutions that are developed for mitigation. A structured overview like this has outlined the technical and ethical considerations necessary for developing robust, responsible cognitive computing systems.

7. Future Prospects and Research Directions

The field of cognitive computing stands at the cutting edge of technological evolution and promises to transform industries with systems that think, learn, and adapt in ways similar to human intelligence. This chapter discusses the trajectory of cognitive computing, emerging trends, integration with advanced technologies, anticipated ethical and social implications, and key areas ripe for future research. Indeed, as cognitive computing matures, it will be able to enhance everything from personalized medicine and predictive analytics to intelligent decision-making systems spread across finance, education, and beyond. But speed brings complexity and ethical consideration challenges that researchers and practitioners must address to responsibly reap the benefits of this emergent field.

7.1. Emerging Trends in Cognitive Computing

One of the most dominant trends in cognitive computing is the increasing reliance on multimodal learning, where systems integrate various types of data—such as visual, audio, and textual information—to develop more accurate and robust insights. This approach mimics human learning, allowing cognitive systems to understand and interpret complex data by fusing inputs from multiple sources. [28]. Examples abound from health-care applications deploying multimodal learning to diagnose patient records and medical imaging coupled with genomic information. Similarly, retail is enhancing customer experience in the service domain via multimodal systems, whereby data, voice, video, and transactional data coalesce to deliver smooth experiences. Another fundamental trend is the adoption of explainable AI, or XAI, by cognitive systems. Since cognitive computing will invade important sectors, such as finance and health, maximum transparency and interpretability in decisions produced by a cognitive system are absolutely necessary. The methodological endeavors of XAI seek to interpret machine learning models so they could be understood by the layperson or even just to show them the trail followed from any given cognitive-system decision in an attempt to bring it down to factors upon which decisions have been made. This trend points to user trust and regulatory requirements, particularly in high-stakes applications - such that stakeholders can understand, challenge, or correct system outputs when necessary.

The trend is toward ethics-based AI design principles for cognitive computing. As public awareness of the impact that AI has on society, developers are increasingly focused on ethics considerations and infusing cognitive systems with fairness, accountability, and transparency. This proactively serves to minimize potential side effects, such as algorithmic bias and violation of privacy, which often result when the data being used to train models lacks the representational nature or does not mirror the diversity required in its data sources. Ethical frameworks are now being incorporated very early in the development cycle, ensuring that cognitive systems actually do good and no harm in such applications as hiring, lending, and enforcement in the event of incorrect and biased decisions. Lastly, distributed cognitive computing is a trend that represents the shift from the centralized data center models toward edge and cloud-based models, which enable real-time processing closer to the data source. This approach supports applications where low latency is of utmost importance, like autonomous driving, IoT, and smart cities. Distributed cognitive computing makes responsiveness and scalability much possible so that cognitive systems could be deployed more widely and effectively, even in resource-constrained environments.

7.2. Integration with Other Advanced Technologies (e.g., IoT, Quantum Computing)

One of the most exciting areas of development relates to the convergence of cognitive computing with other emerging technologies. The integration of cognitive computing with the Internet of Things (IoT) allows systems to gather and analyse data from an enormous network of sensors and devices in real time. For example, IoT-enabled cognitive systems can track and learn user preferences in order to automate lighting, temperature, and security settings in smart homes. For instance, industrial cognitive IoT can now help optimize performance and reduce the cost by anticipating breakdowns in machinery based on the analysis of machine data. Another technology anticipated to revolutionize cognitive computing is quantum computing, which significantly accelerates the processing power available for complex computations. Quantum computing is still in developmental stages, but it does have the potential to handle vast datasets and optimize complex algorithms, especially in fields like cryptography, pharmaceuticals, and financial modeling.

These focus directionally in the inclusion of cognitive systems with quantum computers, promising to overcome all problems otherwise computationally not feasible by classical machines-that is, massive scale patterns recognition, optimization and simulations. This would have immense implications pushing cognitive capabilities so far beyond current bounds towards actual deliverables of breakthrough in analysing data, cryptography, and discoveries of new drugs [29].

Table 2.5. Integration of cognitive computing with advanced technologies

Technology	Integration Benefits	Example Applications	Challenges
Internet of Things (IoT)	Enables real-time data collection and analysis, enhances decision-making, and improves automation	Smart cities, predictive maintenance in manufacturing, healthcare monitoring systems	Managing data security, handling large data volumes, ensuring interoperability
Quantum Computing	Offers exponential processing power, allowing complex problem-solving capabilities	Drug discovery, financial risk modeling, cryptography	Limited availability, high costs, integration complexity
Blockchain	Enhances data security and transparency, ensures data integrity in decentralized networks	Secure healthcare records, supply chain management, fraud detection	Scalability issues, high energy consumption, regulatory hurdles
Augmented Reality (AR)	Enhances user interaction and contextual data visualization in real-time environments	Training simulations, retail virtual try-ons, remote maintenance	High computational demands, limited AR-compatible infrastructure
Robotics	Enhances automation and efficiency, especially in repetitive or hazardous tasks	Autonomous vehicles, robotic process automation (RPA) in manufacturing	Safety concerns, high initial investment, adaptability to complex environments

Table 2.5 presents a vignette of how cognitive computing interacts with the other advanced technologies, including IoT, quantum computing, blockchain, AR, and robotics. For each of these technologies, this table outlines some benefits of integration, examples of applications, and challenges encountered. Integration would enable organizations to enhance data processing, automation, and decision-making, though it cuts across technical, financial, and regulatory hurdles. This integration leads to more efficient, safe, and intelligent systems in various industries.

Further convergence with IoT and quantum computing also shows synergy with the development of cognitive computing. AR and VR technologies have emerged as the most immersive technology with which cognitive systems interact and engage in highly realistic user environments. For instance, the applications developed for AR and VR are fueled by cognitive computing and can serve purposes like individualized education experiences, virtual therapy for health, and simulated learning environments for aeronautics and surgery. Coupling cognitive computing with AR/VR can also promote better user engagement through timely responses that evolve in response to the user's behavior; thus, this brings new horizons of personal and immersive engagements to multiple sectors. More than this, cognitive computing is also being integrated with blockchain to improve data security, transparency, and accountability. Blockchains' decentralized and tamper-proof ledgers could be used to secure sensitive data in cognitive applications involving personal or financial information. This integration can further provide data integrity and trust within healthcare, where data from patients must be safe and secure. Cognitive blockchain systems may allow for safer and more transparent decision-making in such multi-stakeholder settings.

7.3. Anticipated Ethical and Social Impacts

Serious ethical and social problems arise in this era of rapid growth in cognitive computing related to privacy, accountability, and bias. Cognitive systems may be granted such degrees of autonomy that it will challenge, for example, who ought to participate in deciding upon matters that could end in human lives being determined or affected. Cognitive computing also can have serious applications, including in the sectors of law and healthcare. These latter sectors can bring potentially influential life-altering decision outcomes, making a redefinition of ethical guidelines quite pressing. The ethical integrity of ensuring public trust requires that these systems be transparent, and traceable decisions return to specific rules or data inputs.

Another pressing issue that shows up in cognitive systems is the bias that these can demonstrate. Models in machine learning may inherit any biases from their training data, meaning that the applications may go on to give unfair or discriminatory results, for instance, in the hiring process or lending, policing, etc. Bias needs to be taken care of from various directions, such as selection of carefully curated training data, continuous monitoring of the model, and using fairness metrics in evaluation [30]. Researchers and policymakers are actively developing frameworks such as the development of standards to ensure responsible design and deployment of cognitive computing systems. Yet another significant social connotation connected with cognitive computing is changing the nature of employment and jobs because of the capacities these systems embody. In one way, these systems are able to replace boring, monotonous work. In doing so, they may potentially undermine the old occupations: the ones that can be called traditional - manufacture, services, and even data handling. The risk of damage is less likely if measures are taken so that workers can better fit into an entirely new range of tasks in relation to jobs much more driven by AI. Such involves reskilling and upskilling in which one equips workers with relevant skills that are to be developed while working along cognitive systems or performing complex human-centric functions.

Data privacy is also another ethical concern, where cognitive systems are supposed to capture and analyse personal data to a great extent. With many cognitive applications requiring very sensitive data, such as in healthcare and finance sectors, the information has been a cause of concern to be stored, accessed, or protected. Thus, very strong data governance policies, advanced encryption techniques, and compliance to privacy laws such as GDPR are all necessary to ensure personal data is protected. There is a growing demand for transparency, where users know what data is being collected and how it is being used. These are critical concerns for building public trust and ensuring that cognitive systems operate in a manner that respects the privacy of individuals and data security.

7.4. Future Research Areas

Future research in the area of cognitive computing should be centered on enhancing the systems with improved capabilities, reliability, and availability.

Developing adaptive learning models with a cognitive system that auto-updates itself autonomously as more data arrives seems to be an area of importance. Thus, so designed cognitive systems will resist faults, be robust toward change, and learn on the fly. Realistic scenarios are dynamic environments, examples being autonomous driving, financial markets, etc. Emotional intelligence in improving cognitive systems is another trend that gained much attention. Emotional intelligence in AI is the recognition, interpretation, and suitable action on human emotions with their application in healthcare, mental health support, and applications regarding customer service. Enhanced emotional intelligence in cognitive systems could bring users closer to having a deeper and more personal interaction, which will, in turn, lead toward greater user satisfaction and involvement.

Another promising area of research relates to the development of cognitive computing systems that can take ethical decisions autonomously. This domain will contribute significantly in high-stakes applications, including autonomous vehicles and healthcare diagnostics, where such ethical reasoning may be encountered by a cognitive system. Researchers are studying the creation of ethical frameworks and decision models wherein cognitive systems would be able to discern what not to do and in what situation, and they are going to use such moral reasoning like fairness and no harm principle. These cognitive systems might make them liable and dependable in complex scenarios that would provide safety applications in an ethically aligned direction toward the applications of society. This, in turn, extends towards more accessibility and further lower costs for even small business companies and other under-qualified industries. The open development of cognitive frameworks and general availability of various AI-based cloud services help to facilitate this accessibility. Future will come from further cost minimization and the smoothing of this process by the streamlining of the deployment process between these systems and their relatively easy integration.

8. Case Studies in Cognitive Computing Implementation

Basically, cognitive computing is the mingling of AI and machine learning that has radically transformed all boundaries in industries since systems now imitate human thought, so, with massive datasets to be processed in real time, the scope of healthcare, finance, education, customer service, transportation, manufacturing, and human resource has been broadened. The case studies for all these areas are presented below with a minute detail from where it has been explored that by making what kind of changes did cognitive computing improve efficiency, accuracy, and predictability.

Table 2.6 presents the implementations of cognitive computing in various industries- how cognitive systems result in efficiency and decision improvement. Key applications in health, finance, education, customer service, and transportation are explained by highlighting how cognitive tools such as AI-driven systems, smart platforms, and autonomous technologies transform these sectors.

These case studies illustrate very interesting features of cognitive computing and the benefits, challenges, as well as considerations that each respective industry faces. It ranges from medical condition diagnostics to managing risks in financial markets to realize innovation and decrease operational costs and improve decision-making accuracy.

8.1. Healthcare: Cognitive Systems in Medical Imaging and Diagnosis

Advances in healthcare cognitive systems have permitted breakthroughs in medical imaging and diagnostics that are now possible to speed up with more accuracy the assessment of patient health. Cognitive computing models can analyse medical images with high precision over patterns that may be too subtle to be interpreted by a human: for example, patterns indicating early stages of cancer that can be used by physicians to intervene promptly, therefore improving the outcome for patients [31].

- *Enhanced Diagnostics*: Cognitive systems utilize machine learning models to differentiate between many conditions, thus offering a probability score on potential diagnoses. This will assist in informed decisions by radiologists, reduce errors in diagnostics, and increase the accuracy of medical imaging.
- *Reduced Time for Image Analysis*: Cognitive systems will enable healthcare providers to treat more cases more efficiently by automation of parts of the image analysis process. This is the prime requirement of emergency centers, in which a late diagnosis can be fatal.

Table 2.6. Case Studies in cognitive computing implementation

Industry	Cognitive Computing Application	Key Benefits	Example Impact
Healthcare	Cognitive Systems in Medical Imaging and Diagnosis	Improved diagnostic accuracy, faster image analysis, personalized treatment	Early detection of diseases like cancer, reduced human error in diagnoses
Finance	Cognitive Tools in Algorithmic Trading and Risk Management	Enhanced predictive capabilities, automated trading, better risk assessment	Optimized trading strategies, reduced financial risks, faster decision-making
Education	Smart Tutoring and Adaptive Learning Platforms	Personalized learning experiences, real-time progress tracking, scalability	More effective education for diverse learners, reduced teacher workload
Customer Service	AI-driven Chatbots and Virtual Assistants	24/7 support, increased customer satisfaction, faster query resolution	Enhanced customer experience, reduced operational costs, efficient handling of large volumes of inquiries
Transportation	Cognitive Systems in Autonomous Vehicles and Traffic Management	Increased safety, optimized traffic flow, reduced accidents	Safer roads, more efficient transportation systems, reduced congestion

- *Patient-Centric Care:* Apart from diagnostics, cognitive computing in health care also assists in providing tailored treatments by use of patient history, lifestyle aspects, and genetic analysis, thus propelling a personalized approach to delivering health services [32].

Figure 2.4 llustrates how cognitive computing in health care enhances the accuracy of diagnosis and enhances care to patients. The procedure initiates with Patient Data Input. Later, it involves Medical Image Analysis, where the medical images are analysed and fine patterns in it can be detected with the assistance of cognitive systems. Then, Reduced Time for Analysing Images means that the time required for the analysis of images can be reduced faster to enable prompt decision-making as it is more crucial in emergent cases. Information is then used for Personalized Patient-Centric Care, such as tailoring treatments based on patient history and lifestyle.

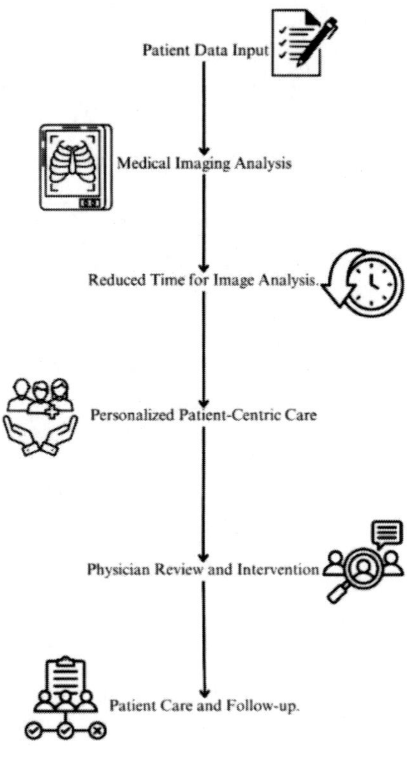

Figure 2.4. Cognitive Computing Workflow in Healthcare for Enhanced Diagnostics and Patient-Centric Care.

Subsequently, there is Physician Review and Intervention wherein healthcare providers check the cognitive insights for accuracy and to advance treatment plans. The process ends in Patient Care and Follow-up by continuously monitoring the patient and thus improving the patient outcome.

8.2. Finance: Cognitive Tools in Algorithmic Trading and Risk Management

In finance, cognitive computing is refreshing algorithmic trading and risk management with speedily driven decisions based on data. Financial markets generate high volumes of data daily. A cognitive system could process real-time data to indicate patterns and risks. In the historical data assessment, the prediction of market flow, and making trades with minimal human engagement, cognitive systems in algorithmic trading maximize profitability.

- *Algorithmic Trading*: Cognitive tools automatically facilitate trading strategies by identifying trends and making predictions on the future price movement. They are sensitive to market changes, making swift decisions in a split of a second to maximize the possibility of successful trades.
- *Risk Assessment*: Cognitive systems include market, credit, and operational risks in risk management. These systems learn constantly from past data and enhance their ability to predict and better prevent the effects of market volatility.
- *Compliance and Fraud Detection*: Cognitive systems also detect fraud through analysing strange kinds of transactions and alerting crimes to the compliance teams followed by compliance with regulatory standards to fight fraud.

8.3. Education: Smart Tutoring and Adaptive Learning Platforms

Education and personalized learning have been revolutionized by cognitive computing; in that it has facilitated the development of smart tutoring systems as well as adaptive learning platforms. These systems assess student performance data and provide such students with tailored educational content as well as support. For instance, cognitive tutoring adjusts the lesson difficulty based on individual responses from the students before they are moved forward on topics.

- *Personalized Learning Paths*: The adaptive platforms provide student-centered curricula, thereby enabling learners to learn at any speed. The systems actually adapt content in real time; they can produce additional resources or give some exercises if the need arises to enhance them [33].
- *Intelligent Feedback*: Instant feedback also takes place when using smart tutoring systems, and this helps the learners correct mistakes even during the learning process. Targeted feedback enhances learning outcomes and provides teachers with the chance to know where the learners need more support.
- *Assessment and Analytics*: Cognitive platforms also support educators by offering detailed insights on student achievements, participation, and progress, facilitating data-driven decisions to improve educational outcomes [34].

8.4. Customer Service: AI-driven Chatbots and Virtual Assistants

Cognitive computing is revolutionizing the face of customer services. Virtual assistants and AI-driven chatbots work way more efficiently and effectively in customer services. They respond to any query a customer has very quickly, thus reducing wait times and making users satisfied. Cognitive chatbots scan the customer's queries to identify intent and give an appropriate response or route complex problems to human agents.

- *Natural Language Processing*: Leverage NLP, so that cognitive chatbots can read into many tones and languages and contextualize for more human-like responses - thus bettering the experience for users and allowing more personalized service.
- *24/7 Customer Support*: Chatbots offer around-the-clock support, reducing dependency on human agents for basic queries. This ensures consistent availability, enhancing customer satisfaction and loyalty [35].
- *Data Collection and Insights*: The cognitive systems collect information from the interchange to highlight common issues and

customer preference, through which a company can better services but also make tactical decisions on customer engagement strategies.

8.5. Transportation: Cognitive Systems in Autonomous Vehicles and Traffic Management

Cognitive computing in transport aids driverless vehicle mobility along with traffic management for efficient safer mobility. Systems developed cognitively will facilitate for the vehicle the process involved in the interpretation of sense data received from surroundings or environment real-time decisioning for driving through different kinds of road conditions in travel. Traffic management systems employing cognition use these computations in determining flow and concentrating efforts at its reduction in conjunction with improving road utilization.

- *Object Detection and Navigation:* Cognitive systems in autonomous vehicles detect and classify objects (e.g., pedestrians, vehicles) in real-time, ensuring safe navigation. They also predict object movements, allowing for proactive decision-making [36].
- *Predictive Maintenance*: Cognitive systems monitor vehicle performance, identifying potential issues before they result in breakdowns. This predictive maintenance reduces downtime and improves vehicle longevity.
- *Traffic Optimization*: In urban areas, cognitive systems analyse traffic data to manage traffic lights and reroute vehicles in case of congestion, improving travel times and reducing emissions.

Conclusion

In this chapter, we discussed the fundamental components of cognitive computing and how it differs from the traditional approaches to computing. The study of such key concepts as natural language processing, machine learning, and human-computer interaction will illustrate how the cognitive system enables machines to simulate processes in the thought procedure. The chapter also reviewed various applications of cognitive computing across health, finance, and education sectors, making it more evident how such technology has the potential to transform the way decisions are made, automated, and personalized services are offered. Scalability and ethical considerations were other important factors for understanding limitations and areas that cognitive computing needs to change to satisfy real-world needs.

Looking back, it is evident that the evolution of cognitive computing moved from simple automation to highly sophisticated systems that add value and augment human potential and allow us to move forward into future opportunities with emerging concepts like the Internet of Things and quantum computing. This innovation brings along with it all those difficult problems related to data privacy and accountability in ethics, thus calling for strong, scalable solutions. To overcome this successfully, innovation will continuously take place while upholding standards of ethics, such that society continues to benefit in responsible ways from cognitive computing.

References

[1] Nalini, M., Prasanth, A., Gopu, A., & Lakshmi, D. (2022). Introduction to cognitive computing. In *Cognitive computing for Internet of Medical Things* (pp. 23–44). Taylor & Francis Group. https://doi.org/10.1201/9781003256243-2.

[2] Hemalatha, J. J., Chokkalingam, B. S., Vivek, V., & Mohan, S. (2023). Cognitive computing: A deep view in architecture, technologies, and artificial intelligence-based applications. In *Principles and applications of socio-cognitive and affective computing* (pp. 1–14). IGI Global. https://doi.org/10.4018/978-1-6684-3843-5.ch001.

[3] Stepney, S. (2009). Non-classical hypercomputation. *International Journal of Unconventional Computing, 5*, 267–276.

[4] Liu, J. (2021). Cognitive computing integrated methodology for smart decision-making and problem-solving. *ResearchSquare*. https://doi.org/10.21203/RS.3.RS-927958/V1.

[5] Beena, T. L. A., & Vijaykumar, V. (2022). Influence of cognitive computing in healthcare applications. In *Cognitive intelligence and big data in healthcare* (pp. 121–143). Wiley Online Library. https://doi.org/10.1002/9781119771982.ch5.

[6] Monteiro, A. C. B., França, R. P., Arthur, R., & Iano, Y. (2022). An artificial intelligent cognitive approach for classification and recognition of white blood cells employing deep learning for medical applications. In *Deep learning for medical applications with unique data* (pp. 53–69). ScienceDirect. https://doi.org/10.1016/b978-0-12-824145-5.00012-5.

[7] Velankar, M. R., Mahalle, P. N., & Shinde, G. R. (2024). Cognitive computing. In *Cognitive computing for machine thinking* (pp. 55–70). Springer. https://doi.org/10.1007/978-981-97-0452-1_5.

[8] França, R. P., Monteiro, A. C. B., Arthur, R., & Iano, Y. (2022). An overview of the computational cognitive from a modern perspective, its techniques, and application potential in healthcare systems. In *Cognitive intelligence and big data in healthcare* (pp. 145–168). Wiley Online Library. https://doi.org/10.1002/9781119771982.ch6.
[9] Sumari, A. D. W., & Ahmad, A. S. (2018). Cognitive artificial intelligence: Concept and applications for humankind. *InTech.* https://doi.org/10.5772/intechopen.72764.
[10] Wang, G., Widrow, B., Hoare, C. A. R., Pedrycz, W., Berwick, R. C., Plataniotis, K. N., Rudas, I. J., & Kacprzyk, J. (2023). The odyssey to next-generation computers: Cognitive computers (κC) inspired by the brain and powered by intelligent mathematics. *Frontiers in Computer Science, 5*, Article 1152592. https://doi.org/10.3389/fcomp.2023.1152592.
[11] Zheng, N. (2023). Cognitive computing of visual and auditory information: State of the art. In *Cognitive computing of visual and auditory information* (pp. 29–40). Springer. https://doi.org/10.1007/978-981-99-3228-3_2.
[12] Reddy, C. K. K., Rangarajan, A., Rangarajan, D., Shuaib, M., Jeribi, F., & Alam, S. (2024). A transfer learning approach: Early prediction of Alzheimer's disease on US healthy aging dataset. *MDPI Mathematics, 12*(14), 2204. https://doi.org/10.3390/math12142204.
[13] Sowmya, B. J., Kumar, D. P., Hanumantharaju, R., & Srinivasa, K. G. (2023). DAMIAN - Data accrual machine intelligence with augmented networks for contextually coherent creative story generation. *International Journal of Business Intelligence and Data Mining, 22*, 115–130. https://doi.org/10.1504/IJBIDM.2022.10045744.
[14] Kantipudi, M. V. V. P., Aluvalu, R., Maheswari, V. U., & Raisinghani, M. S. (2022). Insights on implications of cognitive computing in leveraging online education systems. *International Journal of Online Pedagogy and Course Design, 12*(1), 1–16. https://doi.org/10.4018/ijopcd.302082.
[15] Srivani, M., Murugappan, A., & Mala, T. (2023). Cognitive computing technological trends and future research directions in healthcare — A systematic literature review. *Artificial Intelligence in Medicine, 138*, 102513. https://doi.org/10.1016/j.artmed.2023.102513.
[16] Mohanty, M. N. (2019). Design of cognitive healthcare system for coronary cardiac disease detection. In *Emerging trends and applications in cognitive computing* (pp. 1–34). IGI Global. https://doi.org/10.4018/978-1-5225-5793-7.CH001.
[17] Jain, A., Jain, N., Verma, A., & Jain, A. (2024). Cognitive computing's role in shaping the future landscape of healthcare. In *2024 IEEE International Students' Conference on Electrical, Electronics and Computer Science (SCEECS)* (pp. 1–5). IEEE. https://doi.org/10.1109/sceecs61402.2024.10482075.
[18] Kliman, R., & Arinze, B. (2019). Cognitive computing: Impacts on financial advice in wealth management. In *Aligning business strategies and analytics* (pp. 11–23). Springer. https://doi.org/10.1007/978-3-319-93299-6_2.
[19] Faccia, A. (2023). National payment switches and the power of cognitive computing against fintech fraud. *Big Data and Cognitive Computing, 7*(2), 76.
[20] Gao, J. (2022). Cognitive computing for decision-making and choice modeling of the interactive relationship between local higher education development and

regional economics. *Journal of Interconnection Networks, 22*, 2144013:1–214. https://doi.org/10.1142/s0219265921440138.

[21] Yang, H., Shankar, A., & Velliangiri, S. (2023). Artificial intelligence-enabled interactive system modeling for teaching and learning based on cognitive web services. *International Journal of e-Collaboration, 19*(2), 1–18. https://doi.org/10.4018/ijec.316655.

[22] Sudhakar, A. V. V., Tyagi, A., Patil, P., Kumar, K. S., Sathe, M., & Geetha, B. T. (2024). Cognitive computing in intelligent traffic management systems. In *2024 International Conference on Advances in Computing, Communication and Applied Informatics (ACCAI), India* (pp. 1–6). IEEE. https://doi.org/10.1109/ACCAI61061.2024.10602427.

[23] Vidwans, A. S. (2021). Cognitive computing in autonomous vehicles. In *Cognitive computing for human-robot interaction: Cognitive data science in sustainable computing* (pp. 121–146). ScienceDirect. https://doi.org/10.1016/B978-0-323-85769-7.00008-2

[24] Sultanuddin, S. J., Sudhee, D., Satve, P. P., Sumithra, M., Sathyanarayana, K. B., Kumari, R. K., Narasimharao, J., Reddy, R. V. K., & Rajkumar, R. (2023). Cognitive computing and 3D facial tracking method to explore the ethical implication associated with the detection of fraudulent system in online examination. *Journal of Intelligent & Fuzzy Systems, 45*(5), 8449–8463. https://doi.org/10.3233/jifs-235066.

[25] Kavak, A. (2024). Ethical considerations and privacy concerns in AI-enabled libraries. In *Advances in library and information science (ALIS)* (pp. 45–77). IGI Global. https://doi.org/10.4018/979-8-3693-1573-6.ch003.

[26] Mittal, S. (2017). Cognitive computing architectures for machine (deep) learning at scale. *Proceedings, 1*(3), 186. https://doi.org/10.3390/IS4SI-2017-04025.

[27] Appel, A. P., Candello, H., & Gandour, F. L. (2017). Cognitive computing: Where big data is driving us. In *Handbook of big data technologies* (pp. 807–850). Springer. https://doi.org/10.1007/978-3-319-49340-4_24.

[28] Jiang, Q.-Y., Chi, Z., & Yang, Y. (2024). Multimodal classification via modal-aware interactive enhancement. *arXiv.* https://doi.org/10.48550/arxiv.2407.04587.

[29] Hassan, N., Gaur, A. H., Jadaun, Y., & Bhasney, A. (2024). IoT-enabled medicine dispenser for pills and liquid medication. In *2024 2nd International Conference on Advancement in Computation & Computer Technologies (InCACCT).* IEEE. https://doi.org/10.1109/incacct61598.2024.10550973.

[30] Singh, T. M., Reddy, C. K. K., Murthy, B. V. R., Nag, A., & Doss, S. (2025). AI and education: Bridging the gap to personalized, efficient, and accessible learning. In *Internet of behavior-based computational intelligence for smart education systems* (pp. 131–160). IGI Global.

[31] Reddy, K. K., Reddy, P. A., Janapati, H., Assiri, B., Shauib, M., Alam, S., & Sheneamer, A. (2024). A fine-tuned vision transformer (FTVT)-based enhanced multi-class brain tumor classification using MRI scan imagery. *Frontiers in Oncology: Cancer Imaging and Image-Directed Interventions.* https://doi.org/10.3389/fonc.2024.1400341.

[32] Singh, T. M., & Lippert, K. (2024). Digital twins in human activity prediction on gait using extreme gradient boosting local binary pattern: Healthcare 6.0. In

Exploring the advancements and future directions of digital twins in healthcare 6.0 (pp. 240–261). IGI Global.

[33] Meghla, R. T., Deowan, M. E., Nuhel, A. K., Sazid, M. M., Ekbal, M. N., & Mahamud, M. H. (2022). An Internet of Things (IoT)-based smart automatic medication dispenser with an integrated web application for patient diagnosis. In *2022 5th International Conference of Computer and Informatics Engineering (IC2IE)* (pp. 16–21). IEEE. https://doi.org/10.1109/IC2IE56416.2022.9970073.

[34] Reddy, K. K., Daduvy, A., Mohana, R. M., Assiri, B., Shauib, M., Alam, S., & Sheneamer, A. (2024). Enhancing precision agriculture and land cover classification: A self-attention 3D convolutional neural network approach for hyperspectral image analysis. *IEEE Access.* https://doi.org/10.1109/ACCESS.2024.3420089.

[35] Singh, T. M., & Lippert, K. (2024). Advancing human-centric solutions: The future trajectory of soft computing in modern society. *IGI Global.*

[36] Sreelatha, G., Reddy, C. K. K., Hanafiah, M. M., & Madana Mohana, R. (2024). Hybrid electro search beetle optimization-based task scheduling and game theory SOA-based resource allocation in multi-cloud computing. *Journal of Software: Practice and Experience.* https://doi.org/10.1002/spe.3370.

Chapter 3

Automatic Image Segmentation in Medical Imaging Using Machine Learning and Cognitive Computing

Anamika Ahirwar[1,*], PhD
Shital R. Shegokar[2,†]
and Naresh Marwal[3,‡]
[1]Department of Computer Science and Engineering,
Compucom Institute of Technology and Management, Jaipur, Rajasthan, India
[2] Department of Electrical and Electronics Engineering, Poornima University, Jaipur, India
[3]Department of Computer Science and Engineering,
Anand International College of Engineering, Jaipur, Rajasthan, India

Abstract

Multiple Sclerosis (MS) is a chronic autoimmune disease that affects the central nervous system–he analysis and monitors the mind closely on magnetic resonance imaging (MRI). MS lesions quantify the mind shrinkage and call for tracking. The progresses in computer vision, cognitive, and leveraging deep learning technology have made monitoring through medical images possible. Deep learning models enable automatic and effective extraction and segmentation of MS images, providing captures accuracy. Deep learning models achieve high accuracy (Dice coefficient: 0.85-0.95), improved lesion detection

* Corresponding Author's Email: aanamika77@gmail.com
† Corresponding Author's Email: shital1703@gmail.com
‡ Corresponding Author's Email: nareshkumarmarwal18@gmail.com

In: Building Intelligent Systems for the Future
Editors: Anamika Ahirwar, Neelesh Jain and Sumitha Elayaperumal
ISBN: 979-8-90134-050-9

(sensitivity: 0.90-0.95), and enhanced brain atrophy quantification (correlation coefficient: 0.80-0.90).
The integration of deep learning architectures like LSTM and GRU captures sequential dependencies across MRI slices, while models like U-Net, SegNet, and ResNet provide efficient segmentation using encoder-decoder structures. The lesions, though artificial, are yet realistic and are useful in training robust models, through generative models like Pix2Pix and CycleGAN that provide enriched datasets. To overcome the difficulties caused by a lack of annotated datasets and class imbalances, transfer learning, data augmentation, and ensemble techniques further enhance model performance.
Cognitive computing approaches (attention mechanisms, expert systems) lower false positives and improve segmentation accuracy, which enables automated lesion segmentation and accurate brain atrophy measurement. These cognitive models, when combined with a deep learning framework, facilitate adaptive, customized disease monitoring, empowering medical professionals to customize treatment regimens and make better judgments based on patient-specific information.
The proposed framework offers a robust and scalable solution for MS image segmentation, with potential applications in clinical trials where clinicians can make informed decisions and improve patient outcomes, disease monitoring, and personalized medicine. A DL-based architecture for involuntary subdivision of MS lesions, incorporating cognitive computing techniques to improve segmentation outcomes assessment focuses on clinical MRI data, with comparisons to current to best practices and insights gained through transfer across multiple MS Datasets. The methodology includes gathering and preprocessing data, creating CNN-based architectures (U-Net, SegNet, ResNet), integrating expert systems and attention mechanisms, training and testing, and evaluating the results using the Dice coefficient, sensitivity, specificity, precision, and recall.

Keywords: multiple sclerosis, U-Net, SegNet, ResNet, cognitive computing, magnetic resonance imaging, deep learning

1. Introduction

Medical imaging is becoming increasingly important in advancing care delivery. Methods such as magnetic resonance imaging, computed tomography, ultrasound and positron emission tomography generate large volumes of image data that must be carefully analysed to obtain relevant information. [1,2]. Segmentation refers to the task of dividing the valid portion of an image into discrete regions, e.g. a segment of a CT image contains a region for brain and another region for tumors in case of brain tumors [3], etc., and this is one of the fundamental challenges that are always present in medical images analysis. Accurate segmentation is critical for tasks such as tumor detection, organ delineation, and monitoring disease progression [4].

Old ways of image segmentation usually depend on manual or partly automated methods, which take a lot of work, take much time, and are often subject to differences between observers and within the same observer [5]. The increasing complexity and volume of medical imaging data exacerbates these issues, demanding the development of reliable and efficient automated segmentation techniques.

The introduction of data-driven approaches such as machine learning (ML) and cognitive computing has transformed the medical imaging field and provided higher accurate and efficient solutions. Machine learning, and deep learning [6] has shown great promise in recognizing complex patterns in high-dimensional data and seems like an ideal candidate for medical image segmentation. Notable models such as CNN, U-net architectures, and Transformers are commonly employed for the segmentation of different medical images with great accuracy [7]. Unsupervised segmentation has been addressed by several models that learn from ground-truth segmented datasets to detect and segment complex structures, solving difficulties like low contrast or image noise [8].

Cognitive computing provides additional support for machine learning systems by adding components that emulate human decision-making, allowing systems to consume context and reason why decisions are made between different scenarios. Segmentation results can be increasingly interpretable and reliable with cognitive systems, which use techniques such as natural language processing, knowledge representation, and decision-making. With the fusion of cognitive computing, machine learning, and cognitive search systems, automated systems can reach higher levels of accuracy, robustness, and adaptability, bridging critical gaps in the practices today.

In this chapter, we describe the use of ML and cognitive computing to automate image segmentation in images used in medical imaging. This provides a brief overview of state-of-the-art approaches in these fields, along with the advantages and limitations of these approaches and the possible future directions. These systems will combine the numerical power of machine learning, the contextual intelligence of cognitive computing, and the advanced medical imaging technology to address needs in this sector that no single company can do alone; to change the way healthcare workflows are optimized to solve patient needs to improve clinical outcomes.

1.1. Overview of Multiple Sclerosis

MS is a chronic autoimmune illness that causes inflammation, demyelination, and neurodegeneration in the central nervous system. MS can cause a vast array of symptoms, such as visual problems, cognitive impairment, sensory abnormalities, and motor weakness. What makes the disease is the development of lesions in the brain and spinal cord that vary in size, location, and severity. These lesions can be detected through medical imaging, are critical to the finding and follow-up of MS.

1.1.1. Reasons and Hazards

Multiple sclerosis is considered to be caused by a mix of eco-friendly and genetic aspects, but the particular cause is leftover unidentified. Risk factors for MS include living far from the equator, smoking, viral infection, poor vitamin D levels, and a family history of the condition. The illness primarily affects women and is typically diagnosed between the ages of 20 and 40.

1.1.2. Types of Multiple Sclerosis

MS progresses in different ways, classified into four main types:

- *Relapsing-Remitting MS (RRMS):* This is the most prevalent type, characterized by symptom flare-ups interspersed with recuperation intervals [8].
- *Secondary Progressive MS (SPMS):* This condition progresses from RRMS and causes symptoms to gradually worsen over time.
- *Primary Progressive MS*: This kind of MS is characterized by consistent symptom progression from the beginning without noticeable relapses.
- *Progressive-Relapsing MS:* An uncommon form of the disease in which relapses can be severe and symptoms gradually worsen.

1.1.3. Symptoms

Depending on which nerves are impacted, multiple sclerosis symptoms can vary greatly. Fatigue, numbness, muscle weakness, vision issues, poor coordination, cognitive challenges, and bladder or bowel dysfunction are typical symptoms.

1.1.4. Diagnosis and Treatment

There is no single test for MS, so doctors use a combination of MRI scans, spinal fluid analysis, and neurological exams to diagnose the condition. Although there is no cure, treatment focuses on slowing disease progression, reducing relapses, and managing symptoms. Medications, physical therapy, and lifestyle adjustments can help improve quality of life [8].

1.1.5. Prognosis

MS affects individuals differently—some experience mild symptoms, while others may develop disabilities over time. Early diagnosis and treatment can help manage the condition effectively and maintain mobility and independence for longer.

1.2. Imaging is Crucial for MS Diagnosis and Monitoring

MRI remains the gold standard for MS diagnosis and monitoring. Detailed images of the brain and spinal cord enable clinicians to detect lesions and assess their activity, as well as to track the course of diseases. Myelination, neurotransmission, excitability, and regional interconnectivity may all contribute to explaining how multiple sclerosis manifests, specifically the development of these advanced imaging methods, such as diffusion tensor imaging and fMRI, which can pinpoint small changes in the microstructure and connectivity of the brain [9]. Imaging plays a key role, not only in early diagnosis but also in guiding treatment decisions and assessing handling response, and is thus an important tool in the management of MS.

1.3. Challenges in MS Image Segmentation

Although several imaging technologies have been developed, segmentation of MS lesions is still very challenging. The lesions vary considerably in size [10], shape, and intensity, and frequently merge with, or encompass, normal brain tissue or other pathological findings [11]. Manual segmentation is the gold standard, but it is time-consuming and can vary between observers. Promising automated segmentation methods exist, but are still challenged by low-contrast lesions, artifacts, and differences in imaging protocol [12]. If a general ML algorithm can provide a good result for each subproblem, it should hopefully reach the global optimal solution when all subproblems are solved [13].

1. *Variability in Image Quality*
   The quality of medical images can vary substantially even for images captured using the same imaging modality, owing to differences in imaging protocols, patient motion, noise, etc. Such changes can result in differences in the appearance of MS lesions, complicating the process of achieving reproducible segmentation results. Moreover, intra- and inter-observer variability add to this problem, where different radiologists read the same images differently [14], resulting in differences within lesion identification and measurement.
2. *Complex Lesion Characteristics*
   MS plaques can take on many shapes, sizes, and locations in the brain. This makes segmentation a challenging task, as these lesions are heterogeneous and may be poorly segmented relative to the background. Also, lesions are sometimes located neighbouring to other morphological structures or overlap with healthy tissue, making it more difficult to separate.
3. *Insufficient Annotated Data*
   Image segmentation is a subdivision of computer vision that helps to determine a pixel's classification on an image. However, as manual annotation is time-consuming and needs expert intervention, retrieving such datasets in the medical realm is often difficult [15]. Such limited availability of pixel-accurate, high-quality annotated data can cause models to overfit and subsequently lead to poor generalization of models on new, unseen images.
4. *Evaluation Metrics*
   There are no universal metrics that can effectively summarize the virtue or defects of segmentation algorithms. Widely used metrics such as Dice coefficient may not always convey clinical relevance or acknowledge human visual interpretation of lesion margins [16]. Thus, they commonly require subjective evaluation methods or expert feedback alongside quantitative measures.

5. *Algorithm Robustness*
   Segmentation algorithms must be robust enough to handle variations in imaging conditions such as contrast, brightness, and noise levels. Many traditional methods struggle under these conditions, leading to inaccuracies in segmentation results. Recent advances using deep learning techniques have shown promise [17]; however, they still face challenges related to computational demands and the need for extensive training data.
6. *Real-Time Processing Requirements*
   In clinical settings, there is often a need for real-time processing capabilities to assist radiologists during examinations. Balancing the computational efficiency required for real-time applications with the precision needed for accurate lesion segmentation remains a significant challenge

2. Fundamentals of MS Image Segmentation

2.1. MRI Modalities in MS (T1, T2, FLAIR, etc.)

We then explore how these metrics can be derived from MRI modalities, which are a cornerstone of imaging and analysis for MS. Different MRI features provide complementary information on the disease process. T1-weighted images are useful for evaluating structural anatomy and chronic lesions, whereas T2-weighted images accentuate areas of high-water content, including edema and inflammation [18]. FLAIR imaging allows the suppression of cerebrospinal fluid, which increases its sensitivity to detect lesions located around the ventricles and on the cerebral cortex. Integration of multiple modalities allows clinicians and researchers to develop a more complete picture of disease pathology and progression. The Multimodal Brain tumor Segmentation Challenge 2017 (brats2017) was established [19].

1. *T1-weighted MRI*
   - Purpose: T1-weighted images are primarily used for anatomical details and assessing brain structure.
   - Lesion Visualization: These images can show lesions as hypointense (dark) areas, particularly useful for identifying chronic lesions that have undergone atrophy.

- Limitations: T1-weighted images may not be sensitive enough to detect new or active lesions.

2. *T2-weighted MRI*
   - Purpose: T2-weighted images are sensitive to water content and highlight edema, making them effective for visualizing active lesions.
   - Lesion Visualization: Lesions appear hyperintense (bright) on T2-weighted scans, which helps in identifying both new and old lesions.
   - Limitations: While T2-weighted images are good for detecting lesions, they can sometimes overestimate lesion burden due to the presence of nonspecific hyperintensities.
3. *FLAIR (Fluid-Attenuated Inversion Recovery)*
   - Purpose: FLAIR is designed to suppress cerebrospinal fluid (CSF) signals, enhancing the visibility of lesions adjacent to the ventricles.
   - Lesion Visualization: Lesions appear hyperintense on FLAIR images, making it particularly useful for detecting periventricular lesions that may be missed on T1 or T2 images.
   - Advantages: FLAIR is highly sensitive for detecting MS lesions and is often preferred in clinical practice.
4. *MP2RAGE (Modified Look-Locker Inversion Recovery)*
   - Purpose: This technique provides high-resolution images with improved contrast between Gray and white matter.
   - Lesion Visualization: MP2RAGE can effectively visualize cortical and white matter lesions, offering a detailed view that aids in accurate segmentation.
   - Clinical Relevance: Studies have shown that combining MP2RAGE with other sequences like FLAIR enhances the overall accuracy of lesion detection.

2.2. Traditional Segmentation Techniques (Thresholding, Edge Detection, etc.)

Conventional image segmentation methods have set the foundation for automated analysis. Thresholding techniques are commonly used for segmentation by dividing images based on their intensity value [20]. Such boundaries can be detected by edge detection algorithms, which include Sobel and Canny operators, that recognize abrupt changes in intensity. Methods are based on region-growing segments that adjacent areas according to some predefined criteria, such as similarity in intensity or texture. Although computationally efficient, they do not generalize well to complex medical images such as low contrast and noisy backgrounds, indicating that these approaches are only marginally useful for MS segmentation.

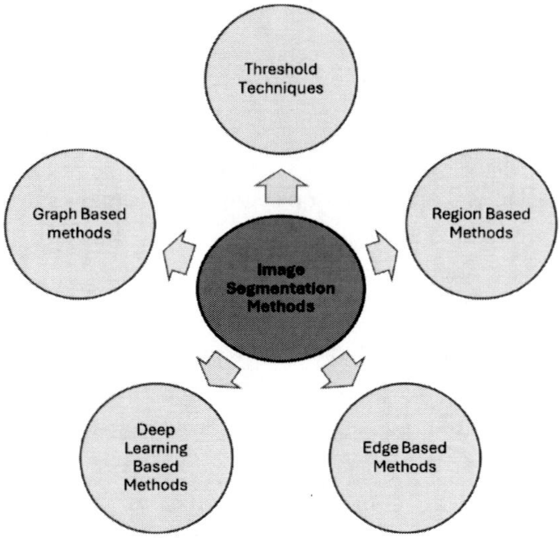

Figure 3.1. Image Segmentation Method.

Some basic customary division methods are:

1. *Thresholding*
   - Introduction: Thresholding is one of the simplest and most used techniques for image segmentation. It is the process of choosing a particular intensity value (threshold) for the separation of pixels foreground and background.
   - Method: Assign pixels with intensity values greater than the threshold foreground and call rest as the background. Examples of implemented methods include, for example, Otsu [21], which finds an optimal threshold as a maximum of inter-class variance.
   - Applications: Useful in applications like document image analysis and medical imaging, where clear distinctions between objects and backgrounds exist.

2. *Edge Detection*
   - Overview: Edge detection methods find sudden changes in pixel brightness, which usually match object edges in an image.
   - Common Algorithms:
   - Sobel Operator: Detects edges based on gradient magnitude.
   - Canny Edge Detector: A multi-stage algorithm that provides good noise reduction and edge detection accuracy.
   - Laplacian of Gaussian: Combines Gaussian smoothing with Laplacian edge detection to find regions of rapid intensity change.
   - Applications: Widely used in object detection and recognition tasks where precise boundary delineation is required.
3. *Region-Based Segmentation*
   - Overview: This technique segments an image into regions based on predefined attributes such as colour, intensity, or texture.
   - Methods:
   - Region Growing: Begins at seed points and grows areas by including nearby pixels that fit similarity rules.
   - Split-and-Merge: Divides the image into smaller regions and merges similar adjacent regions based on attributes like colour or texture.
   - Applications: Particularly effective in medical imaging for identifying organs or tumors due to its ability to handle noise and irregularities.
4. *Clustering-Based Segmentation*
   - Overview: Clustering techniques group pixels with similar characteristics into clusters, effectively segmenting the image based on these groupings.
   - Common Algorithms:
     - K-means Clustering: An unsupervised algorithm that partitions pixels into *k* clusters based on their features (e.g., colour or intensity).
   - Gaussian Mixture Models: Assumptions that data points come from a mix of several Gaussian distributions, leading to more complicatedcluster shapes.
   - Applications: Frequently used in scenarios where objects share similar features but may not have distinct boundaries.

5. *Watershed Segmentation*
   - Overview: This technique treats the image as a topographical map where pixel intensities represent elevation. The watershed lines are identified based on pixel connectivity.
   - Method: The algorithm "floods" the topographical map from seed points until water from different sources meets, effectively segmenting the image into distinct regions.
   - Applications: Useful in separating touching or overlapping objects in images, such as cells in microscopy images.

2.3 Evaluation Metrics for Segmentation (Accuracy, Precision, Recall, etc.)

Evaluating the effectiveness of separation methods is crucial for ensuring their reliability and effectiveness [24]. Common metrics include:

- *Accuracy*: Measures the proportion of correctly classified pixels out of the total pixels.
- *Precision:* Assesses the proportion of true positive segmentations relative to all predicted positive segmentations.
- *Recall (Sensitivity):* Evaluate the proportion of true positive segmentations relative to the actual positives in the ground truth.
- *Dice Similarity Coefficient (DSC):* Quantifies the overlap between the predicted segmentation and the ground truth.
- *Intersection over Union (IoU):* Measures the ratio of the intersection area to the union area between the predicted and ground truth regions.
- *Use Case:* Useful in scenarios where both false positives and false negatives are critical, such as in medical diagnostics

3. Machine Learning for MS Image Segmentation

3.1. Convolutional Neural Networks (CNNs) for Lesion Segmentation

CNNs have proven highly effective in medical image segmentation, particularly for MS lesion detection. By leveraging layers of convolutional filters, CNNs extract hierarchical features from input images, enabling the detection of subtle lesion patterns. Advanced architectures, such as 3D CNNs, further improve performance by capturing spatial dependencies across image slices.

3.2. Deep Learning Architectures (U-Net, SegNet, etc.)

The performance of MS image segmentation has greatly advanced with the use of DL architectures. There are already a lot of popular models on the semantic segmentation task, such as U-Net, which is built on an encoder-decoder structure, using skip connections to maintain spatial information whilst up-sampling [23]. Another recently published architecture, Seg-Net, uses a symmetric encoder-decoder structure and pooling indices to gain accuracy in segmentation. Those architectures effectively learn representative and spatial embeddings, which is a reason why U-Nets architectures are well-suited for heterogeneous MS lesions segmentation.

3.3. Transfer Learning and Fine-Tuning for MS Imaging

The application of transfer learning uses knowledge gained from the analysis of images on one task to improve segmentation on another (e.g., MS lesion detection [24]). Researchers achieve high accuracy with limited annotated data by fine-tuning these models on MS-specific datasets [25]. This mission achieves a balance between minimizing calculation expenses and improving the prediction accuracy while preserving good accuracy.

3.4. Case Studies: Successful ML-Based MS Segmentation Applications

Some notable case studies show successful ML-based methods for MS segmentation. One study applied CNN-based models to achieve highly developed lesion segmentation accuracy on large-scale MS datasets [26]. Likewise, U-Net and its variants have shown impressive segmentation results for challenging lesions in multi-modal MRI data. These applications highlight the transformative potential of ML to improve the diagnosis and monitoring of MS.

Here are notable case studies illustrating successful applications of ML techniques for MS segmentation:

1. *Fully Convolutional Neural Networks for Brain Segmentation*
   Gabr et al. (2020) in this study developed a fully FCNN to segment brain tissues, including T2-hyperintense lesions, from MRI scans of approximately 1000 relapsing-remitting MS patients [27]. The model achieved high accuracy with a DSC of 0.95 for white matter, 0.96 for gray matter, and 0.82 for T2 lesions. The approach demonstrated robust performance across multiple centres, indicating its potential for clinical applications in the automated segmentation of MS lesions.
2. *CNN-based Segmentation Solutions*
   McKinley et al. (2021) in this research explored CNN architectures, including a 3D U-Net and a novel 3D-to-2D architecture called Deep SCAN [28], for simultaneous segmentation of white matter lesions and deep gray matter structures and as a result The study highlighted the effectiveness of these models in providing fast and reliable segmentations, particularly when applied to out-of-center data [29]. Performance was quantified using Dice coefficients and lesion-wise F1 scores, demonstrating the models' adaptability to different datasets.
3. *Consensus Algorithms for Lesion Segmentation*
   De Rosa et al. (2024) evaluated consensus-based approaches using multiple segmentation algorithms to improve lesion detection accuracy in MS. As a result, majority voting method outperformed individual algorithms [30], achieving higher DSC scores for both low and high lesion loads. This approach effectively enhanced the robustness and reproducibility of lesion segmentation across varying datasets
4. *Mask R-CNN for Lesion Detection*
   Yıldırım et al. (2020) proposed an automatic detection method of MS lesions on MRI scans based on Mask R-CNN [31]. The Mask R-CNN yielded promising results in accurately identifying the lesions, thus illustrating the potential of deploying deep learning frameworks in clinical scenarios to increase diagnostic capabilities [31].
5. *Predictive Models for Disability Progression*
   De Brouwer et al. (2024) primarily focused on predicting disability progression in MS patients, this study utilized machine learning models trained on extensive longitudinal data to inform clinical

decision-making [32]. Implication of the integration of such predictive models highlights the broader impact of machine learning beyond segmentation, aiding in treatment planning and patient care.

4. Cognitive Computing for MS Image Analysis

4.1. Introduction to Cognitive Computing

ML, natural language processing, and decision-making are integrated into cognitive computing systems, which strive to replicate human thought processes. They examine and interpret complex data and apply contextual knowledge to increase accuracy and adaptability in decision making. These functions, such as visual analysis, clinical context, and knowledge translation, are relevant to medical imaging, where cognitive computing could at least progress the way, we understand and interpret dynamic and complex pathologies such as multiple sclerosis [33].

4.2. Attention Mechanisms for Lesion Detection

ML, natural language processing, and decision-making are integrated into cognitive computing systems, which strive to replicate human thought processes. They examine and interpret complex data and apply contextual knowledge to increase accuracy and adaptability in decision making. These functions, such as visual analysis, clinical context, and knowledge translation, are relevant to medical imaging, where cognitive computing could at least progress the way, we understand and interpret dynamic and complex pathologies such as multiple sclerosis [33].

4.3. Integration of Domain Knowledge and Expert Systems

Integrating domain knowledge and expert systems with MS imaging will allow the creation of cognitive computing capable of achieving a more accurate MS image. These systems further integrate medical guidelines, imaging protocols, and clinician expertise with segmentation outputs.

Cognitive systems produce clinically relevant and interpretable results by combining data-driven algorithms with human knowledge [34].

4.4. Cognitive Architectures for MS Image Analysis

More complex cognitive architectures like IBM Watson and others are designed to examine the imaging data of physicians, focusing on the appearance of images that signal problems and issues related to treatment specific to MS [35]. Versions of these architectures incorporate multi-modal data integration, progressive learning, and real-time analytics for improved lesion segmentation and disease monitoring. Using cognitive architectures may improve diagnosis and patient outcomes [36].

5. Applications of Automatic MS Image Segmentation

5.1. Lesion Detection and Segmentation

Relying on automatic detection and segmentation, MS lesions were identified in the acquired MR images [37-39]. The automatic segmentation of lesions reduces the dependency on manual techniques, allowing these systems to define the borders of a lesion accurately and improve diagnostic throughput [40]. Improved lesion segmentation also aids in disease surveillance and treatment planning [41].

5.2. Brain Atrophy Measurement

Brain atrophy is a significant marker of MS progression. Automated segmentation techniques enable precise quantification of brain volume changes over time, aiding in the early detection of neurodegeneration and assessment of therapeutic efficacy [42]

5.3. Disease Progression Monitoring

Segmentation tools are critical for monitoring disease progression through the follow-up of lesion evolution and brain atrophy [43]. These insights are a powerful tool for clinicians, enabling them to gauge the success of treatments and inform patient care with data-derived insights.

5.4. Treatment Response Evaluation

Automated segmentation systems assess treatment responses by comparing imaging data before and after treatment [44]. These change metrics (of lesion size, number, and activity) are used as objective measures to inform treatment modification decisions and optimize patient care.

6. Challenges, Limitations, and Forthcoming Directions

6.1. Current Challenges and Limitations

Automatic MS image segmentation continues to face challenges even though substantial progress has been made. The main challenges consist of inconsistent imaging protocols along with the low contrast between lesions and surrounding tissue and various artifacts. Clinical implementation faces challenges because curated annotated datasets are missing and training sophisticated models demands high computational resources. Cross-population and cross-center generalizability and robustness stay central to medical imaging research.

6.1.1. Challenges in Automatic Image Segmentation

1. *Data Scarcity and Quality Issues*
    - Limited Labelled Data: Annotated datasets needed for deep learning training remain scarce which creates significant challenges for developing models to detect rare diseases such as MS. The shortage of data restricts the creation of reliable models that can apply universally to various patient groups.

- Variability in Imaging Protocols: Differences in imaging protocols across institutions lead to inconsistencies in image quality and characteristics, complicating model training and performance.

2. *Noise and Artifacts*
   - Image Noise: Noise and artifacts in medical images often hide essential features that segmentation algorithms need to recognize. Frequent image artifacts such as motion artifacts, partial volume effects along with intensity inhomogeneities appear in medical imaging.
3. *Generalization Across Different Datasets*
   - Model Overfitting: Deep learning models may struggle to generalize when applied to data from different machines or acquisition protocols [40]. This lack of robustness can lead to poor performance when the model encounters new data distributions.
4. *Interpretability and Explainability*
   - Black Box Nature of AI: Lots of machine learning models, especially DL networks, work like "black boxes." This makes it hard for doctors to see how decisions are made. This lack of clarity can reduce trust in automated systems.

6.1.2. Limitations of Current Approaches

1. *Algorithm Specificity*
   - No Universal Solution: There is no one-size-fits-all algorithm for medical image segmentation; each imaging modality has specific limitations. For example, segmentation techniques effective for CT scans may not perform well on MRI data due to differing artifact profiles
2. *Computational Demands*
   - Resource Intensity: Developing advanced deep learning models demands significant computational power which typically takes days or weeks to accomplish. Widespread clinical adoption faces challenges due to the intensive resources and time required for training deep learning models.

3. *Manual Intervention Needs*
    - Need for Expert Oversight: Despite advances in automation, many segmentation processes still require manual corrections by trained professionals, which can be time-consuming and introduce human bias into the results.

6.2. Future Research Directions

Research moving forward must focus on developing advanced algorithms that handle various medical image types and conditions. Segmentation accuracy can be improved through multimodal fusion techniques that merge data from T1, T2, and FLAIR sequences. Longitudinal data integration for tracking disease progression combined with federated learning applications for safeguarding data privacy represents promising research directions.

1. *Development of Robust Algorithms*
    - Adaptive Learning Models: The research community should develop algorithms that continuously learn from incoming data throughout their operation. Models will demonstrate progressive improvement through enhanced performance on varied datasets while minimizing extensive retraining requirements.
    - Hybrid Models: Combining traditional image processing techniques with deep learning approaches can lead to more robust segmentation methods. Hybrid models could leverage the strengths of both paradigms, improving accuracy in challenging scenarios.
2. *Enhanced Data Utilization*
    - Data Augmentation Techniques: The development of sophisticated data augmentation strategies helps to address the challenge of restricted labelled datasets. Generative adversarial networks generate synthetic data to produce realistic training examples which improve model robustness.
    - Federated Learning: Federated learning frameworks enable foundations to cooperate on model training without exchanging sensitive patient data. The technique improves model performance through the use of various datasets without breaching any privacy regulations.

3. *Multi-Modal Imaging Integration*
    - Combining Imaging Modalities: Future research should explore the integration of multiple imaging modalities (e.g., MRI, CT, PET) to provide a comprehensive understanding of anatomical structures and disease processes. Multi-modal approaches can enhance segmentation accuracy by leveraging complementary information from different imaging techniques.
4. *Focus on Interpretability and Explainability*
    - Explainable AI Techniques: Making ways to improve how ML models can be understood is very important for them to be accepted in clinical settings. Research should aim at building tools that explain the reasons behind segmentation choices, which will help clinicians to have faith in and understand the results given by automation.
    - Visualization Tools: Creating effective visualization tools that highlight the regions of interest and decision-making processes within the images can facilitate better communication between AI systems and healthcare professionals.
    - Real-Time Processing Capabilities Efficient Algorithms for Real-Time Applications: Research should aim to develop lightweight algorithms capable of real-time processing in clinical settings. This includes optimizing existing models to run efficiently on standard hardware, enabling timely decision-making during patient care.
5. *Personalized Medicine Approaches*
    - Patient-Specific Models: Future studies could focus on developing segmentation models tailored to individual patients based on their unique imaging characteristics and clinical histories. Personalized models could improve treatment planning and monitoring by providing more accurate assessments of disease progression.
    - Longitudinal Studies and Temporal Analysis Monitoring Sickness Progression: Studies need to emphasize longitudinal studies that examine changes in segmentation over time. Knowledge of how lesions evolve can provide precious insights into ailment progression and remedy efficacy.
    - Dynamic Segmentation fashions: growing fashions able to read temporal sequences of pixel will permit for higher tracking of

lesion activity and modifications in brain structure related to MS.8. Collaboration Across Disciplines.

- Interdisciplinary Research Initiatives: Encouraging cooperation betwixt computer physicists, radiologists, neurologists, and different healthcare artists will support innovative approaches to mechanical figure separation. Interdisciplinary teams can address complex challenges in a more excellent manner by joining knowledge from various fields.

Conclusion

The unification of machine intelligence and cognitive estimating has concreted the way for significant progress in mechanical image separation for healing imaging, specifically in the framework of Multiple Sclerosis. These sciences address critical challenges in wound discovery, disease listening, and situation judgment, offering correct and adept solutions that reinforce patient care. While challenges are pursued, continuous research and innovation promise to further perfect these arrangements, making them necessary finishes in up-to-date healthcare. By combining computational accuracy accompanying human-like reasoning, mechanized separation arrangements represent an example shift in healing imaging, reconstructing effects for cases and clinicians alike.

References

[1] Lundervold, A. S., & Lundervold, A. (2019). An overview of deep learning in medical imaging focusing on MRI. *Zeitschrift für Medizinische Physik, 29*(2), 102–127. https://doi.org/10.1016/j.zemedi.2018.11.002.

[2] Zhu, Y., Cheng, Z., Wang, S., & Zhang, H. (2024). Learning de-biased prototypes for few-shot medical image segmentation. *Pattern Recognition Letters, 183*, 71–77. https://doi.org/10.1016/j.patrec.2024.01.011.

[3] Ker, J., Wang, L., Rao, J., & Lim, T. (2017). Deep learning applications in medical image analysis. *IEEE Access, 6*, 9375–9389. https://doi.org/10.1109/ACCESS.2017.2772518.

[4] Tajbakhsh, N., Jeyaseelan, L., Li, Q., Chiang, J. N., Wu, Z., & Ding, X. (2020). Embracing imperfect datasets: A review of deep learning solutions for medical image segmentation. *Medical Image Analysis, 63*, 101693. https://doi.org/10.1016/j.media.2020.101693.

[5] Ravishankar, H., Sudhakar, P., Venkataramani, R., Thiruvenkadam, S., Annangi, P., Babu, N., & Vaidya, V. (2017). Understanding the mechanisms of deep transfer learning for medical images. *arXiv Preprint* arXiv:1704.06040. https://arxiv.org/abs/1704.06040.

[6] Guo, Z., Li, X., Huang, H., Guo, N., & Li, Q. (2019). Deep learning-based image segmentation on multimodal medical imaging. *IEEE Transactions on Radiation and Plasma Medical Sciences, 3*(2), 162–169. https://doi.org/10.1109/TRPMS.2019.2902957.

[7] Hesamian, M. H., Jia, W., He, X., & Kennedy, P. (2019). Deep learning techniques for medical image segmentation: Achievements and challenges. *Journal of Digital Imaging, 32*, 582–596. https://doi.org/10.1007/s10278-019-00221-0.

[8] Dobson, R., & Giovannoni, G. (2019). Multiple sclerosis–a review. *European Journal of Neurology, 26*(1), 27–40. https://doi.org/10.1111/ene.13746.

[9] Brola, W., Mitosek-Szewczyk, K., & Opara, J. (2014). Symptomatology and pathogenesis of different types of pain in multiple sclerosis. *Neurologia i Neurochirurgia Polska, 48*(4), 272–279. https://doi.org/10.1016/j.pjnns.2014.03.008.

[10] Iqbal, M. S., Heyat, M. B. B., Parveen, S., Hayat, M. A. B., Roshanzamir, M., Alizadehsani, R., & Sawan, M. (2024). Progress and trends in neurological disorders research based on deep learning. *Computerized Medical Imaging and Graphics, 116*, 102400. https://doi.org/10.1016/j.compmedimag.2024.102400.

[11] Kamnitsas, K., Ledig, C., Newcombe, V. F., Simps on, J. P., Kane, A. D., Menon, D. K., & Glocker, B. (2017). Efficient multi-scale 3D CNN with fully connected CRF for accurate brain lesion segmentation. *Medical Image Analysis, 36*, 61–78. https://doi.org/10.1016/j.media.2016.10.001.

[12] Bernard, O., Lalande, A., Zotti, C., Cervenansky, F., Yang, X., Heng, P. A., Cetin, I., Lekadir, K., Camara, O., Ballester, M. A. G., Sanroma, G., Hoogendoorn, C., Konukoglu, E., Sehgal, A., Mohiaddin, R., Pace, D. F., Vitanis, V., Shetty, A. K., Lu, H., & Jodoin, P. M. (2018). Deep learning techniques for automatic MRI cardiac multi-structures segmentation and diagnosis: Is the problem solved? *IEEE Transactions on Medical Imaging, 37*(11), 2514–2525. https://doi.org/10.1109/TMI.2018.2837502.

[13] Pereira, S. R. M. (2018). *Automatic segmentation and classification of brain tumors based on multisequence MRI images with deep learning methods* (Doctoral dissertation, Universidade do Minho, Portugal).

[14] Ramesh, K. K. D., Kumar, G. K., Swapna, K., Datta, D., & Rajest, S. S. (2021). A review of medical image segmentation algorithms. *EAI Endorsed Transactions on Pervasive Health & Technology, 7*(27). https://doi.org/10.4108/eai.17-12-2020.166602.

[15] Rathore, M. M., Shah, S. A., Shukla, D., Bentafat, E., & Bakiras, S. (2021). The role of AI, machine learning, and big data in digital twinning: A systematic literature review, challenges, and opportunities. *IEEE Access, 9*, 32030–32052. https://doi.org/10.1109/ACCESS.2021.3063475.

[16] Zhao, L., Chen, X., Chen, E. Z., Liu, Y., Chen, T., & Sun, S. (2024). Retrieval-augmented few-shot medical image segmentation with foundation models. *arXiv preprint arXiv:2408.08813*. https://arxiv.org/abs/2408.08813.

[17] Hartmann, D., Müller, F., Schulz, C., & Maier, A. (2023). MISM: A medical image segmentation metric for evaluation of weak labeled data. *Diagnostics, 13*(16), 2618. https://doi.org/10.3390/diagnostics13162618.

[18] Milletari, F., Navab, N., & Ahmadi, S. A. (2016). V-net: Fully convolutional neural networks for volumetric medical image segmentation. In *Proceedings of the 4th International Conference on 3D Vision (3DV)* (pp. 565–571). IEEE. https://doi.org/10.1109/3DV.2016.79.

[19] Wang, X., & Zhu, H. (2024). Artificial intelligence in image-based cardiovascular disease analysis: A comprehensive survey and future outlook. *arXiv preprint arXiv:2402.03394*. https://arxiv.org/abs/2402.03394.

[20] Liu, Z., Tong, L., Chen, L., Jiang, Z., Zhou, F., & Zhang, H. (2023). Deep learning-based brain tumor segmentation: A survey. *Complex & Intelligent Systems, 9*(1), 1001–1026. https://doi.org/10.1007/s40747-023-00786-2.

[21] Li, X., Chen, H., Qi, X., Dou, Q., Fu, C. W., & Heng, P. A. (2018). H-DenseUNet: Hybrid densely connected UNet for liver and tumor segmentation from CT volumes. *IEEE Transactions on Medical Imaging, 37*(12), 2663–2674. https://doi.org/10.1109/TMI.2018.2851764.

[22] Liu, X., Song, L., Liu, S., & Zhang, Y. (2021). A review of deep-learning-based medical image segmentation methods. *Sustainability, 13*(3), 1224. https://doi.org/10.3390/su13031224.

[23] Ronneberger, O., Fischer, P., & Brox, T. (2015). U-Net: Convolutional networks for biomedical image segmentation. In *Medical Image Computing and Computer-Assisted Intervention–MICCAI 2015* (pp. 234–241). Springer. https://doi.org/10.1007/978-3-319-24574-4_28.

[24] Azad, R., Asadi-Aghbolaghi, M., Fathy, M., & Escalera, S. (2019). Bi-directional ConvLSTM U-Net with densely connected convolutions. In *Proceedings of the IEEE/CVF International Conference on Computer Vision Workshops* (pp. 0–0). IEEE. https://doi.org/10.1109/ICCVW.2019.00025.

[25] Cadow, J., Manica, M., Mathis, R., Reddel, R. R., Robinson, P. J., Wild, P. J., Zinn, P. O., Huber, F., Schwalbe, M., & Rodríguez Martínez, M. (2021). On the feasibility of deep learning applications using raw mass spectrometry data. *Bioinformatics, 37*(Supplement_1), i245–i253. https://doi.org/10.1093/bioinformatics/btab271.

[26] Wang, W., Wang, G., Wu, X., Ding, X., Cao, X., Wang, L., Zhang, J., & Wang, P. (2021). Automatic segmentation of prostate magnetic resonance imaging using generative adversarial networks. *Clinical Imaging, 70*, 1–9. https://doi.org/10.1016/j.clinimag.2020.10.015.

[27] Rosas-Gonzalez, S., Birgui-Sekou, T., Hidane, M., Zemmoura, I., & Tauber, C. (2021). Asymmetric ensemble of asymmetric U-Net models for brain tumor segmentation with uncertainty estimation. *Frontiers in Neurology, 12*, 609646. https://doi.org/10.3389/fneur.2021.609646.

[28] De Rosa, A. P., Benedetto, M., Tagliaferri, S., Bardozzo, F., D'Ambrosio, A., Bisecco, A., Cocozza, S., Tozza, S., Russo, C., Bonavita, S., & Tedeschi, G. (2024).

Consensus of algorithms for lesion segmentation in brain MRI studies of multiple sclerosis. *Scientific Reports, 14*(1), 21348. https://doi.org/10.1038/s41598-024-28331-2.

[29] Yıldırım, S., & Dandıl, E. (2020). Automatic detection of multiple sclerosis lesions using Mask R-CNN on magnetic resonance scans. *IET Image Processing, 14*(16), 4277–4290. https://doi.org/10.1049/iet-ipr.2020.0591.

[30] Brouwer, H. J., Barry, M., Kluijtmans, M., Damoiseaux, R. A. M. J., & de Groot, E. (2025). Fostering the clinician as teacher: A realist review. *Medical Education, 59*(2), 151–163. https://doi.org/10.1111/medu.13010

[31] Sevakula, R. K., Au-Yeung, W. T. M., Singh, J. P., Heist, E. K., Isselbacher, E. M., & Armoundas, A. A. (2020). State-of-the-art machine learning techniques aiming to improve patient outcomes pertaining to the cardiovascular system. *Journal of the American Heart Association, 9*(4), e013924. https://doi.org/10.1161/JAHA.119.013924.

[32] Wang, R., Lei, T., Cui, R., Zhang, B., Meng, H., & Nandi, A. K. (2022). Medical image segmentation using deep learning: A survey. *IET Image Processing, 16*(5), 1243-1267. https://doi.org/10.1049/ipr2.12171.

[33] Schwid, S. R., Covington, M. M. S. B., Segal, B. M., & Goodman, A. D. (2002). Fatigue in multiple sclerosis: Current understanding and future directions. *Journal of Rehabilitation Research & Development, 39*(2). https://doi.org/10.1682/JRRD.2002.04.0052.

[34] Wei, C., Yang, Y., Guo, X., Ye, C., Lv, H., Xiang, Y., & Ma, T. (2022). MRF-Net: A multi-branch residual fusion network for fast and accurate whole-brain MRI segmentation. *Frontiers in Neuroscience, 16*, 940381. https://doi.org/10.3389/fnins.2022.940381.

[35] Wang, F., Gao, W., Liu, Q., Li, J., Zhao, G., Zhang, Z., & Chen, E. (2024). A survey of models for cognitive diagnosis: New developments and future directions. *arXiv preprint arXiv:2407.05458*. https://doi.org/10.48550/arXiv.2407.05458.

[36] Zhang, N. (2011). Feature selection-based segmentation of multi-source images: Application to brain tumor segmentation in multi-sequence MRI (Doctoral dissertation, INSA de Lyon).

[37] Ahirwar, A., & Jadon, R. S. (2011). Tumor region extraction in cancerous brain MRI images. *International Journal of Computer Information Systems (IJCIS), 2*(4), 72–76. Silicon Valley Publishers.

[38] Ahirwar, A. (2012). Computation of statistical features of brain MR images. *Journal of Global Research in Computer Science (JGRCS), 3*(1), 45–49.

[39] Ahirwar, A., & Jadon, R. S. (2015). FCSOFM technique for medical image segmentation. *International Journal of Bio-Science and Bio-Technology (IJBSBT), 7*(4), 277–282.

[40] Ahirwar, A., & Jadon, R. S. (2013). Effectiveness of soft computing techniques for medical imaging. In *Proceedings of the 5th International Conference on Computational Intelligence & Communication Networks (CICN 2013)* (pp. 336–338). IEEE. https://doi.org/10.1109/CICN.2013.7.

[41] Bakas, S., Reyes, M., Jakab, A., Bauer, S., Rempfler, M., Crimi, A., & Jambawalikar, S. R. (2018). Identifying the best machine learning algorithms for

brain tumor segmentation, progression assessment, and overall survival prediction in the BRATS challenge. *arXiv preprint arXiv:1811.02629*. https://doi.org/10.48550/arXiv.1811.02629.

[42] Dolz, J., Desrosiers, C., & Ben Ayed, I. (2018). 3D fully convolutional networks for subcortical segmentation in MRI: A large-scale study. *NeuroImage, 170*, 456–470. https://doi.org/10.1016/j.neuroimage.2017.12.070.

[43] Rudnicka, Z., Szczepanski, J., & Pregowska, A. (2024). Artificial intelligence-based algorithms in medical image scan segmentation and intelligent visual content generation—A concise overview. *Electronics, 13*(4), 746. https://doi.org/10.3390/electronics13040746.

[44] Khurana, V., Gahalawat, M., Kumar, P., Roy, P. P., Dogra, D. P., Scheme, E., & Soleymani, M. (2021). A survey on neuromarketing using EEG signals. *IEEE Transactions on Cognitive and Developmental Systems, 13*(4), 732–749. https://doi.org/10.1109/TCDS.2021.3054534.

Chapter 4

Cognitive Computing's Theoretical Underpinnings: From Neuroscience to Artificial Intelligence

Shubhra Dixit*
Ajay Sharma†
and Surbhi Gupta‡
Amity University, Noida, Uttar Pradesh, India

Abstract

The theoretical foundations of cognitive computing are examined in this chapter, which links developments in artificial intelligence (AI) with discoveries from neuroscience. The definition of cognitive computing and its multidisciplinary foundations are covered. Examined is the basis of neuroscience, with a focus on Hebbian learning, neural mechanisms and brain plasticity. AI paradigms are then explored, contrasting symbolic reasoning with neural networks and deep learning. Core theoretical concepts, including adaptive learning, pattern recognition, Bayesian inference, and decision-making, are analysed to demonstrate how these ideas drive cognitive computing's development.

The chapter explores multidisciplinary integration, demonstrating how algorithms and computational models inspired by neuroscience are informed by these concepts. Along with technological and ethical issues including bias, interpretability, and system constraints, practical applications in healthcare, robotics and other fields are covered. Finally,

---

* Corresponding Author's Email: sdixit3@amity.edu
† Corresponding Author's Email: asharma3@amity.edu
‡ Corresponding Author's Email: sgupta11@amity.edu

In: Building Intelligent Systems for the Future
Editors: Anamika Ahirwar, Neelesh Jain and Sumitha Elayaperumal
ISBN: 979-8-90134-050-9

future scopes are considered, emphasizing innovations at the intersection of neuroscience and AI, and outlining pathways toward achieving more human-like and generalized intelligence through cognitive computing.

Keywords: cognitive computing, neuroscience, Hebbian learning, neural mechanisms, neural networks, deep learning

1. Introduction

Cognitive computing is thought to represent a transformation in the computer industry, and this maturity is tied to the ability to understand the human brain. First, it would be interesting to understand why the importance of this area of research has been increasing for few years. The chapters of this book presume that cognitive computing is an extension of the capability of artificial intelligence. For instance, the study suggests that the origins of cognitive computing are related to the ability to see, for example, to learn and to adapt. Brain structure, pathways, activity in the brain and how it works have all been studied and created algorithms. Since all the units of deep learning are capable of superior computations of any logical or reasoning nature, the intellect is also capable of mastering. It also involves some complexities and ambiguities. In addition to these conflicts, cognitive ethics of advanced artificial agents raises a deep alarm. In the modern world, many of the issues have been a common concern for all these theorists, philosophers, anthropologists and ethicists. The aim of this chapter and the entire dissertation from an anthropological perspective will be to try to fill this gap.

2. Basis of Neuroscience

The human brain, renowned for its remarkable abilities in learning, reasoning, and adaptation, serves as the primary inspiration for cognitive computing. Neuroscience, a vast repository of knowledge, unveils the mechanisms underlying human cognitive processes, providing the theoretical foundation upon which cognitive computing frameworks are built. Below are some fundamental principles of neuroscience and their connection to computational models:

2.1. Neural Networks: The Blueprint for Intelligence

Neurons, the fundamental building blocks of the brain, communicate within intricate networks where electrical signals pass through synapses. These networks enable parallel and distributed processing, allowing the brain to handle multiple tasks simultaneously such as interpreting sensory inputs while maintaining focus on specific objectives [1].

In cognitive computing, artificial neural networks (ANNs) are inspired by this biological architecture. While artificial neurons are simplified representations, they emulate the interconnected behaviour of biological neurons. Computational units in ANNs process inputs, apply weighted connections to simulate synaptic strengths, and produce outputs that influence subsequent layers, mirroring the brain's information flow [2] (see Figure 4.1).

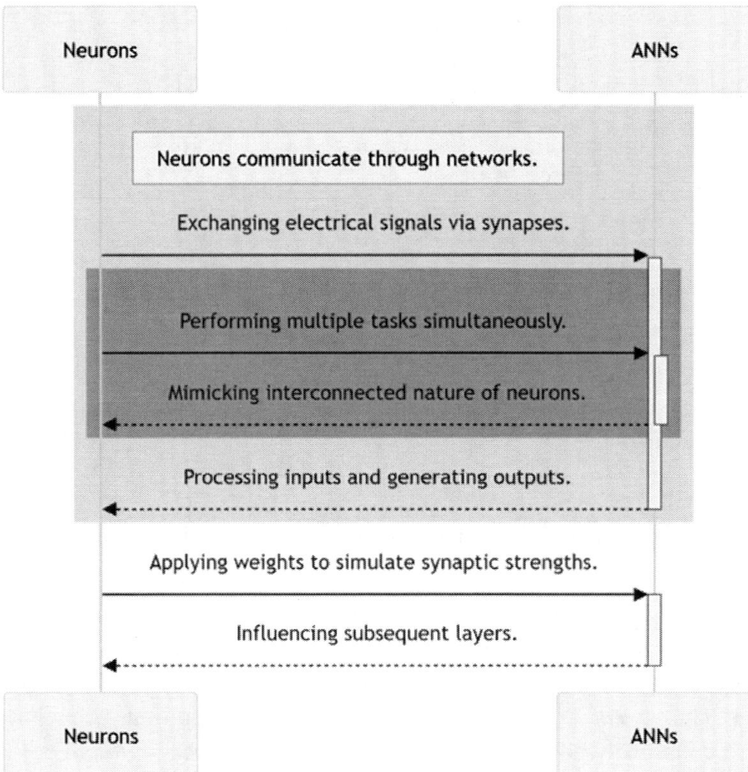

Figure 4.1. Blueprint of sequence of process.

2.2. Synaptic Plasticity and Hebbian Learning

The concept of synaptic plasticity, where synapses strengthen or weaken based on usage, is fundamental to learning in biological systems. Synaptic adjustments enable the formation of long-term memories and the refinement of skills through practice.

Cognitive computing implements these ideas through algorithms like backpropagation in deep learning, where the system iteratively adjusts weights to minimize errors [3]. The biological analogy informs reinforcement learning techniques, where systems improve their behaviour through trial-and-error interactions with their environment. Figure 4.2 represents general distribution of Synaptic Plasticity cognitive computing and Hebbian Learning.

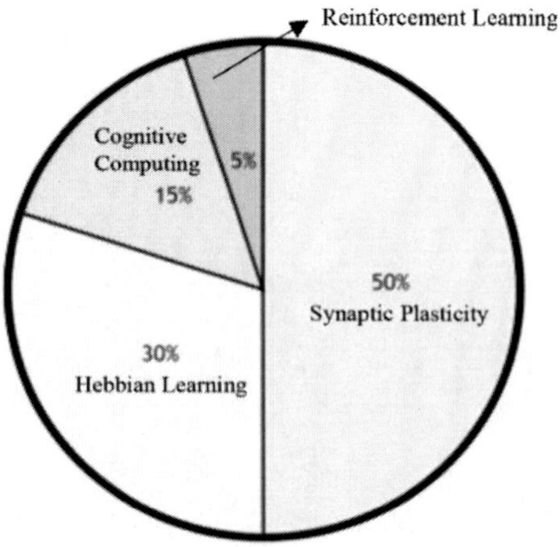

Figure 4.2. General distribution of Synaptic Plasticity cognitive computing and Hebbian Learning.

2.3. Specialized Brain Regions and Cognitive Architectures

Neuroscience has mapped the brain into regions specialized for distinct functions. For example:

- The *visual cortex* processes image data, inspiring convolutional neural networks (CNNs) for tasks like object recognition [4].

- The *hippocampus* plays a critical role in memory formation, influencing memory storage mechanisms in machine learning systems.
- The *prefrontal cortex* governs decision-making and planning, informing AI models designed for strategic reasoning and problem-solving.

Cognitive computing seeks to replicate these specialized functions, often by creating modular systems where different components mimic the distributed nature of the brain (Figure 4.3).

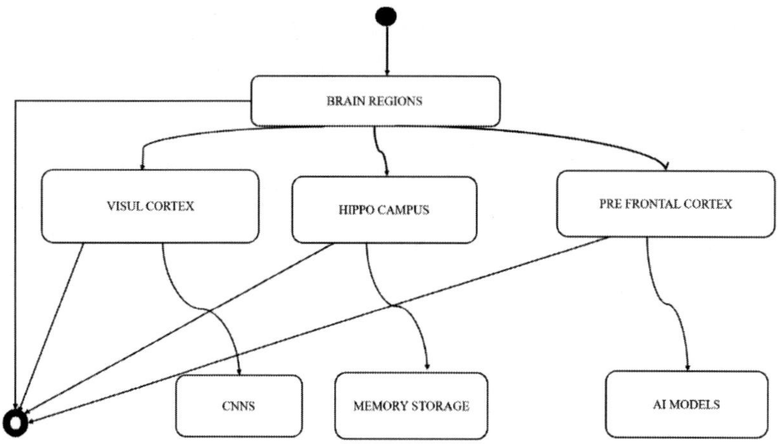

Figure 4.3. State diagram of mapping of brain.

2.4. Neuromodulation and Adaptive Behaviour

The brain's adaptability is further enhanced by neuromodulators like dopamine, which regulate learning and motivation. These mechanisms inspire reward-based learning in AI, such as in reinforcement learning frameworks where agents optimize their actions to maximize cumulative rewards.

2.5. Biological Fidelity vs. Computational Efficiency

While the brain operates with remarkable energy efficiency, processing vast amounts of data with minimal energy, replicating this in computational systems remains a challenge. Cognitive computing often simplifies biological processes into mathematical representations, such as activation functions and gradient-based optimization [5]. These abstractions enable scalability and practical applications but leave room for improvement in mimicking biological efficiency and robustness.

2.6. Cognitive Computing and the Limits of Neuroscience

Despite notable advances in neuroscience, much has still not been fully understood regarding the brain's development of consciousness, creativity, and higher-order reasoning. Therefore, models of cognitive computing must work within the limits of this knowledge base and strive to emulate capabilities in human-like fashion but within the anticipation of further developments in neuroscience.

Having a neuroscientific understanding aid in engineering of cognition so that effective computing systems are built which in turn advises improvements in cognitive systems [6]. On the other hand, this continuous interaction between the two domains also contributes towards the development of intelligent systems with the hope of newer solutions that would blend biological and artificial intelligence.

3. Artificial Intelligence Paradigms

The convergence of artificial intelligence (AI) paradigms creates the basis of cognitive computing which involves understanding, reasoning, and adapting. Artificial neurons form the foundation of neurobiology, neural networks, and deep learning, enabling pattern recognition and learning from data to perform tasks like natural language processing and image recognition. However, logic-based systems that also rely on a set of written rules known as symbolic reasoning also offer an ability to explain and solve formal problems. Bayesian networks, among other probabilistic models, are also effective tools since they facilitate reasoning capability in the face of uncertainty while more evidence is added. All of them contribute to cognitive computing in the sense that they attempt to mimic forms of human intelligence by incorporating, among others, the reasoning processes behind the action although it could be interpreted in a specific time frame [7].

3.1. Neural Networks and Deep Learning

The foundational concepts of artificial intelligence, neural networks and deep learning are greatly influenced by the composition and operations of the human brain. By using artificial neurons layers of interconnected nodes that process and transfer information similarly to biological neurons these methods [8–9] simulate intelligence.

3.2. Neural Networks (ANNs)

Artificial Neural Networks (ANNs) consist of interconnected neurons across input, hidden, and output layers as shown in Figure 4. Weights between neurons determine signal strength, adjusted during training using backpropagation and optimization algorithms like gradient descent. These networks process raw data, perform computations with activation functions, and produce predictions or classifications, enabling tasks like pattern recognition.

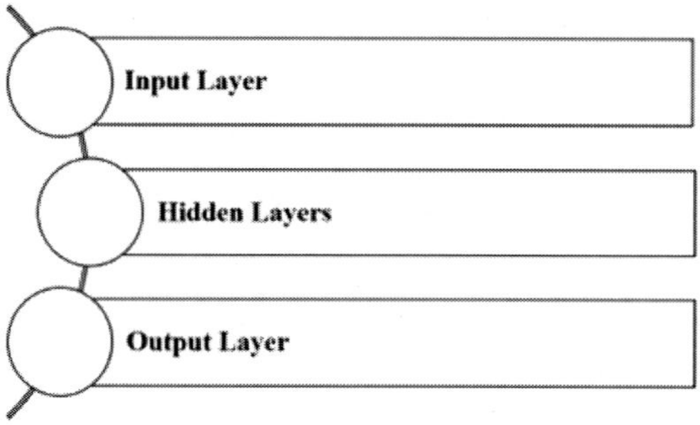

Figure 4.4. Layers of neural network.

3.3. Deep Learning

The word "deep" comes from the fact that Deep Learning (DL) is a type of neural networks that have several hidden layers. These deeper architectures enable the network to learn hierarchical features from data, where each layer extracts more abstract representations [10-11]. For example, in image recognition:

- Lower layers might learn to detect edges.
- Intermediate layers identify shapes or textures.
- These characteristics are combined by higher layers to identify objects.

Common architectures in deep learning include (Figure 4.5):

- *Convolutional Neural Networks (CNNs):* excel at processing grid-like inputs such as images or videos by leveraging convolutional layers to automatically extract spatial feature hierarchies.
- *Recurrent Neural Networks (RNNs):* RNNs) are used for sequential data as they retain memory of prior inputs, making them well-suited for applications.
- *Generative Adversarial Networks (GANs):* consist of two competing networks: a generator and a discriminator. They work together to create new data, making GANs widely used for tasks like image generation and style transfer.

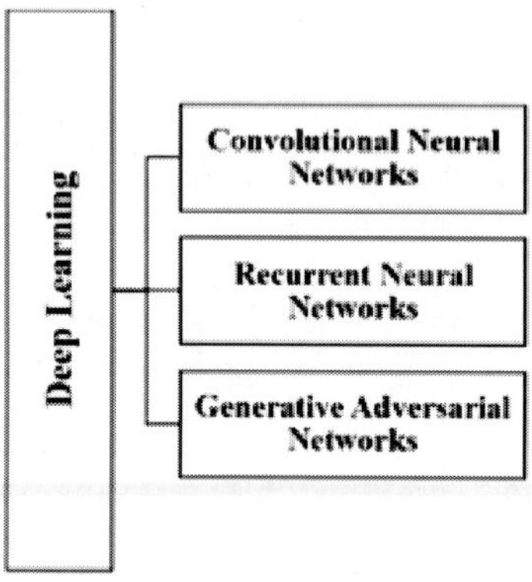

Figure 4.5. Common deep learning techniques.

3.3.1. Training Neural Networks

The process of Training Neural Network includes (Figure 4.6):

- *Forward Pass:* Deep learning model training demands significant computational resources and large datasets. It involves a forward pass to generate predictions and a loss function.

- *Loss Function:* A function, like mean squared error or cross-entropy, to quantify discrepancies between predicted and actual values
- *Backward Pass:* Backpropagation and optimization algorithms like gradient descent, the model adjusts weights to minimize the loss function.

Over time, the network improves its performance as it learns from more data and fine-tunes its parameters. Advanced techniques such as dropout, batch normalization, and transfer learning help improve generalization and speed up training [12].

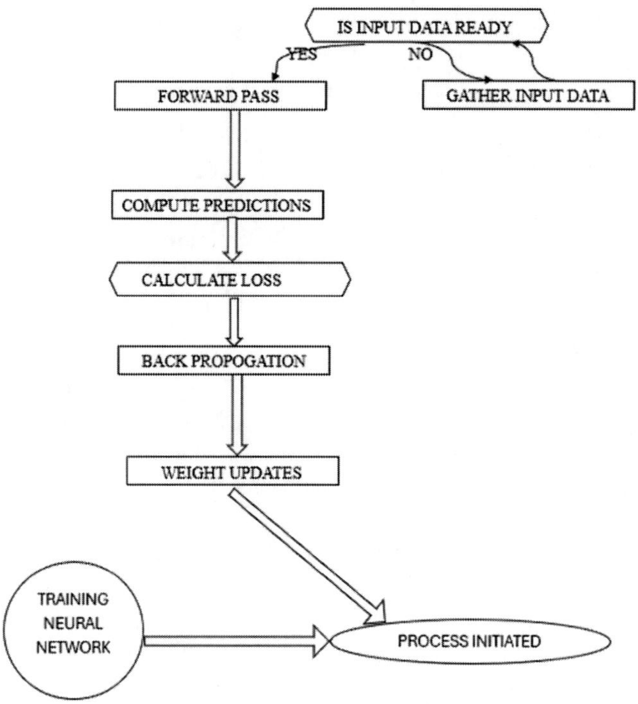

Figure 4.6. Complete process of neural network training.

3.3.2. Neural Networks and Deep Learning in Cognitive Computing

Neural networks and deep learning are central to cognitive computing because they enable systems to process and learn from unstructured data, like how the human brain learns from sensory inputs. These technologies [13] power many cognitive applications, such as:

- *Image and Speech Recognition*: Deep learning models directly learn features, excelling at object detection and speech-to-text.
- *Natural Language Processing (NLP):* Transformers enable language understanding and generation.
- *Autonomous Systems:* Deep learning models process sensor data for navigation.

Overall, neural networks and deep learning represent a significant leap in cognitive computing, enabling AI systems to exhibit high levels of performance in tasks that involve pattern recognition, decision-making, and adaptation, much like the human brain.

3.3.3. Symbolic Reasoning and Probabilistic Models

- *Symbolic Reasoning:* This is the top-down type of artificial intelligence that works with frameworks based on logics to encode and compute with structured knowledge. Its important components include:
- *Knowledge Representation*: Formal structures such as propositional or predicate logic, semantic networks, and ontologies are used in the representation of information. For example, a rule might be written as If A and B, then C.
- *Inference Mechanisms*: To infer new data or even conclusions, algorithms rely on logical processes such as the use of modus ponens or resolution. One such form of reasoning has been expressed in tools like Prologue and rule-based systems.

For explainable AI applications, symbolic thinking works well, particularly in planning, legal analysis, and moral judgement. However, it has scalability problems when handling ambiguity and unstructured data.

3.3.4. Probabilistic Models

By using probability theory, probabilistic models add uncertainty to AI thinking. Major components of such models include:

- *Bayesian Networks:* Bayesian networks are directed acyclic graphs with conditional dependencies and nodes. A conditional probability table (CPT) is linked to every node [14]. Utilizing probabilistic weights, for example, a Bayesian network for medical diagnosis can simulate the connections between symptoms and illnesses.

- *Probabilistic Model Inference:* Models can update their beliefs as new data becomes available by using techniques like Markov Chain Monte Carlo (MCMC) or belief propagation to compute posterior probabilities.

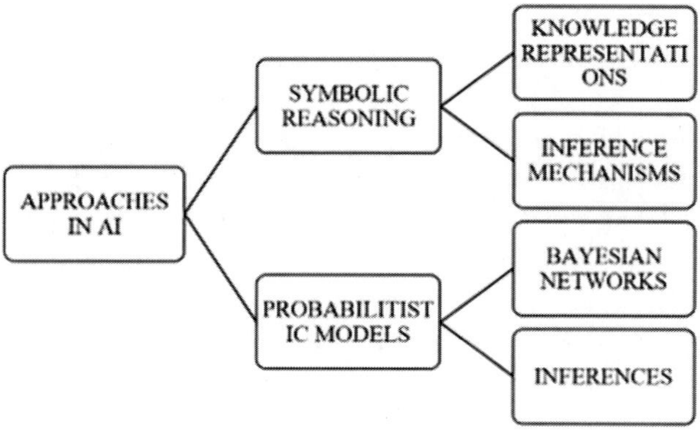

Figure 4.7. General Approaches in AI.

These models are perfect for real-world uses like spam filtering, fault diagnostics, and recommendation systems because they perform exceptionally well when dealing with noisy or missing data (Figure 4.7).

3.3.5. Cognitive Computing Integration

Structure, logical reasoning, and interpretability are made possible by symbolic reasoning. Probabilistic models, on the other hand, are adaptable and useful for handling uncertainty. Combining these paradigms makes cognitive systems more capable of reasoning in the dynamic and unpredictable environment needed to more closely resemble human decision-making and problem-solving.

4. Theoretical Underpinnings

The theoretical foundations of cognitive computing borrow concepts from artificial intelligence and neurology. Hebbian learning underpins reinforcement learning methods in AI that allow systems to adapt their performance with time. Similar to the way humans perceive sensory information, pattern recognition aids in identifying significant structures in data by cognitive systems [15]. Besides this, contextual knowledge makes possible the analysis of data by an AI relative to its environment. So, the systems react according to circumstances and change along with time. All of these concepts are together serving for creating intelligent systems almost like the human brain does.

4.1. Hebbian Learning and Adaptive Systems

Hebbian learning is a fundamental principle in neuroscience and a key concept in developing adaptive systems for both biological and artificial networks. It is based on the idea that "neurons that fire together, wire together," meaning that the synaptic connection between two neurons strengthens when both are activated simultaneously. This idea, which guides the training of artificial neural networks (ANNs), explains how the biological brain adapts and gains knowledge from experience.

4.1.1. Hebbian Learning in Biological Systems

The link between two neurones in biological neurones that permits signal transmission between them is called a synapse. The synaptic strength between two neurones increases when they are engaged concurrently, indicating a greater link between the neurones [16]. The Hebbian learning mechanism is the process that underpins memory and learning. Hebbian learning can be explained mathematically as follows:

$$\Delta w_{ij} = \eta x_i y_j \tag{4.1}$$

where Δw_{ij} denotes synaptic weight change between neurons i and j, η is the learning rate, and x_i and y_j represent activations of neurons i and j, respectively.

According to this equation, the weight update is exactly proportional to the product of the pre- and post-synaptic activations of the two neurones. As a result, when neurones fire together, their connection gets stronger.

4.1.2. Hebbian Learning in Artificial Neural Networks (ANN)

In ANN, Hebbian learning is applied as a very simple unsupervised learning scheme to adjust weights based on input correlations. It is not very popular in deep learning, where backpropagation is the main method, but Hebbian learning is very useful in smaller, simpler networks or when exploring physiologically realistic learning models [17]. It is especially well-suited for modelling associative memory and extracting unsupervised features from these networks.

4.1.3. Adaptive Systems

The behaviour or structure of an adaptive system is known to vary, according to environmental alterations. Within cognitive computing, some of the adaptive systems are based on Hebbian learning; these systems modify internal parameters by fitting synaptic weights for improved performance in changing situations. These systems are known to take advantage of their potential for improvement with time for adaptive changes within new patterns or stimuli. Following are the examples of adaptive system:

- *Reinforcement learning algorithms*: whereby agents learn through modification of their actions in response to rewards and penalties.
- *Self-organizing maps (SOMs):* which are applied using unsupervised learning to identify and represent patterns in data.

These kinds of systems use the Hebbian learning approach as a basis for changing internal structures such as neural weights; adaptation is possible without explicit supervision through experienced patterns.

4.1.4. Practical Applications

Various practical applications include Hebbian learning and adaptive systems defined as follows:

- *Neural Network Training*: In early network models, Hebbian learning is used to create associations between inputs and outputs, particularly in recurrent networks.
- *Robotics and Control Systems*: Robots employ adaptive systems to modify behaviour based on sensory inputs, optimizing actions in real-time.

- *Speech and Image Recognition*: Systems adjust their models to accommodate new patterns in data by reinforcing connections between features during training.

Overall, Hebbian learning provides biologically inspired efficient mechanisms for systems to adapt and learn from experience; adaptive systems use the principle to optimise behaviour in response to their dynamic contexts.

4.1.5. Pattern Recognition and Contextual Understanding

Pattern recognition and contextual understanding are two of the fundamental principles behind cognitive computing and artificial intelligence. These concepts enable systems to understand data and make informed decisions. They draw inspiration from how the human brain is thought to analyse regularities in sensory data and contextual rules to derive meaning from it [18].

4.2. Pattern Recognition and Contextual Understanding

Pattern recognition is the ability to identify regularities, structures, or significant patterns in data. Cognitive computing is based on it; it allows the system to recognise objects, events, or relationships in images, sounds, and text-unstructured data. It provides the framework for applications like as image classification, speech

4.2.1. Recognition and Anomaly Detection

Algorithms are used in pattern recognition to examine input data, extract features, and classify the information using learnt models. The following are the main steps involved:

- *Pre-processing:* Raw data is cleaned and transformed into an appropriate format for analysis, which may include normalising values or extracting pertinent features.
- *Feature Extraction*: Extracts key features that characterise the data, which could be edges in photos and phonemes in voices.
- *Classification or Clustering*: In classification (supervised learning), features extracted help classify the data into the already-defined groups. Clustering (unsupervised learning) finds patterns and groups without the prior definition of categories.

- *Model Training*: The datasets labelled are fed to train the machine learning model, like neural networks and decision trees. Such models learn the relationship between input and output.

Mathematically, pattern recognition frequently requires supervised learning, in which the system learns a function f(x) that maps inputs x to outputs Y:

$$Y = f(x) + \epsilon \tag{4.2}$$

Here, x represents the input features, y denotes the predicted output, and ϵ refers to the error term. Unsupervised learning employs clustering techniques like k-means or hierarchical clustering to group similar data points without predefined labels as shown by Figure 4.8.

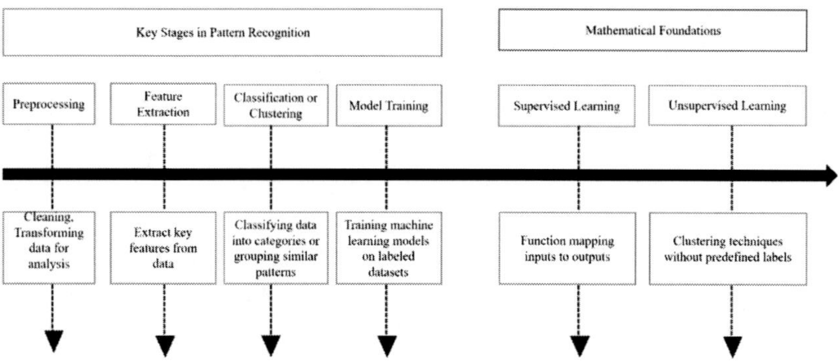

Figure 4.8. Timeline of Pattern recognition in machine learning.

4.3. Contextual Understanding

Contextual comprehension refers to a system's ability to analyse and respond to information based on its context. Just as humans understand meaning from the context of an event or conversation, AI systems must employ contextual signals to make more accurate predictions or choices. Context is critical when dealing with confusing, incomplete, or shifting information.

Key aspects of contextual understanding include:

- *Disambiguation:* Words or acts with various meanings can be resolved with the help of context. For example, the term "bank" could describe a river's edge or a financial institution. The context provided by the surrounding words or acts makes the intended meaning clear.
- *Temporal and Spatial Context:* Understanding when and where an event occurs can significantly influence its interpretation. In autonomous systems, recognizing the context of a specific moment in time (e.g., recognizing that a car is approaching a stop sign) is critical for decision-making.
- *Dynamic Adaptation:* Systems must adapt their responses based on changing contexts [19]. For instance, a chatbot may provide different responses depending on the user's tone, previous interactions, or the current task being discussed.

Contextual understanding in AI typically involves:

- *Natural Language Processing (NLP):* NLP models, such as transformers (e.g., GPT, BERT), analyse text not only at the word level but also at the sentence, paragraph, or even document level, incorporating context to determine meaning.
- *Reinforcement Learning:* In reinforcement learning, agents learn to adapt based on contextual feedback from their environment (i.e., rewards and penalties) rather than simply responding to predefined inputs.

Mathematically, contextual understanding often involves sequential models like Recurrent Neural Networks (RNNs) or transformers, which maintain context over time and process sequential data:

$$h_t = f(h_{t-1}, x_t) \tag{4.3}$$

Here, h_t represents the hidden state, which reflects the system's understanding at time t, while x_t denotes the input at time t. The function f, such as an RNN or LSTM, updates the hidden state by incorporating the new input and the previous context.

4.3.1. Pattern Recognition and Contextual Understanding in Cognitive Computing

Together, pattern recognition and contextual understanding empower cognitive systems to function similarly to human cognition, where recognition of patterns is influenced by the context in which they occur [20-22]. For example:

- *In image recognition*, a system may recognize a face (pattern recognition) and understand the context (e.g., detecting a smile suggests happiness).
- *In speech recognition*, contextual understanding helps disambiguate words based on the surrounding words or the speaker's tone.

These principles allow cognitive systems to make more accurate, adaptive decisions and interactions, such as understanding intent in language, predicting future events, or making recommendations based on past behaviour and current context.

5. Implementations and Ethical Issues

Cognitive computing, aiming to replicate human thought, advances through AI technologies, presenting technical and ethical challenges.

5.1. Implementations of Cognitive Computing

Cognitive computing systems have been implemented across various industries, leveraging AI to improve decision-making, automate tasks, and enhance human-computer interactions [23-26]. Key implementations (Figure 4.9) include:

- *Healthcare:* Cognitive systems analyse medical data such as patient records, genetic information, and diagnostic images. AI-powered tools like IBM Watson assist doctors in making personalized treatment recommendations based on vast amounts of medical literature and patient data.

- *Finance:* AI in finance is used for algorithmic trading, fraud detection, and risk analysis. Cognitive computing models can analyse market trends, detect anomalies in transactions, and predict market behaviours, enhancing financial decision-making.
- *Autonomous Vehicles:* Self-driving cars are powered by cognitive computing systems, which process sensor data, identify objects, and make judgements in real time based on contextual information. These systems utilize deep learning models to understand traffic patterns, road conditions, and pedestrian behaviour.
- *Customer Service:* Virtual assistants and chatbots use NLP and cognitive computing to offer 24/7 help, answer questions, and personalize interactions. These technologies understand context, recognize purpose, and give natural language responses, therefore improving the consumer experience.
- *Retail and Marketing:* In retail and marketing, AI is used in giving customized recommendations, in inventory management, and even in the segmentation of customers. Cognitive computing models analyse the behaviour of consumers, preferences, and purchasing history to serve targeted marketing and product optimisation.

Despite the success of these applications, implementing cognitive computing presents significant obstacles, including data privacy concerns, scalability issues, and the necessity for robust models that generalise effectively across domains.

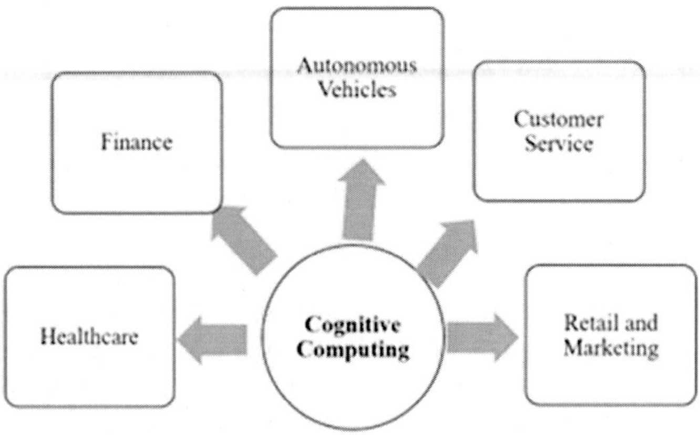

Figure 4.9. Implementation Areas of Cognitive Computing.

5.2. Ethical Issues in Cognitive Computing

As cognitive systems develop, a number of ethical concerns like accountability, privacy, transparency, bias, and human effect come up. These consist of:

1. *Privacy and Data Security*: In order to work properly, cognitive computing systems primarily depend on vast volumes of personal data, including user behaviour, financial transactions, and medical information. The procedures for gathering, storing, and safeguarding data have come under scrutiny. Unauthorised access or data processing may result in security and privacy issues. Ethical guidelines are desperately needed to guarantee informed consent and appropriate data management procedures.
2. *Fairness and Bias*: Cognitive systems, especially machine learning-based systems, are prone to biased data in training. The system would thus perpetuate or exacerbate prejudice if the past data indicate human judgments or social injustices skewed by bias. AI systems could inadvertently favour some races or groups over others for recruiting or law enforcement processes, for instance. Ensuring that the developers address these issues through reducing biases and ensuring fairness involves such approaches as using different types of data during training and periodically assessing the AI systems.
3. *Transparency and Explainability*: A lot of cognitive systems, especially deep learning models, operate as "black boxes." It is hard to understand how a decision is being made. In high-stakes applications like healthcare, where comprehending the logic behind an AI's advice is essential, this lack of interpretability can be problematic. Systems that make judgements without giving people a reason raise ethical questions because they undermine responsibility.
4. *Responsibility and Accountability*: It gets harder to assign blame for judgements made by cognitive systems that are becoming more and more independent. Who is responsible if an AI system causes injury (for example, in accidents involving autonomous driving) the AI itself, the manufacturer, or the developer? To define responsibilities and guarantee that systems function within reasonable limitations, legal frameworks and ethical standards are necessary.
5. *Job Displacement and Human Impact*: The far-reaching adoption of cognitive computing across industries such as manufacturing,

logistics, and customer service may lead to huge job losses. The fact that technology is likely to displace human labor in a few jobs raises serious issues of economic inequality and labor in the future. To ensure equitable distribution of benefits from AI and assistance for displaced workers, social safety nets and retraining have to be integral to driving ethical values in its use.

6. *Decision-making and Autonomy*: For instance, cognitive computing systems deployed in the health and law enforcement spaces can determine the lives of other people. There are issues surrounding autonomy in cases where important decision-making power rests within such systems. Deciding on human finances, law, or health matters can be delegated to machines? Decisions with so much significance in humans should not solely rest on the machines but require due deliberation with human interests in mind.

Conclusion

In an attempt to close this gap between artificial intelligence and neurology, this chapter analyses the theoretical foundations of cognitive computing. We have here noticed how the ideas in the neural networks, Hebbian learning, pattern recognition, and contextual awareness power forward the creation of intelligent systems with reasoning, learning, and adaptability.

During perception, learning, and decision-making, this cognition aims to impressively replicate the features of the human brain. In order to replicate some parts of human cognition, neural networks with layered architecture and the capacity to learn intricate patterns have proven quite successful. These networks have also made notable strides in the areas of picture identification and natural language processing, to mention a few. However, there is still more work to be done before cognitive computing is completely realised. Although a lot has been done, there are still problems with achieving full general intelligence, creating AI in an ethical and responsible manner, and handling the social and economic repercussions of widespread AI adoption.

Future Scope

The future of cognitive computing looks bright. Advances in neuroscience will continue to be important for the better understanding of how human cognition functions. These advancements will guide increasingly complex and physiologically accurate AI models. Some research directions that could help us reach the full potential of cognitive computing and create a future where AI is smoothly integrated into our lives, thereby enhancing our abilities and expanding our understanding of the world and ourselves are:

- *Developing more biologically plausible neural networks*: Exploring alternative architectures and learning algorithms that more closely mimic the brain's structure and function.
- *Improving Explainability and transparency*: Enhancing our understanding of how deep learning models make decisions to improve trust and accountability.
- *Addressing ethical concerns*: Developing frameworks for responsible AI development, ensuring fairness, privacy, and human oversight.
- *Exploring the intersection of AI and other disciplines*: Integrating AI with fields like cognitive science, psychology, and philosophy to gain a deeper understanding of human intelligence and its implications.
- *Developing AI for social good*: Leveraging cognitive computing to address global challenges such as climate change, healthcare, and poverty.

References

[1] Shao, Y., Zhang, C., Xing, L., Sun, H., Zhao, Q., & Zhang, L. (2024). A new dust detection method for photovoltaic panel surface based on Pytorch and its economic benefit analysis. *Energy and AI, 16*, 100349. https://doi.org/10.1016/j.egyai.2024.100349.

[2] Maity, R., Alam, M. S., & Pati, A. (2020). An approach for detection of dust on solar panels using CNN from RGB dust image to predict power loss. In *Proceedings* (pp. 41–48). https://doi.org/10.1007/978-3-030-48118-6_4.

[3] S. M., Murugappan, A., & T., M. (2023). Cognitive computing technological trends and future research directions in healthcare—A systematic literature review. *Artificial Intelligence in Medicine, 138*, 102513. https://doi.org/10.1016/j.artmed.2023.102513.

[4] Irfan, M. T., & Gudivada, V. N. (2016). Cognitive computing applications in education and learning. In *Proceedings* (pp. 283–300). https://doi.org/10.1016/bs.host.2016.07.008.

[5] Gudivada, V., Raghavan, V., Govindaraju, V., & Rao, C. R. (2016). *Cognitive computing: Theory and applications.*

[6] Wang, M., Yin, X., Zhu, Y., & Hu, J. (2022). Representation learning and pattern recognition in cognitive biometrics: A survey. *Sensors, 22*(14), 5111. https://doi.org/10.3390/s22145111.

[7] Perconti, P., & Plebe, A. (2020). Deep learning and cognitive science. *Cognition, 203*, 104365. https://doi.org/10.1016/j.cognition.2020.104365.

[8] Da, K., Dalmau, M., & Roose, P. (2011). A survey of adaptation systems. *International Journal on Internet and Distributed Computing Systems, 2.*

[9] Oliva, A., & Torralba, A. (2007). The role of context in object recognition. *Trends in Cognitive Sciences, 11*(12), 520–527. https://doi.org/10.1016/j.tics.2007.09.009.

[10] Amato, G., Carrara, F., Falchi, F., Gennaro, C., & Lagani, G. (2019). Hebbian learning meets deep convolutional neural networks. In *Proceedings* (pp. 324–334). https://doi.org/10.1007/978-3-030-30642-7_29.

[11] Herz, A., Sulzer, B., Kühn, R., & van Hemmen, J. L. (1989). Hebbian learning reconsidered: Representation of static and dynamic objects in associative neural nets. *Biological Cybernetics, 60*(6), 457–467. https://doi.org/10.1007/BF00204701.

[12] Kuriscak, E., Marsalek, P., Stroffek, J., & Toth, P. G. (2015). Biological context of Hebb learning in artificial neural networks: A review. *Neurocomputing, 152*, 27–35. https://doi.org/10.1016/j.neucom.2014.11.022.

[13] ElKalaawy, N., & Wassal, A. (2015). Methodologies for the modeling and simulation of biochemical networks, illustrated for signal transduction pathways: A primer. *Biosystems, 129*, 1–18. https://doi.org/10.1016/j.biosystems.2015.01.008.

[14] Parashar, J., Kushwah, V. S., & Rai, M. (2023). Determination human prediction supported by cognitive computing-based neural network. In *Proceedings* (pp. 431–441). https://doi.org/10.1007/978-981-19-9858-4_36.

[15] Collobert, R., & Weston, J. (2008). A unified architecture for natural language processing. In *Proceedings of the 25th International Conference on Machine Learning (ICML '08)* (pp. 160–167). ACM Press. https://doi.org/10.1145/1390156.1390177.

[16] Janiesch, C., Zschech, P., & Heinrich, K. (2021). Machine learning and deep learning. *Electronic Markets, 31*(3), 685–695. https://doi.org/10.1007/s12525-021-00475-2.

[17] Zhang, C., Bengio, S., Hardt, M., Recht, B., & Vinyals, O. (2021). Understanding deep learning (still) requires rethinking generalization. *Communications of the ACM, 64*(3), 107–115. https://doi.org/10.1145/3446776.

[18] Montesinos López, O. A., Montesinos López, A., & Crossa, J. (2022). Fundamentals of artificial neural networks and deep learning. In *Multivariate Statistical Machine Learning Methods for Genomic Prediction* (pp. 379–425). Springer International Publishing. https://doi.org/10.1007/978-3-030-89010-0_10.

[19] Ghosh, S., Das, N., Das, I., & Maulik, U. (2020). Understanding deep learning techniques for image segmentation. *ACM Computing Surveys, 52*(4), 1–35. https://doi.org/10.1145/3329784.

[20] Ben-Gal, I. (2007). Bayesian networks. In *Encyclopedia of Statistics in Quality and Reliability.* Wiley. https://doi.org/10.1002/9780470061572.eqr089.

[21] Kriegeskorte, N., & Douglas, P. K. (2018). Cognitive computational neuroscience. *Nature Neuroscience, 21*(9), 1148–1160. https://doi.org/10.1038/s41593-018-0210-5.

[22] Talbot, T. B. (2013). Balancing physiology, anatomy, and immersion: How much biological fidelity is necessary in a medical simulation? *Military Medicine, 178*(10S), 28–36. https://doi.org/10.7205/MILMED-D-13-00212.

[23] Grill-Spector, K., & Weiner, K. S. (2014). The functional architecture of the ventral temporal cortex and its role in categorization. *Nature Reviews Neuroscience, 15*(8), 536–548. https://doi.org/10.1038/nrn3747.

[24] Song, S., Miller, K. D., & Abbott, L. F. (2000). Competitive Hebbian learning through spike-timing-dependent synaptic plasticity. *Nature Neuroscience, 3*(9), 919–926. https://doi.org/10.1038/78829.

[25] Shaneman, S., Moore, A. W., & Hebert, M. (2018). The AI stack: A blueprint for developing and deploying artificial intelligence. In *Ground/Air Multisensor Interoperability, Integration, and Networking for Persistent ISR IX* (T. Pham, M. A. Kolodny, & D. M. Wiegmann, Eds.). SPIE. https://doi.org/10.1117/12.2309483.

[26] Adrowitzer, A., Temper, M., Buchelt, A., Kieseberg, P., & Eigner, O. (2024). Safeguarding the future of artificial intelligence: An AI blueprint. In *Artificial Intelligence for Security* (pp. 3–22). Springer Nature Switzerland. https://doi.org/10.1007/978-3-031-57452-8_1.

Chapter 5

Financial Applications of Cognitive Computing: Improving Risk Assessment and Decision-Making

V. Umadevi*, PhD

PG and Research Department of Computer Science,
Nehru Memorial College (Autonomous), Puthanampatti, Tiruchirappalli, India

Abstract

The advantages of the Cognitive computing method primarily stem from the ability to leverage equity market indices to anticipate stock trends, while actual market metrics, such as initial and final prices, can serve to authenticate those forecasts. The proposed Generative Adversarial Network method forecasts the data with remarkable precision. While the generator uses long short-term memory to forecast stock data, the discriminator uses a Convolutional Neural Network to distinguish between actual and predicted data as precisely as feasible. Within this investigation, the Convolutional Neural Network Procedure was adopted for feature extraction. The effectiveness of the model's results is scrutinized. The assessment metrics utilized include Mean Absolute Error, Mean Square Error, Root Mean Square Error, Mean Absolute Percentage Error, and R-squared. Based on the results, the proposed method outperforms the other models.

Keywords: cognitive computing, stock prediction, CANs, feature extraction, CNN

---

* Corresponding Author's Email: yazh1999@gmail.com

In: Building Intelligent Systems for the Future
Editors: Anamika Ahirwar, Neelesh Jain and Sumitha Elayaperumal
ISBN: 979-8-90134-050-9

1. Introduction

A stock market forecast is an assessment of the upcoming value of company stocks or other financial assets that are bought and sold on an exchange. Accurately predicting stock value can lead to substantial gains and long-term success. In the efficient-market theory, stock prices reflect all accessible information, and any price changes not based on recently revealed data are fundamentally unpredictable. However, there is contention regarding this issue, as advocates of differing perspectives utilize various techniques and technologies that allegedly provide them with an understanding of future price trends.

Stock prices are affected by various factors, such as the broader economic environment, market trends, significant interpersonal and fiscal occurrences, Fund contributor inclinations, and directorial choices crafted by companies [1]. Stocks have three main characteristics: (1) Non-returnability: once stocks are sold, they cannot be returned and cannot be repurchased or refunded by the company; they can solely be resold to other entities via the secondary market; investors must bear increased risks because of the following factors: (2) The speculative aspect of the stock market, resulting in volatility and susceptibility to speculation; (3) Earnings uncertainty: gains and losses in stocks depend on the company's operations and the Shareholder Equity market, both of which are unpredictable and erratic. Due to their significant volatility and speculative characteristics, stocks entail a notable risk of loss [2].

2. Limitations in the Existing Method

Predicting the stock market is an intriguing and demanding task. As more information emerges, new challenges arise in gathering and assessing data to draw conclusions and determine their impact on stock prices. Traders, analysts, and researchers often prioritize short-term stock price predictions over longer-term forecasts, including weekly or monthly projections based on historical data. Due to the complexity and dynamism of financial markets, accurately quantifying and forecasting the data with existing methods is difficult, making it hard to consistently attain high precision.

3. Advantages of the Proposed Method

The advantages of the intended strategy primarily stem from the ability to use stock market indexes to assess stock market prices, while actual market metrics, such as initial and final prices, can be utilized to verify those predictions. The proposed generative adversarial network method predicts the data with remarkable precision. The discriminator employs a Convolutional Neural Network to distinguish real from anticipated data as accurately as possible, while the generator predicts stock data utilizing Persistent memory. In this study, Features were extracted and performed utilizing the Convolutional Neural Network method. The effectiveness of the model's results is assessed. The assessment metrics used include Mean Absolute Error, Mean Square Error, Root Mean Square Error, Mean Absolute Percentage Error, and R-Squared. The results indicate that the intended method outperforms the other models.

4. Literature Review

Neural Networks equipped with Deep Learning features are ideal for engaging with nonlinear functions. As mentioned in [3] and [4], many are interested in the plan to use a Deep Neural Network to forecast stock prices and their results. To achieve a more precise Stock Price forecast, [5] combine Contextual Memory Neural Network with Convolutional Neural Network, focusing on the characteristics of chronological financial data and the price prediction using high-order information of time series [6]. The hybrid prediction method have created a forward-thinking approach that harnesses a Convolutional Neural Network to analyze the spatial organization and motifs (recurring patterns) of noisy financial time series to break them down. [7] Discussed a similar study that offers a cohesive method for predicting stock prices by combining persistent memory with grouped Empirical Mode Decomposition. The intricate chronological stock data prices were divided into multiple subsequences employing the comprehensive Empirical Mode Decomposition method. Subsequently, every subsequence was trained and predicted utilizing the long short-term memory method. By aggregating the forecasted values from several subsequences, the predictions of the original Stock Price time series were ultimately achieved. [8] A Deep Learning system known as Convolutional Neural Network was utilized by [9] to predict c changes. Furthermore, the parameters of the Convolutional Neural Network approach were notably refined by implementing the Genetic Algorithm.

5. Stock Price Prediction

This section outlines the suggested generative adversarial network method for accurately anticipating stock price movements. Contextual memory leverages historical basic indicator data to generate new instances; Convolutional Neural Network evaluates whether the forecasts from contextual memory are real or anticipated; Convolutional Neural Network captures the temporal qualities of the data; long short-term memory predicts the data; and by maximizing the chronological order of stock price data, it can yield more precise predictions. The contextual memory, which serves as a generative model for adversarial training to forecast the stock market, is integrated with the Convolutional Neural Network, a boundary-drawing model, to create the generative adversarial network. The prediction process consists of the steps: preprocessing, evaluation, prediction, and feature extraction. As illustrated in Figure 5.1, the task is structured.

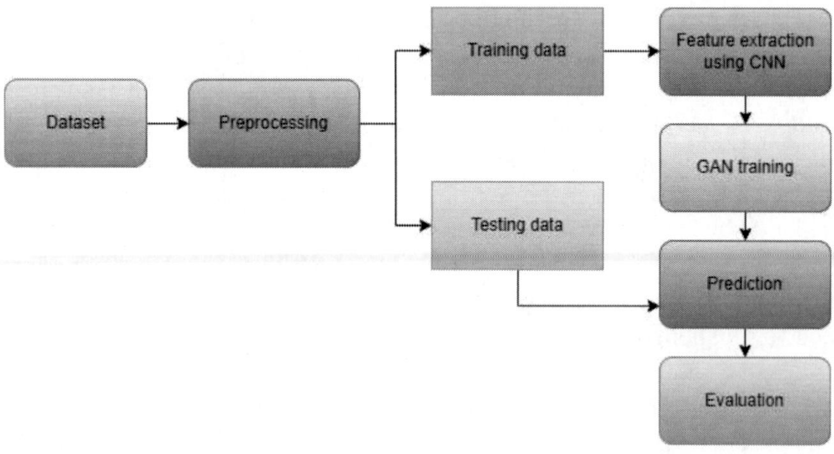

Figure 5.1. Flow of the proposed work.

- *Data Preparation*
  Every dataset is characterized by several anomalies, such as duplicate entries, absent indicators, and additional hurdles. To address this

problem, a technique known as data processing is required. A pre-processing step is necessary to address these issues.

- *Verify for Null Values*
  Reviewing the data frame is performed to confirm that there are no null values present. Since null values behave like outliers and significantly enhance process volatility, including them in the dataset creates challenges during training.
- *Managing Incomplete Data*
  Instances of data loss included unrecorded data changes, incorrectly entered data, data overlooked during input, and data that conflicted with information from other records. Lacking values were detected, and the sufficiently lowered when certain stocks or indices were recorded as null on specific days.
- *Expansion*
  Normalize the stock value to a range of 0 to 1 scale down to the expense of pertaining the data presented in Table 5.1. This decreases the amount of all pertinent data, thus lowering the memory utilized. Diminishing the scale can likewise enhance accuracy since the data is not dispersed across vast amounts.
- *Diminishing noise in Chronological stock data*
  Owing to the intricate nature of stock market fluctuations, random noise is often incorporated into stock prices, resulting in heightened volatility and issues with over-fitting. To decrease noise in time series data, it is necessary to adjust functions to eliminate numerous small oscillations found in the source data. This method preserves the primary volatility trend while smoothing the curve of the original data. The wavelet transform is a widely used method for reducing noise since it effectively manages non-stationary chronological stock data and maintains the essential features of the first-hand information. It serves as a powerful tool for predicting financial conditions.

Table 5.1. Parameters of long short-term memory architecture

Layer Name	Values
LSTM layer	2
Output Layer	1
Units	200

In the context of wavelet transformation, signals that exceed the defined threshold are considered to hold significant information and should be retained. Signals falling below the threshold are considered noise and should be disregarded. In this procedure, the basic wavelet functions as the simulation component. It entails filtering out noise from the signal and obtaining pertinent information. To improve the preservation of original information, signals can be fragmented into both high-frequency and low-frequency components through the wavelet transform. In contrast to conventional high-pass or low-pass filters that directly handle the data without any breakdown, the wavelet method analyzes the original signal through processes such as stretching and shifting the basic wavelet [10].

6. Data Feature Identification Using Convolutional Neural Network

Convolutional Neural Networks excel at automatically extracting features. For instance, the initial convolutional layer of a dog image identifies edges, the next one identifies circles, and the third one identifies a nose. Similarly, small trends created by data points eventually develop into larger trends, which then result in patterns. By leveraging the attributes recognition competencies of Convolutional Neural Networks, insights about trends in stock price fluctuations, like those of GS, can also be obtained.

Convolutional Neural Network is an excellent option as it performs effectively with spatial data. This indicates a more robust connection among nearby data points compared to those that are more distant. This concept should likewise pertain to chronological data, where every observation (for each feature) corresponds to daily. It is sensible to think that the couple of a day becomes increasingly connected as they draw nearer.

Features related to the n-days change are obtained through a preliminary variable filter. The commonly utilized 3x3 image filter is employed, and a more complex feature matrix can be generated by combining these filters. This layer aids in the formation of assorted combinations of host variables. By changing the filter weights, the network can also remove irrelevant variables. Consequently, the layer serves as a module for selecting features. Subsequently, the chronological term memory system employs the characteristics of Convolutional Neural Networks to predict the stock price. Higher-level features arise by merging temporal data over time through convolution and pooling methods, whereas foundational-level features are consolidated from their inputs into superior-level inputs.

7. Generative Adversarial Network

The generative adversarial network category of generative models has demonstrated noteworthy effectiveness in various chores, such as image generation and picture-to-image translation.

By differentiating between valid and deceptive trading behavior, the discriminator employs the PLR/generator of a generative adversarial network to create and predict daily trading actions. The experiment results demonstrate that the suggested frameworks based on generative adversarial networks outshine the LSTM network. The generator converts the random noise vector $z \in Z$, where $z \sim p(z)$, to create “fake” samples, with Z denoting the latent space and p(z) indicating the random noise distribution (Generally a uniform or Gaussian distribution).

The generator’s goal is to mislead the discriminator into thinking the generated sample is authentic, while the discriminator’s task is to classify and differentiate between genuine and fake data samples (that is, to identify the traits of the actual data distribution). Consequently, a scalar $D(a) \in [0, 1]$ is generated, indicating the chance that the discriminator perceives the sample (a) as belonging to the authentic distribution. In a formal context, the value function V (G, D) serves to train G and D as follows:

$$\underset{G}{min}\ \underset{D}{max}\ V(G,D) = E_{x-p(r)}[\log D(x) + E_{z-p(z)}[\log\left(1 - D\big(G(z)\big)\right)] \tag{5.1}$$

Here’s the description of how to break it down:

- V(G,D)V(G, D)V(G,D): The objective function, typically used in Generative Adversarial Networks (GANs), describing the competition between the generator GGG and discriminator DDD.
- Ex~p(r)[log⁡D(x)]E_{x \sim p(r)} \left[\log D(x) \right]Ex~p(r) [logD(x)]: The expectation over the real data distribution p(r)p(r)p(r), where xxx is a real sample, and D(x)D(x)D(x) is the probability the discriminator assigns to it being real.

- Ez~p(z)[log(1−D(G(z)))]E_{z \sim p(z)} \left[\log (1 - D(G(z))) \right]Ez~p(z)[log(1−D(G(z)))]: The expectation over the noise distribution p(z)p(z)p(z), where G(z)G(z)G(z) is the generated sample, and D(G(z))D(G(z))D(G(z)) is the probability the discriminator assigns to it being real.

The genuine data distribution of the sample x is shown by the symbol p(r). Equation (3.1) can be rewritten as follows if it indicates the generator's output with x͂=G (z) x~=G (z).

$$\min_{G} \max_{D} V(G,D) = E_{x-p(r)}[\log D(x) + E_{\tilde{x}-p(g)}[\log(1 - D(\tilde{x}))] \quad (5.2)$$

- $\min_G \max_D$: Represents the adversarial nature of GANs, where G (the generator) seeks to minimize the objective, while D (the discriminator) seeks to maximize it.
- V(G,D)V(G, D)V(G,D): The value function or objective function that measures the performance of G and D.
- $E_{x\sim p(r)}$[logD(x)]: The expectation over real data samples xxx drawn from the real data distribution p(r). It reflects the discriminator's ability to correctly classify real samples as real.
- $E_{x\sim\sim p(g)}$[log(1−D(x̄): The expectation over generated data samples x̄ produced by GGG from the noise distribution p(g). It reflects the discriminator's ability to correctly classify generated samples as fake.

Where can the generator's distribution be found within data p(g)? The generator might be capable of understanding the adversarial nature of the game since it aims to classify false samples as true in Eq. 3.2, second term, conversely, the main objective of the discriminator is to correctly classify fake samples. Every network supports the others' growth by offering training. The next two rules establish the update at iteration n+1, with θD and θG denoting the settings of the generator and discriminator, respectively.

$$\theta_{n+1}^{D} \leftarrow \theta_{n}^{D} + \eta_{D}\left(\nabla_{\theta^{D}} \frac{1}{m} \sum_{i=1}^{m} [log(D(x^{i})) + log(1 - D(\tilde{x}^{i}))]\right), \theta_{n+1}^{G} \leftarrow \theta_{n}^{G} + \eta_{G}\left(\nabla_{\theta^{G}} \frac{1}{m} \sum_{i=1}^{m} [log(1 - D(\tilde{x}^{i}))]\right) \quad (5.3)$$

These are calculated by sampling m authentic and counterfeit samples, with the learning rates of the generator and discriminator represented as $\eta\_G > 0$ and $\eta\_D > 0$, respectively.

8. Convolutional Neural Network

A representative framework of a Convolutional Neural Network consists of the input layer, pooling layer, convolutional layer, fully connected layer, and an output layer. A Convolutional Neural Network contains additional hidden layers compared to a standard Neural Network, indicating that it possesses greater capacity [11]. The network can more effectively extract and recognize features from the input with a greater number of hidden layers. In tasks related to computer vision, such as recognizing faces and classifying images, Convolutional Neural Networks are frequently used.

For example, the convolutional layer uses convolutional kernels to perform convolution operations on inputs, producing outputs for the next layer. The pooling layer is significant in Convolutional Neural Networks because it efficiently decreases the parameter count of the model and operational level of difficulty while preserving essential insight in the aspect maps [12]. By employing a systematic approach involving pooling and convolution, this algorithm examines the input and identifies features. The quantity of input data and the necessity to extract features are two factors that can impact the filter's dimensions, which subsequently affect the window size and sliding step of the process.

9. Stock Price Using Generative Adversarial Network

9.1. The Generator

Employing a model based on generative adversarial networks enhances the training effectiveness due to the demonstrated performance of the generative adversarial network structure. Let $Xt= \{Xt-n+1,\ldots,Xt-1,Xt\}$ denote data provided in the form of sequential time data, where each element reflects chronicle information from the respective day, beginning n-1 days prior and concluding at the present. It is crucial to note that Xt is a vector encompassing all daily schedule items for day t. As a result, Stock Prices for day t+1 were computed utilizing the LSTM model, which was trained to forecast price data based on the previous n days. The generative model, denoted as G, employs the LSTM network. The generator model consists of three layers: an embedding layer, a fully connected layer, and an LSTM layer. In our application, a label is transformed into a dense vector and embedded in the latent space via an embedding layer before it merges with the input matrix of historical pricing data. To achieve the desired result, an LSTM layer is subsequently adopted. To enhance generalization and decrease the chances of overfitting, a dropout layer may be placed between two long short-term memory layers [13]. The authentic target data (Xt+1) and the pseudo data generated by an FC layer utilizing a ReLU activation function are ultimately very similar. Here's a description of the output produced by our generator:

$$\widetilde{X}_{t+1} = G(X_t|Z_t) \tag{5.4}$$

9.2. The Discriminator

This generative adversarial network model assesses if the input data is authentic or fraudulent through a discriminator that comprises a Convolutional Neural Network. (Table 5.2). The discriminator will be given either the generated data or the original data from the generator. This discriminator contains three 1D convolution layers with 32, 64, and 128 neurons. With the exception of the output layer, which employs the sigmoid activation function, the generative adversarial network applies ReLU as its activation function in every other layer. The sigmoid function generates a single scalar output, either 0 or 1, based on whether the input is genuine or not. The structure of the suggested work is depicted in Figure 5.2.

Table 5.2. List the parameters of Convolutional Neural Network architecture

Layer	Layer Name	Kernel	Kernel size	Stride
1	Convolution	32	1 * 1	1
2	Convolution	64	1 * 1	1
3	Max Pooling	-	2 * 2	2
4	FC	64	-	-

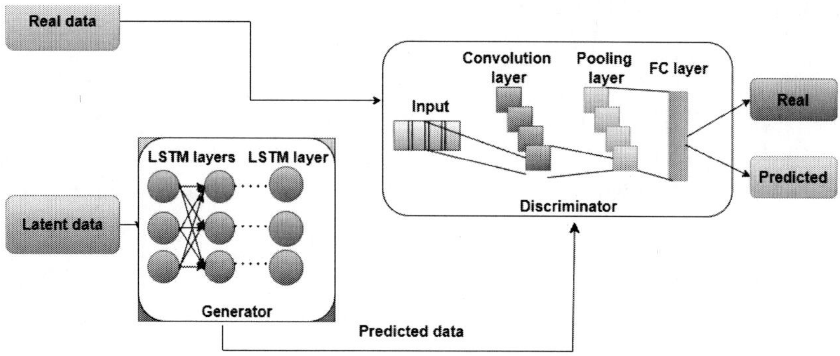

Figure 5.2. Framework of the generative adversarial network model.

9.3. Hyperparameter Tuning

Hyperparameter tuning involves finding an appropriate set of hyperparameter values for a learning algorithm and implementing this refined algorithm on any dataset. That selection of hyperparameters yields improved outcomes with reduced errors by enhancing the model's efficacy and diminishing a specified loss function [14].

One of the key hyperparameters is the learning rate. The optimizer's learning rate is vital in training Neural Networks because it determines the speed of convergence and overall performance of the network. The optimizer can discover efficient solutions by choosing a low learning rate, but the initial speed of convergence will be reduced. By progressively adjusting the learning rate, this compromise can be circumvented. Adam serves as the optimizer applied to enhance the model. It employs epochs ranging from 100 to 200 for training and utilizes batch sizes between 32 and 128 for the Stock Price dataset. Its learning rate is 0.001. Table 5.3 displays the hyper parameters along with their corresponding values.

Table 5.3. Lists the Convolutional Neural Network and LSTM hyper parameter values

Hyperparameters	Initial Learning rate	Batch size	Dropout	Momentum	Activation Function	Epochs
CNN Values	0.001	32	0.5	0.9	ReLU, Sigmoid	100
LSTM Values	0.001	32	0.5	-	Tanh	100

10. Results and Discussion

The experiment's data was supplied by the Wind-Economic database. Listed in Table 5.4, data from the Shenzhen Component Index from October 1, 2000, to October 30, 2020, were employed in the experiment. As certain data points are not particularly helpful for predicting stock values, they are excluded from the dataset. The closing prices of stocks are affected by various factors, including the initial price of the index, the highest rate, the lowest rate, the final rate, trading volume, and turnover.

Table 5.4. Part of the experimental data

Date	Opening price	Highest price	Lowest price	Closing price	Turnover volume	Turnover rate
2020/03/01	364.87	367.42	360.54	333.35	562540	0.0087
2020/03/02	357.67	359.76	348.75	367.23	475772	0.0078
2020/03/03	339.45	352.32	321.34	364.45	439689	0.0074
2020/03/04	325.56	345.45	321.54	358.86	459669	0.0080
2020/03/05	318.45	353.56	311.35	367567	448756	0.0075

Utilizing the chosen stock data, two subsets of data are generated: a training set that comprises 80% and a testing set of 20%. The Stock Price model based on generative adversarial networks is built progressively using training data. Generative adversarial networks utilize data from test samples to generate predictions once they have completed training. This experiment uses the fundamental evaluation metrics of the regression model. The main metrics to assess the regression model include Mean Absolute Error, Mean Squared Error, Mean Absolute Percentage Error, Root Mean Square Error, and R-Squared. These indicators can be utilized to compute the discrepancy between the actual and forecasted metrics.

10.1. Mean Absolute Error

The typical variation of real Stock Prices from estimated prices is frequently determined using the Mean Absolute Error in financial assessments. In financial series, large values are less influenced by the Mean Absolute Error, as it assesses the mean magnitude of the errors rather than their directional aspect. The Mean Absolute Error signifies the average magnitude of the difference between the values observed and the expected data points in the dataset. In this measurement, the average of the dataset's residuals is calculated.

$$MAE = \frac{1}{N}\sum_{i=1}^{N} |y_i - \hat{y}| \quad (5.5)$$

10.2. Mean Squared Error

Mean Square Error is a metric that determines the average squared value of errors. The error in this statistic is the difference between the estimated and real values. Since both the Mean Square Error and Mean Absolute Error use the average of the squared variations among the actual and predicted values, they are equal in all other aspects. It calculates the variance of the residuals.

$$MSE = \frac{1}{N}\sum_{i=1}^{N} (y_i - \hat{y})^2 \quad (5.6)$$

N represents the number of data values; y_i indicates the observed values; $\hat{y} = Predicted\ values$

10.3. Root Mean Square Error

The Root Mean Square Error is simply the square of the mean square error. The standard deviation of the residuals is calculated. Whether during training, cross-validation, or post-deployment evaluation, utilizing a single metric to evaluate a model's performance is highly advantageous. A frequently used measure for this is the Root Mean Square Error. The scoring rule being discussed is suitable, straightforward, and aligns with some commonly accepted statistical assumptions.

$$RMSE = \sqrt{MSE} = \sqrt{\frac{1}{N}\sum_{i=1}^{N} (y_i - \hat{y})^2} \quad (5.7)$$

10.4. Mean Absolute Percentage Error

The Mean Absolute Percentage Error is calculated by taking the total of per period's individual absolute errors and dividing it by the demand. This signifies the average of the percentage mistakes. Given that it expresses the error in percentage form, this metric is commonly utilized as it simplifies the comparison of model accuracy across different use cases and datasets for end users to grasp.

$$MAPE = \frac{1}{N}\sum_{i=1}^{N}\frac{|A_i - F_i|^2}{A_i} \tag{5.8}$$

where A_i represents the Actual value
F_i denotes forecast value
N indicates the total count of observations

10.5. R-Square (R2)

R2 value indicates the proportion of the dependent variable's variation in the linear regression model. Although correlation illustrates the strength of the connection between an independent variable and a dependent variable. R-Square will consistently be below one because correlation is a scale invariant scale-invariant measure.

$$R^2 = 1 - \frac{\Sigma(y_i - \hat{y})^2}{\Sigma(y_i - \bar{y})^2} \tag{5.9}$$

In which y indicates the actual value
$\hat{y}$ represents the anticipated value
$\bar{y}$ denotes the mean value

The suggested model has been evaluated against various algorithms such as LSTM, Autoregressive Integrated Moving Average, and Gated Recurrent Unit to assess its performance. (Table 5.5). Since the generator (LSTM) of the generative adversarial network can accurately predict time series data, it has been observed that the generative adversarial network excels on stock data, illustrated in Figure 5.3.

The present Gated Recurrent Unit-based approach shows elevated error rates across different evaluation metrics, including Root Mean Square Error (7.6894), Mean Absolute Percentage Error (0.0685), and R-Square (0.6545). In comparison, the suggested approach demonstrates a notable decrease in error, yielding values of 4.8684, 0.0325, and 0.3856 for Root Mean Square

Error, Mean Absolute Percentage Error, and R-Square, respectively. This enhancement can be attributed to the proposed method's use of a Convolutional Neural Network for feature extraction, allowing the model to effectively capture important features from the dataset. Consequently, the model attains improved prediction reliability and decreased training durations.

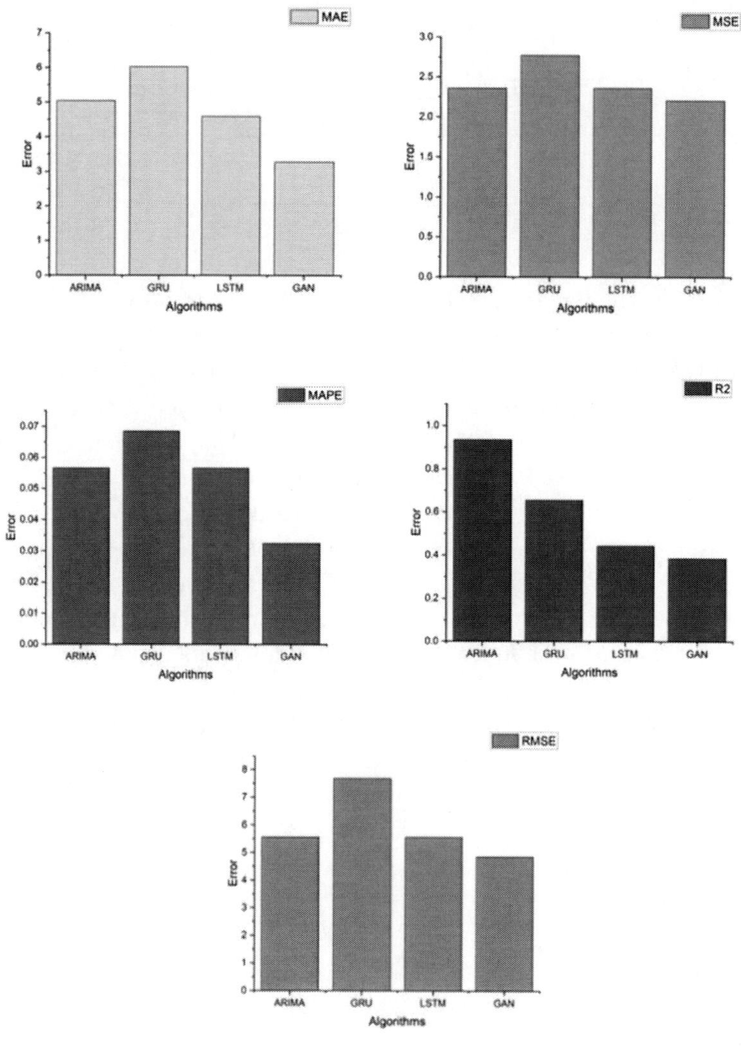

Figure 5.3. Comparative Charts.

Table 5.5. Performance comparison of algorithms

Algorithms	Mean Absolute Error	Mean Square Error	Root Mean Square Error	Mean Absolute Percentage Error	R-Square (R2)
Auto Regressive Integrated Moving Average	5.0465	2.3596	5.5678	0.0567	0.9344
Gated Recurrent Unit	6.0256	2.7729	7.6894	0.0685	0..6545
Long Short-Term Memory	4.5879	2.3612	5.5754	0.0567	0.4435
Generative Adversarial Network	3.2797	2.2064	4.8684	0.0325	0.3856

Conclusion

Financial forecasting and risk assessment can be improved by incorporating cognitive computing techniques, particularly the Generative Adversarial Network (GAN) framework, as this chapter demonstrates. By combining the strengths of Convolutional Neural Networks (CNN) for feature extraction and Long Short-Term Memory (LSTM) networks for temporal prediction, the proposed model achieves significant accuracy improvements in predicting stock price movements. Experimental evaluation against conventional algorithms such as ARIMA, GRU, and standalone LSTM models confirms that the GAN-based approach yields lower error rates and higher prediction reliability. The results show that intelligent, data-driven investment strategies can be built on top of cognitive computing's ability to optimize decision-making in volatile financial markets. In order to further refine predictive capabilities and adaptability to dynamic market conditions, future extensions may include incorporating hybrid ensemble architectures and real-time sentiment analysis.

Reference

[1] Ji, X., Wang, J., & Yan, Z. (2021). A stock price prediction method based on deep learning technology. *International Journal of Crowd Science, 5*(1), 55-72. https://doi.org/xxxx.

[2] Lu, R., & Lu, M. (2021). Stock trend prediction algorithm based on deep recurrent neural network. *Wireless Communications and Mobile Computing, 2021*(1), 5694975. https://doi.org/xxxx.

[3] Rezaei, H., Faaljou, H., & Mansourfar, G. (2021). Stock price prediction using deep learning and frequency decomposition. *Expert Systems with Applications, 169*, 114332. https://doi.org/xxxx.

[4] Kusuma, R. M. I., Ho, T.-T., Kao, W.-C., Ou, Y.-Y., & Hua, K.-L. (2019). Using deep learning neural networks and candlestick chart representation to predict stock market. *arXiv preprint arXiv:1903.12258*. https://arxiv.org/abs/1903.12258.

[5] Wu, J. M.-T., Li, Z., Herencsar, N., Vo, B., & Lin, J. C.-W. (2023). A graph-based CNN-LSTM stock price prediction algorithm with leading indicators. *Multimedia Systems, 29*(3), 1751-1770. https://doi.org/xxxx.

[6] Wen, M., Li, P., Zhang, L., & Chen, Y. (2019). Stock market trend prediction using high-order information of time series. *IEEE Access, 7*, 28299-28308. https://doi.org/xxxx.

[7] Yujun, Y., Yimei, Y., & Jianhua, X. (2020). A hybrid prediction method for stock price using LSTM and ensemble EMD. *Complexity, 2020*(1), 6431712. https://doi.org/xxxx.

[8] Lin, Y., Liu, S., Yang, H., & Wu, H. (2021). Stock trend prediction using candlestick charting and ensemble machine learning techniques with a novelty feature engineering scheme. *IEEE Access, 9*, 101433-101446. https://doi.org/xxxx.

[9] Chung, H., & Shin, K.-S. (2020). Genetic algorithm-optimized multi-channel convolutional neural network for stock market prediction. *Neural Computing and Applications, 32*(12), 7897-7914. https://doi.org/xxxx.

[10] Liang, J., Ma, M., Sadiq, M., & Yeung, K.-H. (2019). A filter model for intrusion detection system in vehicle ad hoc networks: A hidden Markov methodology. *Knowledge-Based Systems, 163*, 611-623. https://doi.org/xxxx.

[11] Staffini, A. (2022). Stock price forecasting by a deep convolutional generative adversarial network. *Frontiers in Artificial Intelligence, 5*, 837596. https://doi.org/xxxx.

[12] Wang, H., Wang, J., Cao, L., Li, Y., Sun, Q., & Wang, J. (2021). A stock closing price prediction model based on CNN-BiSLSTM. *Complexity, 2021*(1), 5360828. https://doi.org/xxxx.

[13] Siddharth, M. (2021, December 6). Stock price using long short-term memory and its implementation. *Analytics Vidhya.* https://www.analyticsvidhya.com/blog/2021/12/stock-price-prediction-using-lstm/.

[14] Navas, J. (2022, February 8). What is hyperparameter tuning? *Anyscale.* https://www.anyscale.com/blog/what-is-hyperparameter-tuning.

Chapter 6

Cognitive Computing's Place in Decision-Making in Uncertain Environments

Anamika Ahirwar*, PhD
and Akash Saxena†, PhD
Department of Computer Science and Engineering,
Compucom Institute of Technology and Management, Jaipur, Rajasthan, India

Abstract

Cognitive computing is a model of computation, which models human cognitive processes in assisting in decision-making when the information is uncertain or incorrect (Gershman, Horvitz, and Tenenbaum, 2015; Zhao, Li, and Xu, 2022). The role of cognitive computing is very crucial in such cases when the necessary role is not correctly conducted by conventional methods because the process of reasoning carried out by the human brain is simulated. This chapter discusses the role of cognitive computing and the key aspect to this chapter is that the cognitive computing is capable of addressing complexity, uncertainty, and ambiguity. The field of cognitive computing has a number of research areas. A short overview of decision-making theories and cognitive problems is presented. We discuss that the cognitive computing systems can utilize NLP, probabilistic reasoning, and machine learning algorithms to assist humans in making decisions (Patel et al., 2024). Real-life examples of how cognitive computing can influence decision-making in the uncertain environment are cybersecurity, healthcare, and the financial sector (Behera, Bala, and Dhir, 2019; Andronie et al., 2021). We go further to analyze the problems and ethical concerns in the

* Corresponding Author's Email: aanamika77@gmail.com
† Corresponding Author's Email: akash27saxena@gmail.com

In: Building Intelligent Systems for the Future
Editors: Anamika Ahirwar, Neelesh Jain and Sumitha Elayaperumal
ISBN: 979-8-90134-050-9

decision-making process when cognitive computing is involved. Having known how cognitive computing plays a role in decision-making, we could possibly use it in order to make better and efficient decisions in complicated and dynamically changing scenarios.

Keywords: cognitive computing (CC), artificial intelligence (AI), cyber security, internet of things (IoT), robotics, chatbot, data analytics

1. Introduction

In the chaos of today's frantic world, where organizations, governments, and industries are imperative with the challenge, "How can I identify who I am? Who will be my partner? Where are the nodes? And how do we keep connected with our base?" making good decisions in an unconcerned environment. Cognitive computing applies artificial intelligence (AI), machine learning (ML), and natural language processing (NLP) for mimicking human-like reasoning and decision-making abilities (Patel et al., 2024; Narne et al., 2024; Zhao et al., 2022; Gupta et al., 2022). When the evidence is incomplete, uncertain, or changing at a great speed, standard models of decision-making usually fail (Gershman et al., 2015; Hafenbrädl et al., 2016; Juárez Ramos, 2018). In sharp contrast, cognitive systems provide adaptive, real-time insights based on the use of pattern recognition, data analytics, and predictive modeling (Ng et al., 2021; Zhu et al., 2020; Herrera-Viedma et al., 2020). Therefore, cognitive computing turns out to be a great asset for improving decision-making in the domains highly impacted by uncertainty, e.g., healthcare and emergency response.

1.1. Comprehension of Cognitive Computing

Cognitive computing is a field of systems that are driven by artificial intelligence and are designed to emulate human cognitive processes, including learning, reasoning, and decision-making (Zhao et al., 2022; Konar, 2018; Patel et al., 2024). To be able to function with exorbitant volumes of unstructured data, these systems use data analytics, machine learning, and natural language processing. Developed by IBM, Watson is one of the leading Cognitive Computing platforms with throughputs above 200 million pages per second (Patel et al., 2024; Gupta et al., 2018). Cognitive computing systems can learn and change over time and deliver up to 20% more decision-making accuracy in certain situations, such as medical diagnostics. According to forecasts, the global market for cognitive computing will be $14 billion in 2023 and will grow by a compound annual growth rate (CAGR) of 30% until 2030 (Ng et al., 2021; Gupta et al., 2018).

1.1.1. Cognitive Systems: Key Concepts and Principles

The basic principles of cognitive systems are how to use the latest technologies to emulate human reasoning and processes of thought. This is shown in Figure 6.1.

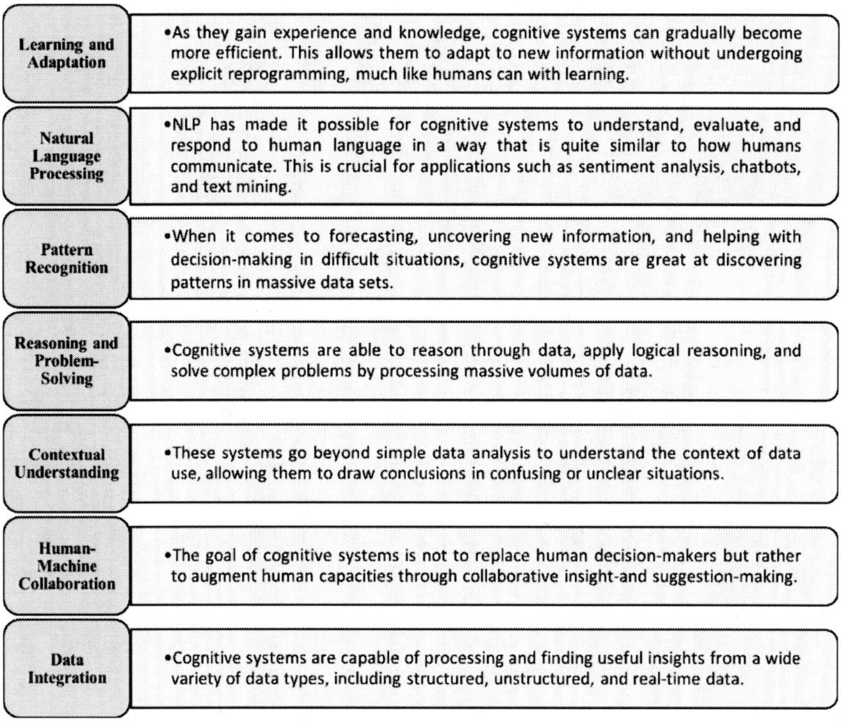

Figure 6.1. Key concepts of cognitive computing.

1.1.2. Explanation of Uncertainty in Various Contexts

The fact that there is uncertainty is a hindrance to strategy and decision-making in a number of industries. Six points in the world GDP growth decrease was the result of the economic instability in 2023 caused by inflation and geopolitical tensions. Misdiagnosis has been reported to be a major cause of medical errors, and the diagnostic ambiguity applies to approximately 15-25% of all medical diagnoses. Climate warming has augmented the uncertainty of natural disasters by half, and it is estimated that the alteration of intense weather patterns will increase four times by the year 2050. Due to unforeseen demand and supply chain shocks such as the COVID-19 pandemic, logistical costs were increased by 3040%. The decline in global stock markets by 30% in 2020, prompted by the COVID-19 pandemic is one of the vivid illustrations of how volatile financial markets can be and consequently, the market can be volatile. These illustrations indicate that complex systems are needed in order to assess and reduce the effects of uncertainty, which is one of the major elements of risk.

1.2. The Need for Decision-Making in Uncertain Environments

The process of decision making in uncertain situations is important because it has a direct effect on the consequences of complex and dynamic situations. Lack of certainty in business, healthcare and crisis management, poses a problem where businesses, healthcare and crisis managers need to predict future outcomes as accurately as possible due to the changing variables like incomplete data, unexpected events and missing data. Indicatively, 60 % of businesses die as a result of bad decision making in the uncertain times economically and businesses have to survive the unstable markets. The causes of diagnostic errors in healthcare are uncertain patient outcomes or poor medical histories, which influence 12 million people every year in the US alone. It has been found out that 30 % of lives could be saved when the decisions are made effectively in the case of a natural disaster. Quick decision making is quite crucial in a disaster management situation when one has to save lives and property during unexpected emergencies. Cognitive computing assists in that huge volumes of data are analyzed, patterns are identified, and probable threats are forecasted to make superior judgments. The Figure 6.2 below demonstrates a well-organized framework that demonstrates the role of cognitive computing in solving uncertainty in decision making in diverse situations.

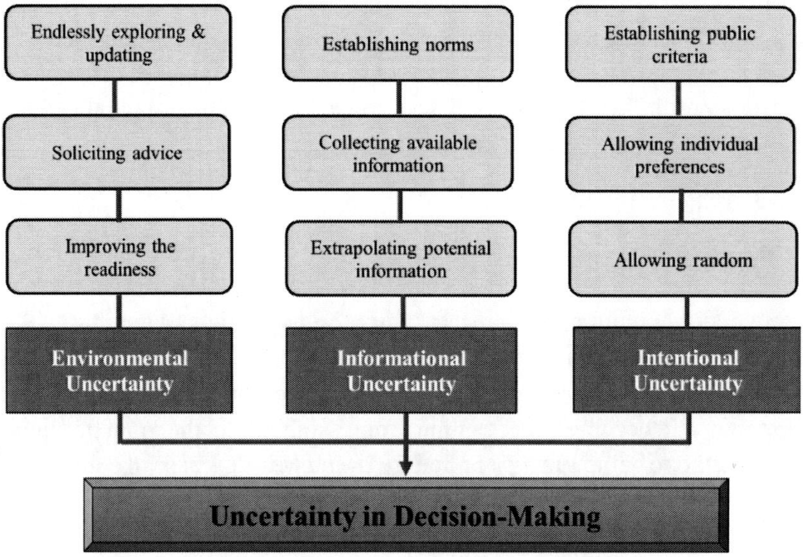

Figure 6.2. Framework for Addressing Uncertainty in Decision-Making.

1.2.1. Decision-Making Complexity in Unpredictable Situations

The situation is extremely hard to make decisions in case of uncertainty, ignorance and rapidly changing circumstances. As a case in point, in healthcare there is a risk of misdiagnosing a patient when the physician does not have sufficient data, in business, unforeseen events such as market crashes, economic crises can be dangerous and in disaster management the authorities have to make decisions on behalf of the population within a natural disaster within a very short time with minimal information. These problems particularly become most noticeable in unsure situations when they require new technology that can assess extensive information and provide pertinent knowledge. In case of a natural disaster, there is a lot of uncertainty and minimal information on which disaster management decisions should be made, at a moment. All this adds to the complexity of the decisions to be made, with the aspect of higher technologies that can filter through a ton of data and give an idea even when there is total uncertainty.

1.2.2. Impact of Uncertainty on Outcomes and Performance

Uncertainty can impact negatively on performance and results as it creates more risks and makes it harder to predict. The failure rate of new product launches is 75% and this may result to poor business strategies. Diagnostic uncertainty in healthcare has been known to misdiagnose millions of people every year. During the financial crisis in 2008 and other unexpected activities, market drops of up to 50% were registered. Ambiguity impedes effectiveness and efficiency in most areas, as it will restrict the decision-making process (Hafenbrädl, Waeger, Marewski, and Gigerenzer, 2016).

1.3. Significance of AI and ML

The cognitive computing systems are based on two pillars; AI and ML. Such technologies assist the robots to be able to replicate human capabilities like seeing, thinking and reasoning. These assist computers to learn through information and become better as time progresses without the input of a human being. Cognitive computing is applied to AI and ML to deal with complex and uncertain situations, through simulating human thought processes. These systems process volumes of data, discover patterns and forecast. They are developed to think and reason as humans through learning and experience. The correlation between CC, AI, and ML is presented in Figure 6.3.

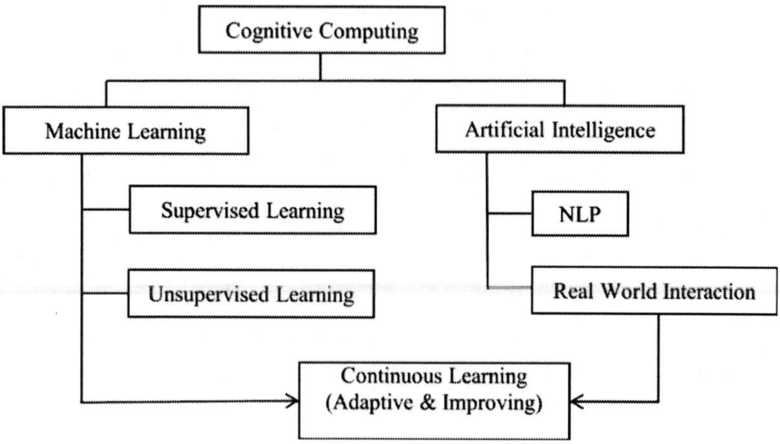

Figure 6.3. Relation between CC, ML, and AI.

2. Fundamentals of Cognitive Computing

Cognitive computing is a new technology that acts like the brain of a human being and assists in enhancing the user interaction, complex problem solving and making better decisions. Conventional mechanisms operate by set rules, but cognitive mechanisms have the ability to reason with ambiguous data, learn with vast information, and become even better with time (Konar, 2018; Gershman et al., 2015; Patel et al., 2024). The systems employ NLP, ML, and AI to replicate human brain. Figure 6.4 demonstrates the essence of cognitive system.

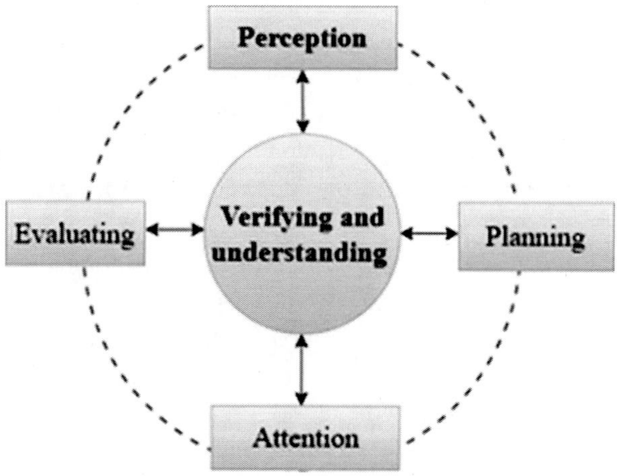

Figure 6.4. Cognitive Core: Understanding and Decision-Making.

2.1. Principles of Cognitive Computing Systems

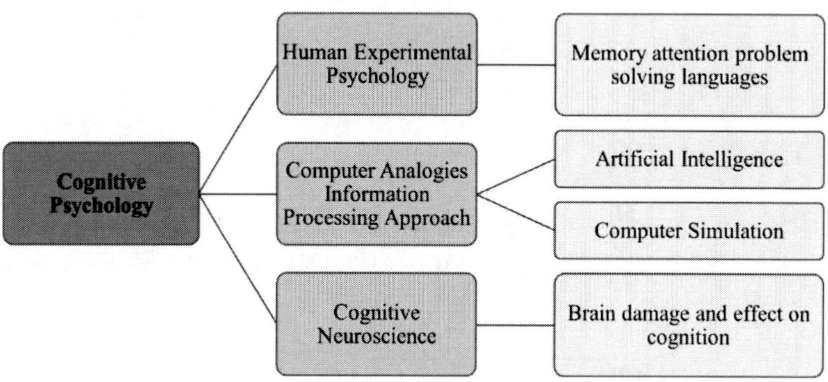

Figure 6.5. Cognitive Computing and its Subsets.

2.1.1. Self-Learning Capabilities

One such kind of system is that of cognition, which is capable of learning. There is no human supervision requirements to enhance their performance in the long-term. These systems apply machine learning to identify patterns of data, store information, and change their behavior in line with these patterns. Modelling is improved to make superior decisions to handle additional data. In practice, such self-learning ability assists them to do well in situations where the data are either incomplete or unclear.

As an example, within the health sector, a cognitive system will be able to diagnose diseases more effectively over time, whereas in finance, it will adapt to alterations in the markets to make better investments. Cognitive systems improve and become more efficient as they learn and keep adapting, which means that human intervention is not needed all the time.

2.1.2. Understanding and Interpreting Natural Language

Cognitive computing aids computer to interact with humans in a significant and natural manner by interpreting and understanding human language. Computers are able to read, analyze and produce text as well as speech using NLP. NLP assists cognitive systems to interpret words as well as the context, emotions and intention. This will assist in answering the questions, dealing with big data and conducting real time discussions with the users. One might give an example of this; in customer service, the intelligent systems would be able to interpret the request of the customers, respond accurately and in case it needs a structured answer, the intelligence systems would be able to suggest solutions that would need structured commands. This links the human communication to the computer communication to enhance the communication between the human and computer.

2.1.3. Simulation of Human-Like Reasoning and Decision-Making

Cognitive computing is able to reason as human beings and hence make decisions (Collins and Koechlin, 2012). In case there is a challenging or sudden event, cognitive computing enables robots and computers to behave as a human brain. They are able to interpret information, give findings and even make judgments as a human being would. Those algorithms are a form of thinking simulation since they compile data, analyze it, think of various possibilities, and make choices based on the information they have studied. The capability to recreate the medical decision-making process of reasoning will be of great help to doctors in determining proper diagnoses (Sarafyazd & Jazayeri, 2019). In most situations, cognitive systems enhance the effectiveness, precision, and flexibility of decisions through simulation of human thought.

2.1.4. The Concept of "Thinking" in Machines

When talking about machines, the word thinking can be applied to define the way computers, and particularly the ones with AI, process information and come to the decision like a human being. People can think, but through artificial intelligence, computers can learn and take a solution. These systems examine data and identify patterns as they acquire new information and become better with time. Although the data is not fully complete, cognitive computing is used to make decisions, analyze the meaning of a language and understand it (Zheng et al., 2017). This enables the computers to decide, resolve issues and forecast, which normally involves human intelligence. The usefulness of machines in assisting people to perform various tasks is on the increase since machines do not have feelings or awareness.

2.1.5. Key Features of Cognitive Computing Systems

- *Adaptive:* This step is the first step towards coming up with a machine learning cognitive system. The solutions must be capable of the human brain learning and adapting to its environment. The systems are incapable of being single-task programmable. They should be dynamic when it comes to the collection of data, comprehension of goals and fulfillment of requirements.
- *Interactive:* The brain, as well as the cognitive solution, should be able to interact with the other components of the system, which are the processor, devices, cloud services and the user. Interactions between the cognitive systems ought to be in both directions. They should learn to use NLP and deep learning to compute the input of human beings and provide related output. This is already a feature of some intelligent chatbots, including Mitsuku. Through these systems, individuals are able to interact with each other in their natural voice, text and gestures.
- *Contextual:* The system must be able to recall some previous interactions in a process and provide information relevant to the application to that instance. It must be capable of formulating the problem either through posing questions or by finding more information. This aspect requires the strict implementation of data

quality and validation processes to make sure that the system is consistently provided with the adequate amount of information as well as so that the data sources on which it works provide reliable and recent input. They perceive the situation through the analysis of various forms of information, the environment, and user requirements to deliver valuable information (Cornelio et al., 2018).

- *Iterative and Stateful*: They have to detect, identify, and elicit contextual information like meaning, syntax, time, location, suitable domain, regulations, user profile, process, task, and goal. They can also make use of various sources of information, such as formalized and non-formalized digital data, and sensory data (sensory, gestural, auditory, sensor-delivered). They use previous experiences, make corrections and better their responses as time progresses.
- *Real-Time Data Processing*: They process large volumes of data fast and aiding in making quick and informed decisions.

This, as seen in Figure 6.6, is because a cognitive computing system has the key attributes of adaptability, interactivity, contextual awareness, iterative learning and real-time data processing.

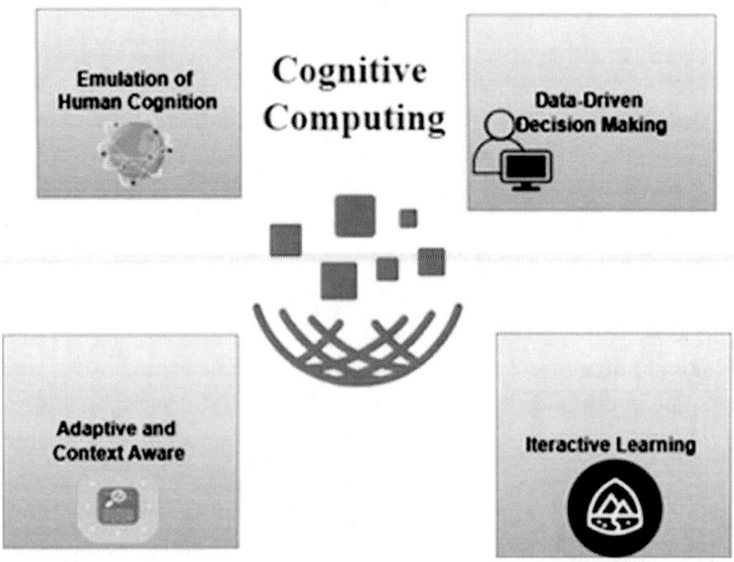

Figure 6.6. Features of Cognitive Computing Systems..

2.2. Core Technologies: NLP, ML, and AI

- *NLP, Role in CC:* Cognitive computing is one area with significant role of NLP. It is an artificial intelligence that assists the machine in interpreting complex language, detect significant information and comprehend context. This enables them to treat individuals as they naturally do. Cognitive computing makes use of NLP in question answering, language translation, emotion analysis, and text summarization. As an example, medical information about a patient can be analyzed through NLP to aid in making a diagnosis. It can be used in the context of customer service, where the chatbots are made to listen by responding to customer queries. The NLP bridges the gap between the operation of human language to the understanding of the machine and makes decision-making and solving problems that are easier in various fields.
- *ML algorithms and techniques used for data-driven decisions:* Machine learning methods and techniques are required to allow for making data-driven decisions without coding it in, because with these methods and techniques, the computer will be able to work with large datasets, find patterns, and estimate (An et al., 2023; Guido et al., 2024). Machine learning algorithms have three categories of algorithms. These are supervised, unsupervised learning, and reinforcement learning (Biswas, Pramanik, & Giri, 2016).

The working principle of supervised learning is founded on the data sets, labeled, and ML algorithms as well as on the techniques of data-driven decisions. Supervised learning employs label data in predictive analytics and classification tasks in predicting results. Unsupervised learning is the one that is used to identify unknown patterns based on the unlabeled data and it also involves clustering of the clients based on their shopping patterns or also uncovers new tendencies in the market. The idea of reinforcement learning is based on the process of decision-making in a dynamic environment and the enhancement of the behavior with time with the help of trial-and-error learning. Decision trees, neural networks, support vector machines, and ensemble techniques were used to improve the accuracy of their predictions, risk identification, and performance in healthcare and financial sectors (Orhan and Kurutkan, 2025; Wijaya et al., 2024; Guido et al., 2024; Chang et al., 2024; Saberironaghi et al., 2025; An et al., 2023). The systems are able to use the data to accumulate knowledge and currently update their knowledge due to the ML algorithms (Wijaya et al., 2024; Chang et al., 2024). This prevents individuals from being at a point of confusion in as much as making snap judgments is concerned, in most cases where the matter is muddled and should not be assumed.

Figure 6.7 demonstrates the iterative process of developing machine learning models within cognitive computing systems, emphasizing continual learning and refinement.

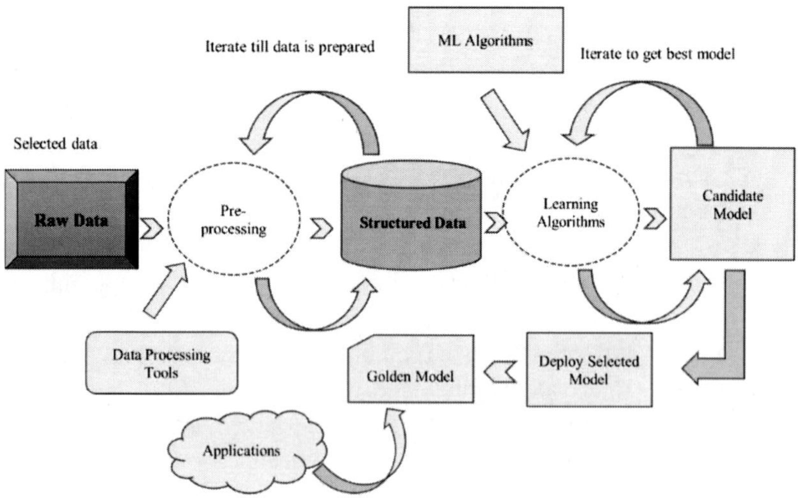

Figure 6.7. Iterative Process of Model Development.

The application of AI in the simulation of human mental processes (reasoning, learning, problem-solving): Artificial Intelligence (AI) systems can perform tasks that require human intelligence as they can imitate human thought processes, learning, and problem-solving. When it comes to evaluation, the AI systems analyze data, take into account a number of options, and perform actions according to what is presented through information. One of the subfields of Artificial Intelligence (AI), popularly referred to as Machine Learning (ML), allows a computer to observe data, learn through errors, and become more and more efficient until it can adjust to new and different conditions.

This power of assimilation and utilization of the knowledge is reliant on the exercise programs, and such is the case in human beings who learn and apply new information. AI can offer strong solutions to the challenging problems in various industries, like real-time optimization of the supply chain and the diagnosis of disease by studying patient information.

2.3. Comparison of Cognitive Computing and Traditional Computing

Aspect	Cognitive Computing	Traditional Computing
Learning Capability	Learns from data dynamically.	Requires explicit programming and updates.
Interaction	Supports natural, intuitive interactions.	Relies on structured inputs like commands.
Decision-Making	Provides probabilistic and contextual insights.	Operates on predefined rules and logic.
Data Handling	Processes unstructured and real-time data.	Primarily focuses on structured data.
Adaptability	Adapts to changes and evolves.	Static in nature, changes require coding.
Purpose	Augments human intelligence.	Automates predefined tasks.

2.3.1. Constraints of Traditional Models in Uncertain Environments

Traditional models face several limitations when operating in uncertain environments (Hubmann, Schulz, Becker, Althoff, & Stiller, 2018). These constraints are illustrated in Figure 6.8.

2.3.2. How Cognitive Systems Improve Upon Traditional Systems?

In some cases, complex and ambiguous conditions are formulated in conventional systems and in that case, the cognitive systems will outperform the conventional approach. Traditional systems operate similarly to the case of the static models, in contrast to the modern technologies, such as NLP and ML that acquire knowledge according to the new information, and their performance improves over time. These advanced systems can analyze structured and unstructured data to determine trends, predict and draw correlations which might be difficult to realise using traditional systems.

Cognitive systems also play a role in situations that have ambiguous or complex situations since they can reason ambiguity in situations when sufficient information is not present or when the available information is contradictory. In that case, medical cognitive systems can be useful when the provider is handling the data of multiple patients, predicting, and prescriptions, and the data is either incomplete or ambiguous.

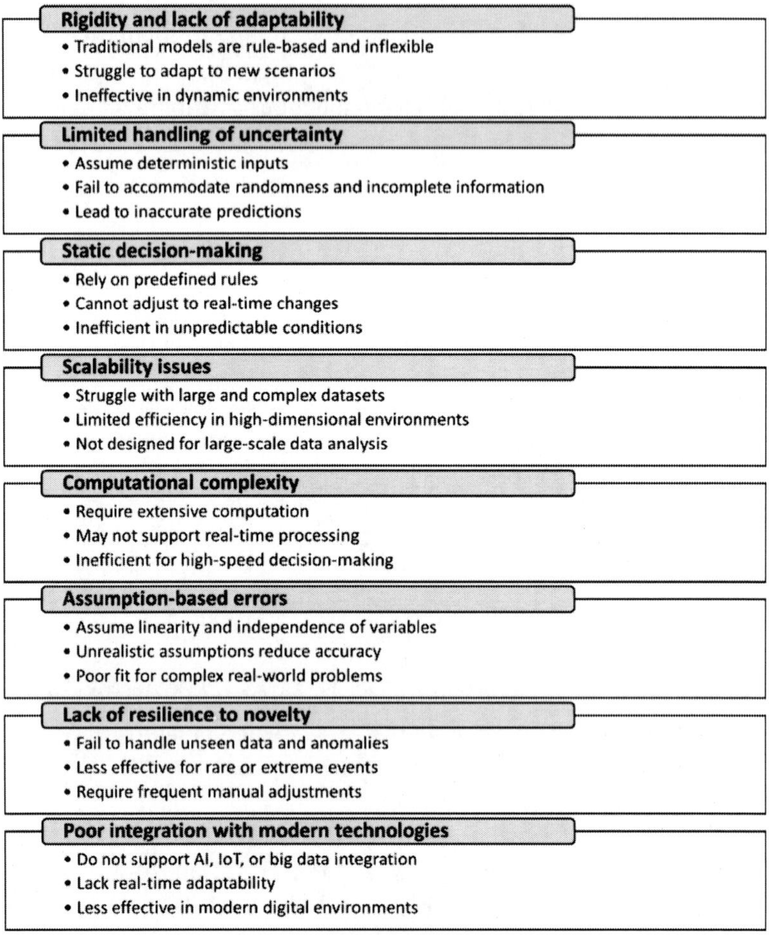

Figure 6.8. Constraints of traditional models in uncertain environments.

Cognitive structures comprise learning and adaptation and permit a more flexible, more accurate and dynamic approach to problem solving. This means that they are far more useful in dealing with real-world problems compared to conventional models of computing.

3. Decision-Making in Uncertain Environments

The cognitive decision-making model is depicted in Figure 6.9. Under this model, there is processing of information, experience-based learning and improved decisions are determined through experience over time. Here, the system interacts with the user and the environment in processing the inputs and verdicts.

First, data is interpreted and compared to the information stored. An enthusiastic learning constituent is never out of date and enhances this knowledge pool to make it current. Depending on decisions, the system will then apply its internal mental model with a set decision policy.

Once the decision is installed in the environment, it will be a continuous learning process of the system based on the results of the choice. Such a dynamic and responsive approach makes civil systems better at responding to complex and uncertain situations as compared to their earlier, more static incarnations.

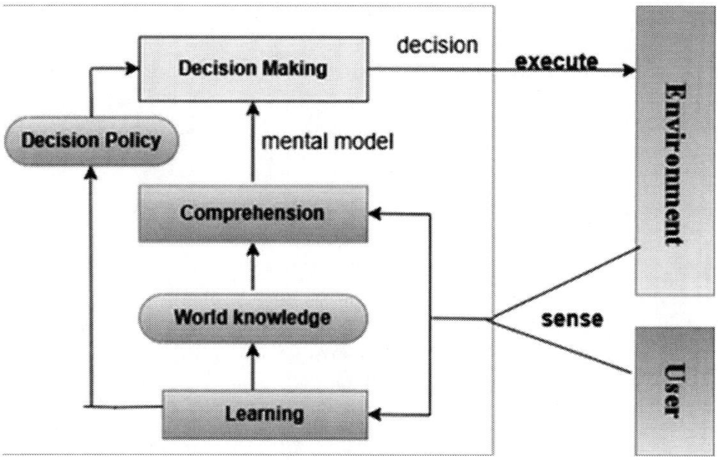

Figure 6.9. Decision-Making in Cognitive AI.

There are three forms of decision-making uncertainties, namely complexity, ambiguity and probabilistic uncertainty. Here we are discussing these.

- *Probabilistic* uncertainty are that cases where the probability of several possible outcomes cannot be known, but can be estimated. The basis of such decisions is probability-based on the historical information or statistical models.
- *Ambiguity* is the state where there is no clear definition of outcomes, and hence it is hard to know the best course to take. As an example,

the ambiguity regarding the implications of a new technology or a new regulation may lead to ambiguity in the circumstances of decision-making. The decision-makers need to make informed decisions even in cases where the information is open to a variety of interpretations.

- *Complexity* entails the situation where one has many interdependent elements that make it difficult to predict the response. The interdependence of variables in such properties as healthcare administration or supply chain management makes the prediction of the outcome especially hard. Complexity Cognitive computing can solve the problem of complexity by examining large volumes of data and uncovering patterns that would be unnoticeable to human decision-makers.

3.1. Challenges in Traditional Decision-Making Models

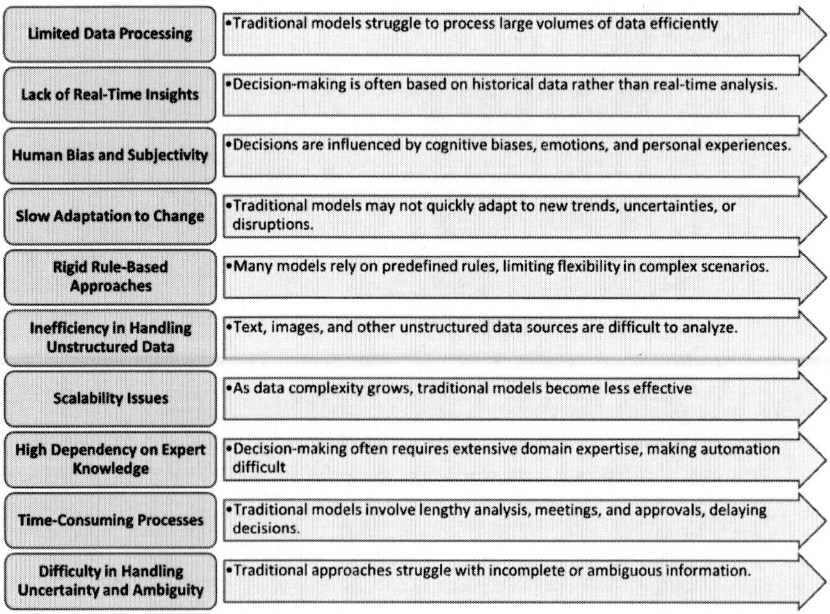

Figure 6.10. Overview of challenges in traditional decision-making models.

Traditional decision-making models faced some challenges, which are summarized in Figure 6.10 (Rizk et al., 2018).

3.2. Cognitive Computing's Approach to Handling Uncertainty

Cognitive computing uses AI and ML technologies to deal with the complexities of uncertainty uniquely. Figure 6.11 presents the cognitive decision-making process, outlining how data interpretation, probabilistic reasoning, and feedback loops interact to manage uncertainty effectively.

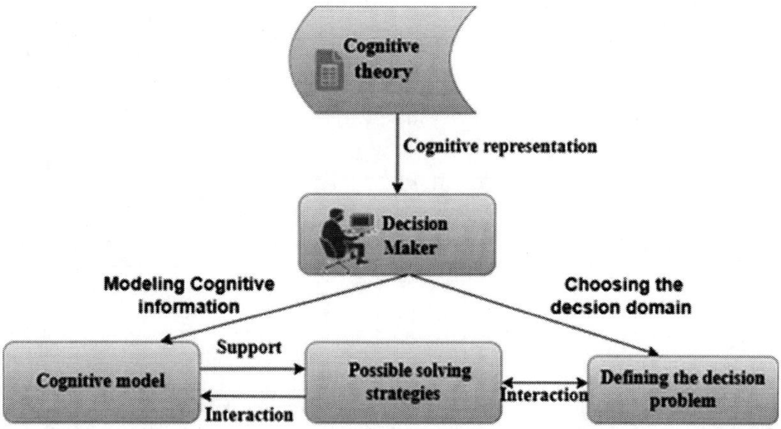

Figure 6.11. Decision-Making Process from a Cognitive Perspective.

A lot of major benefits are mentioned here.

Cognitive computing systems are supposed to deal with uncertainty through simulated human reasoning and responding to any incomplete or ambiguous information. The important approaches will be the following:

1. Probabilistic reasoning is based on using statistical models to evaluate the likelihood of different events, which enables the process of making a decision in an uncertain environment (Gershman et al., 2015; Rodríguez and Martinez, 2013).
2. Machine learning and pattern recognition find trends and relationships in large datasets to predict, even when incomplete information exists.

3. Fuzzy logic can process inaccurate and confusing information because it does not tell whether data is true or false, but it can have many possible truth values (Wang et al., 2017).
4. NLP is the process of reading through ambiguous or context-driven human conversation to get meaningful information.
5. Bayesian networks are probabilistic models applied to update beliefs based on new evidence to enhance decision accuracy (Gershman et al., 2015).

4. Applications of CC in Decision-Making

CC enhances decision-making across various industries using AI, ML, and data analytics to process vast amounts of information and provide intelligent insights. Figure 6.12 illustrates the application of CC in decision-making.

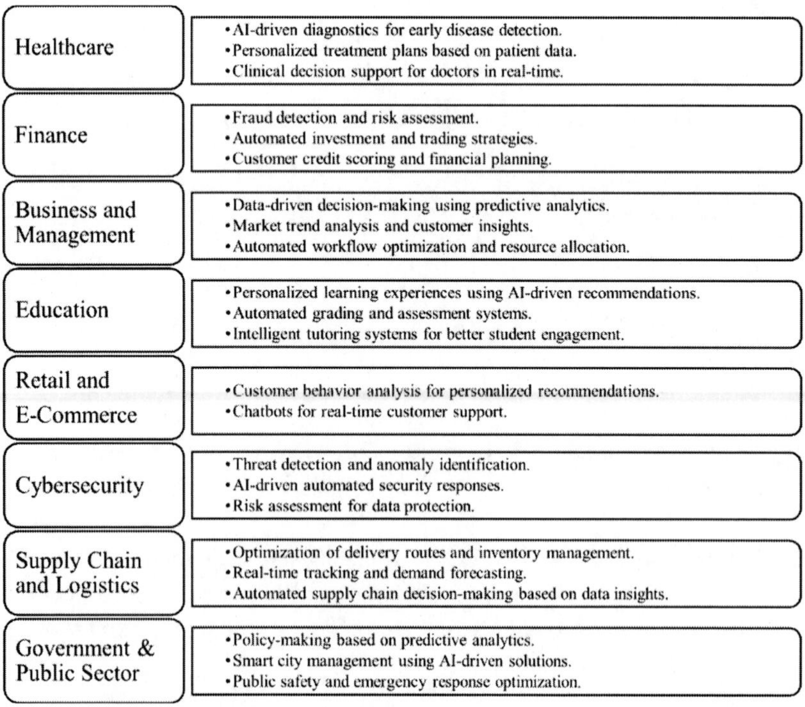

Figure 6.12. Application of CC in decision-making.

5. Architectures and Frameworks for Cognitive Decision-Making

The cognitive decision-making architecture and frameworks enable the efficient processing of complicated data, ensure compatibility with existing systems, and support practical application across a wide range of domains. In this section, we will examine the principles of cognitive systems, their operational mechanisms, and real-world examples demonstrating their effectiveness. Figure 6.13 illustrates the architecture of CC decision-making.

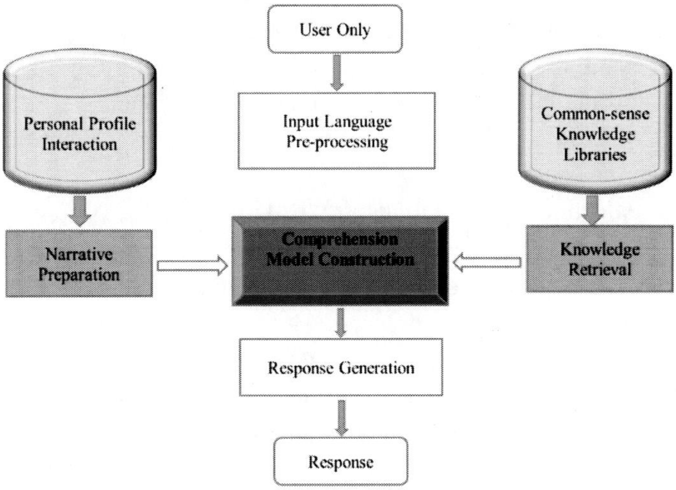

Figure 6.13. Cognitive Decision-Making Architecture.

5.1. Cognitive Systems Workflow for Decision-Making

Cognitive systems use multiple coordinated processes to assimilate and deliver actionable guidance. They are designed to help make decisions when faced with difficult, dynamic, and uncertain problems. The main steps are:

1. *Collection of Data*: Cognitive systems collect data from a variety of sources using real-time sensors, structured and unstructured data, data from databases, and spreadsheets. The data is collected from internal sources (e.g., enterprise) and external sources (e.g., social media, trends in the market).

2. *Data Preprocessing:* Raw data is subjected to removal, cleaning, and transformation in order to improve the raw data quality and to ensure it will be consistent with the original data. For example, it may involve the removal of outliers, imputation of missing data, normalization of data onto a common scale, and, more abstractly, transforming the unstructured data into an explicit format in order to perform an easier analysis.
3. *Knowledge Representation:* Cognitive systems use algorithms to reason from the data. Methods are:
   - Machine Learning to identify patterns
   - Uncertainty Analysis by Probabilistic Models
   - Rule-Based Reasoning to use existing knowledge
   - Natural Language Processing (NLP) to understand and derive meaning from unstructured voice or audio inputs
4. *Inference and Reasoning*: Cognitive systems use algorithms to reason from the data. Methods are:
   - Machine Learning to identify patterns
   - Uncertainty Analysis by Probabilistic Models
   - Rule-Based Reasoning to use existing knowledge
   - Natural Language Processing (NLP) to understand and derive meaning from unstructured voice or audio inputs
5. *Decision-Making or Recommendation Generation*: The system generates conclusions or recommendations from its reasoning. The outputs may be in the form of reports, dashboards, or visualizations, and may facilitate both automatic decisions and human interventions. There are also certain systems that rank or score recommendations by confidence levels.
6. *Action/Execution:* Decisions can lead to automatic action. For instance, a supply chain management cognitive system might automatically adjust stock levels in accordance with demand predictions. Or, it might make suggestions to human decision-makers, who then make the final action.
7. *Learning and Feedback:* Cognitive systems constantly learn new facts and past decisions. Feedback loops improve models, update knowledge bases, and improve accuracy over time. The system gets better by learning iteratively, with improved performance in the future.

Through this learning process, cognitive systems retain their flexibility, tolerance for uncertainty, and ability to improve (Tomic et al., 2012). Their final objective is to provide correct, timely, and data-based insights that support or supplement human decision-making in complex environments.

5.2. Integration with Existing Decision Support Systems

The incorporation of cognitive computing in traditional Decision Support Systems (DSS) truly enhances their effectiveness and efficiency in general, allowing organizations to better manage uncertainty, complexity, and variability of information. Cognitive systems bring adaptive intelligence, context-based learning, and real-time insights to traditional DSS systems.

The key integration methods include:

- *API Connectivity*: Application Programming Interfaces (APIs) enable seamless communication between cognitive technologies and legacy systems. This integration facilitates the smooth transfer of data and functionalities, allowing systems to operate cohesively without extensive restructuring.
- *Middleware Solutions*: Middleware acts as an intermediary layer, bridging compatibility gaps between traditional DSS and cognitive platforms (Rizk, Awad, & Tunstel, 2019). It allows real-time data exchange, interoperability, and enhanced data analysis without disrupting existing workflows. This modular approach is comparable to multi-agent cooperative systems (Rizk et al., 2019).
- *Modular Architectures:* Modular design supports the incremental integration of cognitive components into traditional DSS. This approach reduces the risk of operational disruptions and provides flexibility for gradual system upgrades based on specific needs.
- *Scalability:* Cognitive computing systems are inherently scalable, capable of adapting to organizational growth and managing increasingly complex and large-scale datasets.

For instance, in the financial services sector, cognitive computing can be integrated with risk assessment systems to generate more accurate, dynamic risk profiles (Hu et al., 2020). This enhances decision-making under conditions of uncertainty and evolving market conditions.

By incorporating these methods, organizations can transform conventional decision support systems into intelligent, adaptive platforms capable of learning, reasoning, and improving over time, thereby enabling better decision outcomes in complex environments.

6. Advantages of Cognitive Computing in Uncertainty Management

Artificial intelligence, machine learning, and natural language processing are used in cognitive computing to enhance decision-making in uncertain environments. Figure 6.14 presents a brief overview of the advantages of cognitive computing in uncertainty management.

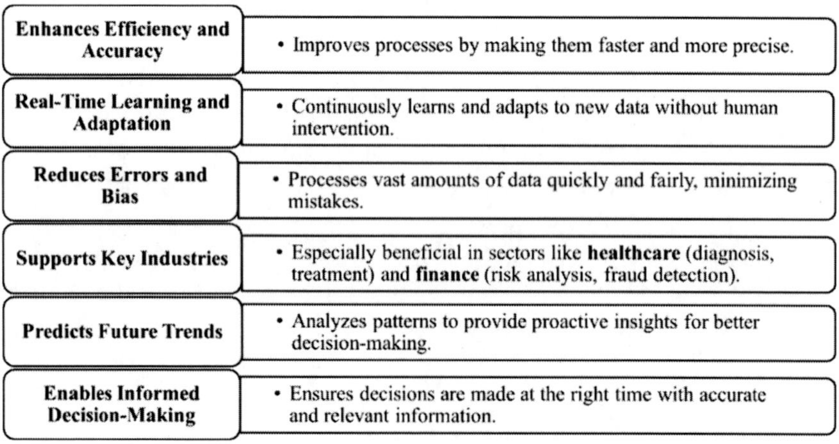

Figure 6.14. Advantages of cognitive computing in uncertainty management.

7. Challenges and Limitations

Cognitive computing has the power to transform a broad array of industries through enabling intelligent automation, adaptive learning, and improved decision-making. But its application and use are diluted by some technical, ethical, and operational hurdles. These need to be given thoughtful attention by organizations seeking to deploy cognitive technologies successfully.

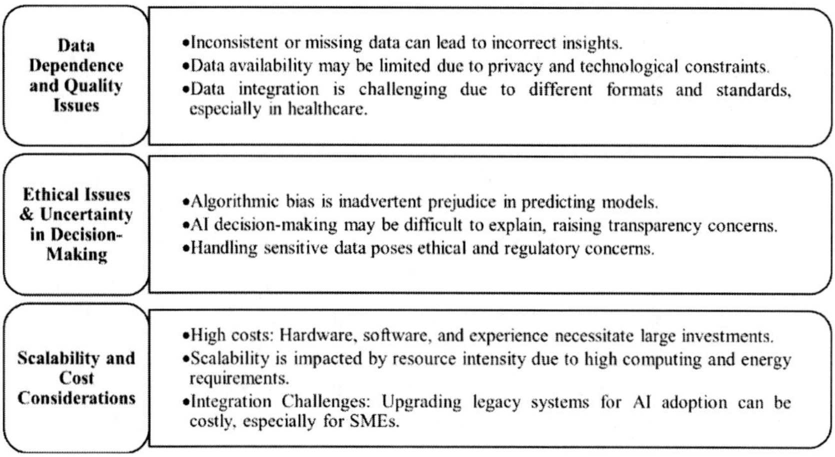

Figure 6.15. CC challenges.

Figure 6.15 depicts these challenges in depth to allow stakeholders to comprehend where strategic planning and mitigation are needed to facilitate effective deployment of cognitive computing solutions.

8. Future Trends and Opportunities

8.1. Emerging Innovations in Cognitive Computing

Cognitive computing has significantly advanced due to the evolution of machine learning algorithms, enabling systems to more effectively recognize patterns, generate accurate predictions, and make intelligent decisions. One major breakthrough lies in the ability to process multimodal data, including text, images, and video, allowing machines to interpret complex and varied sources of information with enhanced precision (Zhao et al., 2022).

Cognitive learning systems have made their mark in automation and are being utilized in almost all industries (Skagerlund et al., 2022). Connecting almost all examples of automation are efficient cognitive learning systems that minimize the amount of reliance on human operators and create efficiencies in robustness and reliability in almost all industries, from transportation to robotics to manufacturing. Most probably, the most significant aspect of cognitive learning systems is the advancements made in natural language understanding and processing in recognizing elements of language nuance and contextual semantics beyond just word associations, as well as delivering intended meanings more accurately and naturally when presented with human-oriented tasks such as sentiment analysis, language translations, or chatting with intelligent assistants.

Furthermore, with the integration of emotional intelligence in cognitive learning systems in industries such as education, healthcare, or customer service, the human emotional aspect of capturing and responding to new means could imply a considerably enhanced user experience (Tran & Pham, 2024; Hess & Bacigalupo, 2011; Helfat & Peteraf, 2015). Finally, autonomous cognitive systems, which are systems that self-learn as it relates to autonomously adapting to ever-changing conditions in dynamic environments while relying on minimal human intervention, are opening new fronts in multiple industries, such as logistics, predictive healthcare, and financial services, and allowing organizations the ability to enable predictive analytics via cognitive systems or the capability to implement autonomous decisions.

8.2. Impacts of Quantum Computing and Edge AI

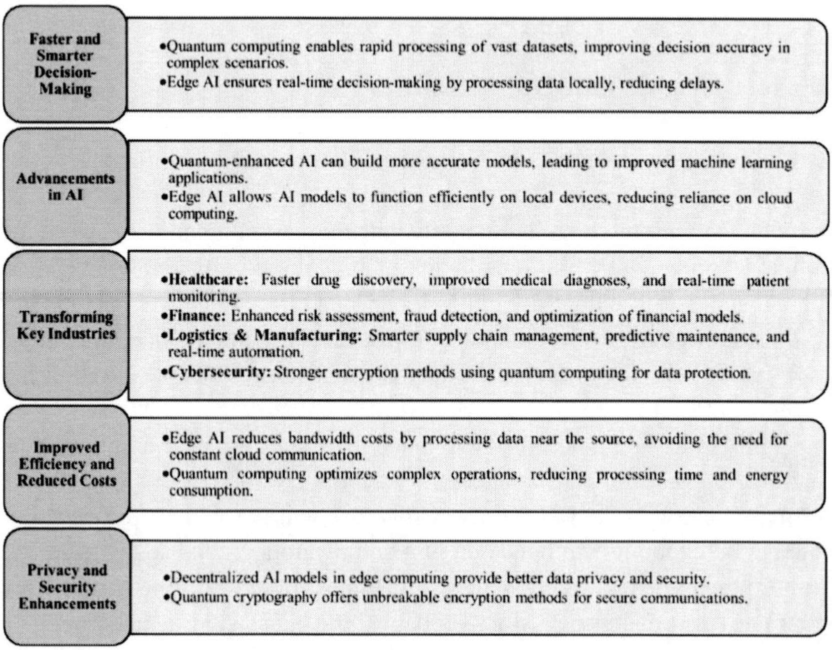

Figure 6.16. Impact of Quantum Computing and Edge AI.

Quantum computing and edge AI will revolutionize industries by making decisions faster, smarter, and more securely (Pejovic & Musolesi, 2015). Their combined potential with AI, healthcare, financial services, logistics, cybersecurity, and beyond will bring new directions in AI and influence the future of technology (Zhao et al., 2012). The overview in Figure 6.16 offers a rudimentary basis for their impact.

8.3. Cognitive Computing in Global and Complex Decision-Making

Cognitive systems can provide organizations and governments with advanced data analytics and decision-making to help organizations take smart, timely business actions in challenging, often fast-changing environments (Visvizi et al., 2018). These systems can provide coordination and planning collectively across multiple dimensions of decision-making that will help simplify action and gain better outcomes in difficult situations. In addition, cognitive computing can be used to assist in processing and analyzing large amounts of data, identify and interpret patterns formed in complex situations, and make decisions. These cognitive systems will enable decision-making in many areas throughout the world with the three related applications of AI, ML, and Natural Language Processing. Figure 6.17 shows some of the major dimensions of CC and its substantial value to global decision-making.

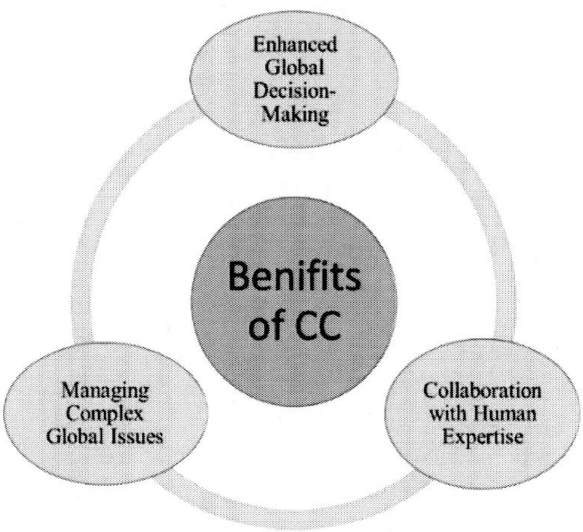

Figure 6.17. Benefits of CC in Global Decision-Making.

Cognitive computing is revolutionizing global decision-making by offering deeper insights, enhancing efficiency, and enabling proactive responses to complex challenges (Wu et al., 2014). Its impact spans across various industries, making it an indispensable tool for navigating the complexities of the modern world.

Conclusion

Cognitive computing has emerged as a transformative technology for decision-making, particularly in uncertain environments. It enhances predictive analytics, risk assessment, and problem-solving across diverse sectors such as healthcare, banking, disaster management, and supply chain logistics. These systems can process vast amounts of both structured and unstructured data, identify patterns, and provide real-time insights, enabling more informed and efficient decision-making (Gershman et al., 2015). While cognitive computing offers numerous benefits, it also presents challenges, including data dependency, ethical concerns, scalability issues, and the need for seamless integration. Organizations leverage this technology to ensure fair decisions, uphold data privacy, and address high startup costs. However, advancements in quantum computing and edge AI are poised to elevate cognitive computing, enhancing decision-making accuracy and adaptability. As edge AI progresses, it will revolutionize industries globally, driving smarter decision-making and unlocking new opportunities. With ongoing innovation and ethical application, cognitive computing holds immense potential to reshape decision-making processes, paving the way for smarter, more adaptive systems in the future.

References

An, Q., Rahman, S., Zhou, J., & Kang, J. J. (2023). A comprehensive review on machine learning in healthcare industry: Classification, restrictions, opportunities and challenges. *Sensors, 23*(9), 4178. https://doi.org/10.3390/s23094178.

Andronie, M., Lăzăroiu, G., Iatagan, M., Uță, C., Ștefănescu, R., & Cocoșatu, M. (2021). Artificial intelligence-based decision-making algorithms, Internet of Things sensing networks, and deep learning-assisted smart process management in cyber-physical production systems. *Electronics, 10*(20), 2497. https://doi.org/10.3390/electronics10202497.

Behera, R. K., Bala, P. K., & Dhir, A. (2019). The emerging role of cognitive computing in healthcare: A systematic literature review. *International Journal of Medical Informatics, 129*, 154–166. https://doi.org/10.1016/j.ijmedinf.2019.04.024.

Biswas, P., Pramanik, S., & Giri, B. C. (2016). TOPSIS method for multi-attribute group decision-making under single-valued neutrosophic environment. *Neural Computing and Applications, 27*, 727–737. https://doi.org/10.1007/s00521-015-1891-2.

Chang, V., Sivakulasingam, S., Wang, H., Wong, S. T., Ganatra, M. A., & Luo, J. (2024). Credit risk prediction using machine learning and deep learning: A study on credit card customers. *Risks, 12*(11), 174. https://doi.org/10.3390/risks12110174.

Collins, A., & Koechlin, E. (2012). Reasoning, learning, and creativity: Frontal lobe function and human decision-making. *PLoS Biology, 10*(3), e1001293. https://doi.org/10.1371/journal.pbio.1001293.

Cornelio, O. M., Ching, I. S., Gulín, J. G., & Rozhnova, L. (2018). Competency assessment model for a virtual laboratory system at a distance using the fuzzy cognitive map. *Investigación Operacional, 38*(2), 170–178.

Gershman, S. J., Horvitz, E. J., & Tenenbaum, J. B. (2015). Computational rationality: A converging paradigm for intelligence in brains, minds, and machines. *Science, 349*(6245), 273–278. https://doi.org/10.1126/science.aac6076.

Guido, R., Ferrisi, S., Lofaro, D., & Conforti, D. (2024). An overview on the advancements of support vector machine models in healthcare applications: A review. *Information, 15*(4), 235. https://doi.org/10.3390/info15040235.

Gupta, S., Kar, A. K., Baabdullah, A., & Al-Khowaiter, W. A. A. (2018). Big data with cognitive computing: A review for the future. *International Journal of Information Management*, *42*, 78–89. https://doi.org/10.1016/j.ijinfomgt.2018.06.005.

Gupta, S., Modgil, S., Bhattacharyya, S., & Bose, I. (2022). Artificial intelligence for decision support systems in the field of operations research: Review and future scope of research. Annals of Operations Research, 308(1), 215–274. https://doi.org/10.1007/s10479-020-03856-6.

Hafenbrädl, S., Waeger, D., Marewski, J. N., & Gigerenzer, G. (2016). Applied decision making with fast-and-frugal heuristics. *Journal of Applied Research in Memory and Cognition*, *5*(2), 215–231. https://doi.org/10.1016/j.jarmac.2016.04.011.

Helfat, C. E., & Peteraf, M. A. (2015). Managerial cognitive capabilities and the microfoundations of dynamic capabilities. *Strategic Management Journal, 36*(6), 831–850. https://doi.org/10.1002/smj.2247.

Herrera-Viedma, E., Cabrerizo, F. J., Pérez, I. J., Alonso, S., & Chiclana, F. (2020). Revisiting fuzzy and linguistic decision making: Scenarios and challenges for making wiser decisions in a better way. *IEEE Transactions on Systems, Man, and Cybernetics: Systems, 51*(1), 191–208.

Hess, J. D., & Bacigalupo, A. C. (2011). Enhancing decisions and decision-making processes through the application of emotional intelligence skills. *Management Decision, 49*(5), 710–721. https://doi.org/10.1108/00251741111130805.

Hubmann, C., Schulz, J., Becker, M., Althoff, D., & Stiller, C. (2018). Automated driving in uncertain environments: Planning with interaction and uncertain maneuver prediction. *IEEE Transactions on Intelligent Vehicles, 3*(1), 5–17. https://doi.org/10.1109/TIV.2017.2788208.

Hu, J., Niu, H., Carrasco, J., Lennox, B., & Arvin, F. (2020). Voronoi-based multi-robot autonomous exploration in unknown environments via deep reinforcement learning. *IEEE Transactions on Vehicular Technology, 69*(12), 14413–14423. https://doi.org/10.1109/TVT.2020.3034800.

Juárez Ramos, V. (Ed.). (2018). *Analysing the role of cognitive biases in the decision-making process.* IGI Global. https://doi.org/10.4018/978-1-5225-3952-0.

Konar, A. (2018). *Artificial intelligence and soft computing: Behavioural and cognitive modelling of the human brain.* CRC Press. https://doi.org/10.1201/9781315219738.

Narne, S., Adedoja, T., Mohan, M., & Ayyalasomayajula, T. (2024). AI-driven decision support systems in management: Enhancing strategic planning and execution. *International Journal on Recent and Innovation Trends in Computing and Communication, 12*(1), 268–275. https://ijritcc.org/index.php/ijritcc/article/view/10252.

Ng, K. K., Chen, C. H., Lee, C. K., Jiao, J. R., & Yang, Z. X. (2021). A systematic literature review on intelligent automation: Aligning concepts from theory, practice, and future perspectives. *Advanced Engineering Informatics, 47*, 101246. https://doi.org/10.1016/j.aei.2021.101246.

Orhan, F., & Kurutkan, M. N. (2025). Predicting total healthcare demand using machine learning: Separate and combined analysis of predisposing, enabling, and need factors. *BMC Health Services Research, 25*, 366. https://doi.org/10.1186/s12913-025-12502-5.

Patel, R., Goswami, A., Mistry, H. K. K., & Mavani, C. (2024). Cognitive computing for decision support systems: Transforming decision-making processes. *Educational Administration: Theory and Practice, 30*(6), 1216–1221. https://doi.org/10.53555/kuey.v30i6.5473.

Pejovic, V., & Musolesi, M. (2015). Anticipatory mobile computing: A survey of the state of the art and research challenges. *ACM Computing Surveys, 47*(3), 1–29. https://doi.org/10.1145/2693843.

Rizk, Y., Awad, M., & Tunstel, E. (2018). Decision making in multi-agent systems: A survey. *IEEE Transactions on Cognitive and Developmental Systems*. Advance online publication. https://doi.org/10.1109/TCDS.2018.2840971.

Rizk, Y., Awad, M., & Tunstel, E. W. (2019). Cooperative heterogeneous multi-robot systems: A survey. *ACM Computing Surveys, 52*(2), 1–31. https://doi.org/10.1145/3303848.

Rodríguez, R. M., & Martínez, L. (2013). An analysis of symbolic linguistic computing models in decision making. *International Journal of General Systems, 42*(1), 121–136. https://doi.org/10.1080/03081079.2012.710442

Saberironaghi, M., Ren, J., & Saberironaghi, A. (2025). Stock market prediction using machine learning and deep learning techniques: A review. *Applied Mathematics, 5*(3), 76. https://doi.org/10.3390/appliedmath5030076.

Sarafyazd, M., & Jazayeri, M. (2019). Hierarchical reasoning by neural circuits in the frontal cortex. *Science, 364*(6441), eaav8911. https://doi.org/10.1126/science.aav8911.

Skagerlund, K., Forsblad, M., Tinghög, G., & Västfjäll, D. (2022). Decision-making competence and cognitive abilities: Which abilities matter? *Journal of Behavioral Decision Making, 35*(1), 2242. https://doi.org/10.1002/bdm.2242.

Tomic, T., Schmid, K., Lutz, P., Domel, A., Kassecker, M., Mair, E., & Burschka, D. (2012). Toward a fully autonomous UAV: Research platform for indoor and outdoor urban search and rescue. *IEEE Robotics & Automation Magazine, 19*(3), 46–56. https://doi.org/10.1109/MRA.2012.2206473.

Tran, T. D., & Pham, T. V. (2024). The relationship between thinking ability, emotional intelligence, and decision-making. *Emerging Science Journal, 8*(2). https://doi.org/10.28991/ESJ-2024-08-02-017.

Visvizi, A., Lytras, M. D., Damiani, E., & Mathkour, H. (2018). Policy making for smart cities: Innovation and socially inclusive economic growth for sustainability. *Journal of Science and Technology Policy Management, 9*(2), 126–133. http://dx.doi.org/10.1108/JSTPM-07-2018-079.

Wang, J. Q., Cao, Y. X., & Zhang, H. Y. (2017). Multi-criteria decision-making method based on distance measure and Choquet integral for linguistic Z-numbers. *Cognitive Computation, 9*, 827–842. https://doi.org/10.1007/s12559-017-9493-1.

Wijaya, R., Saeed, F., Samimi, P., Albarrak, A. M., & Qasem, S. N. (2024). An ensemble machine learning and data mining approach to enhance stroke prediction. *Bioengineering, 11*(7), 672. https://doi.org/10.3390/bioengineering11070672.

Wu, Q., Ding, G., Xu, Y., Feng, S., Du, Z., Wang, J., & Long, K. (2014). Cognitive Internet of Things: A new paradigm beyond connection. *IEEE Internet of Things Journal, 1*(2), 129–143. https://doi.org/10.1109/JIOT.2014.2311513.

Zhao, G., Li, Y., & Xu, Q. (2022). From emotion AI to cognitive AI. *International Journal of Network Dynamics and Intelligence, 1*(1), 65–72. https://www.sciltp.com/journals/ijndi/articles/2504000020.

Zhao, P., Chen, J., Song, Y., Tao, X., Xu, T., & Mei, T. (2012). Design of a control system for an autonomous vehicle based on adaptive-PID. *International Journal of Advanced Robotic Systems, 9*(2), 44. https://doi.org/10.5772/51314.

Zheng, N. N., Liu, Z. Y., Ren, P. J., Ma, Y. Q., Chen, S. T., Yu, S. Y., & Wang, F. Y. (2017). Hybrid-augmented intelligence: Collaboration and cognition. *Frontiers of Information Technology & Electronic Engineering, 18*(2), 153–179. https://doi.org/10.1631/FITEE.1700053.

Zhu, G. N., Hu, J., & Ren, H. (2020). A fuzzy rough number-based AHP-TOPSIS for design concept evaluation under uncertain environments. *Applied Soft Computing, 91*, 106228. https://doi.org/10.1016/j.asoc.2020.106228.

Chapter 7

Smart Learning and Flexible Frameworks in Cognitive Computing for Education

S. Chitra[1,*], PhD
and N. Vasunthira Devi[2], PhD
[1]SRM Trichy Arts and Science College, Trichy, Tamil Nadu, India
[2]Annai Vailankanni Arts and Science College, Thanjavur, Tamil Nadu, India

Abstract

Cognitive computing means a system that simulates the human brain to analyze complex data. This computing unites all advanced technologies like Artificial Intelligence, ML-Machine Learning, NLP-Natural Language Processing, and so on. These technologies help enable machines to understand, reason, and learn from experience. The machine mimics the process as a human. Cognitive computing in education refers to transforming education by providing personalized, data-driven learning experiences and improving both teaching and administrative processes. Cognitive computing addresses complex learning challenges and personalizes education. In this chapter, smart learning and flexible frameworks play pivotal roles in reshaping traditional educational models by enabling dynamic, adaptive, and individualized learning experiences. It also investigates how cognitive computing can drive the development of smart learning environments, particularly through flexible educational frameworks that adapt to students' needs and cognitive profiles. By integrating all three technologies like AI, ML, and NLP, cognitive systems to create more efficient, effective, and accessible educational environments.

In this chapter, six sessions are included. First session states about the definition of Cognitive Computing in Education, secondly, the basic

* Corresponding Author's Email: chithismca@gmail.com

In: Building Intelligent Systems for the Future
Editors: Anamika Ahirwar, Neelesh Jain and Sumitha Elayaperumal
ISBN: 979-8-90134-050-9

concept of smart learning will be discussed, next, it discuss about the flexibility of cognitive computing in education, further, the Cognitive Frameworks in Smart Learning Systems are described, next, it states about the implementation of smart learning and flexible frameworks with Cognitive Computing and finally, it conclude the session with the Case Studies such as Real-World Applications of Cognitive Computing particularly in Education field.

Keywords: cognitive computing, artificial intelligence, machine learning, natural language processing

1. Introduction to Cognitive Computing in Education

Cognitive computing refers to systems that act like the human brain and process information. The key components include AI, ML, and NLP, used to imitate the human thought process, as shown in Figure 7.1.

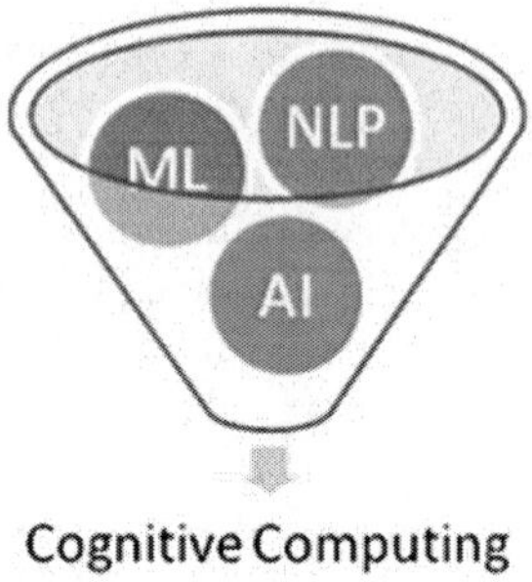

Figure 7.1. Key components of Cognitive Computing.

These technologies work together to construct systems that can analyze knowledge, solve problems, and provide solutions similar to human reasoning [2]. These advanced technologies are considered the backbone of cognitive computing, enabling systems to study, recognize, reason, and communicate in ways similar to human processes. The various applications of cognitive computing include education, healthcare, business, and more. Cognitive computing in education uses various technologies to enhance personalized learning, function as intelligent tutoring systems, facilitate communication between learners and technologies, help educators make data-driven decisions, analyze learner behavior, streamline administrative tasks such as grading and scheduling, and create smart, interactive e-content tailored to the needs of learners [2].

2. Differences Between Traditional Education and Cognitive Education

Table 7.1 represents the difference between Traditional education and Cognitive education.

Table 7.1. Difference between traditional education and cognitive education

S. No	Traditional Education	Cognitive Education
1.	The focus of traditional education is on the acquisition of knowledge, facts, and skills.	It is focused on the development of the thinking process.
2	The teacher is the main source in traditional education.	In cognitive education, the teacher act as a facilitator to guide the students.
3	It is typically passive learning where students participate as per the teacher's instruction.	It is active learning that is used to engage the students with critical thinking and problem-solving.
4	The assessment will follow the summative evaluation, such as exams, quizzes, and assignments.	Assessment focuses on formative evaluation, like a project or evaluates their thinking performance.
5	The learning environment is typically a systematic format and one-way direction, i.e., teacher direction only.	It is a more flexible, collaborative and interactive manner.

3. Importance of Smart Learning and Flexible Frameworks

In modern education, smart learning and flexible frameworks have become increasingly important due to advancements in technology. Cognitive systems can:

- Adapt to new input data, contexts, and environments.
- Personalize output based on user preferences.
- Handle a huge volume of data to identify patterns and create predictions efficiently.
- Make decisions and provide accurate predictions.

- Interact, collaborate, and integrate with other systems or technologies across various industries.
- Ensure efficiency and reduce costs while scaling.

These elements combine to enable systems that operate dynamically, functioning similarly to human beings. This ensures the provision of real-time, actionable insights, personalized experiences, and effective decision-making in ever-changing environments.

4. Definition of Cognitive Computing in Education

4.1. Define Cognitive Computing

It is a technology that imitates the process of thinking and decision-making like humans. These systems are considered to analyze, learn, and decide from the vast amount of data, like human cognition, such as understanding language, recognizing patterns, and adapting to new information. It combines techniques like AI, ML, NLP, data analytics, and neuroscience to create systems that can process huge volumes of unstructured data (e.g., text, speech, images) and provide insight, predictions, or suggestions [3].

Characteristics of Cognitive Computing:

- *Learning*: The Cognitive system learns and improves its performance based on its inputs, such as data, behavior, or experiences.
- *Reasoning:* The problems can be resolved by applying logic, identifying patterns, and systematic approaches.
- *Natural Language Understanding*: The system can recognize and produce human language as output; it also interacts with users in a more instinctive manner.
- *Adaptability:* These systems can adapt to new situations or data by adjusting their approach to solve problems in an effective way.
- *Interactivity:* These systems can interact with humans or other systems to provide valuable information according to their needs.

For instance, IBM Watson refers to a common example of cognitive computing. It uses AI and NLP to analyze large datasets and provide answers or recommendations in fields like healthcare, finance, and customer service. It can simulate human thought processes to make better, faster, and more informed decisions based on data.

4.2. Function of AI

It is an important transformation in the field of education. It offers new and innovative methods to enhance both teaching and learning environments. AI is a powerful tool in educational practices by automating the process from personalized learning experiences to administrative duties [4]. It also has the potential to analyses huge amounts of data in an efficient, adaptable, and inclusive learning environment. Figure 7.2 shows the functions of AI in education field.

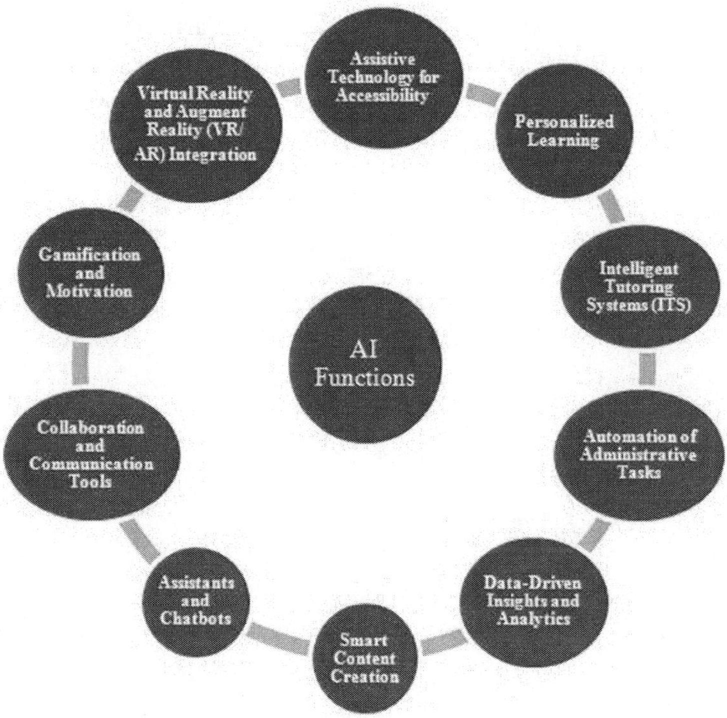

Figure 7.2. Functions of AI in education field.

4.2.1. Personalized Learning

Particularly in education, AI produces more advantages by personalizing learning experiences based on individual student requirements. Traditional methods follow one common approach for all students, but this raises the challenge for students who vary in learning speeds and styles [5]. AI overcomes by customizing educational content according to each student's pace and learning style. For instance, DreamBox and Knewton create types of curriculum (Easy, Intermediate, Advanced), changing the difficulty level (easy, moderate, advanced) of lessons based on students individual requirements. Additionally, AI also provides resources, such as videos, problems, and quizzes, to achieve the specific needs of each learner [6]. It can also customize the speed of learning based on the needs of each learner.

4.2.2. Intelligent Tutoring Systems (ITS)

AI-ITS can mimic like a personal tutor by offering guidance and support in subjects like mathematics, science, and languages. It also acts like real-time assistance to explain difficult concepts and guide them to solve difficult problems. It gives continuous feedback to correct their students' mistakes and fosters independent learning. It works 24/7 to support the students who need to enhance learning flexibility.

4.2.3. Automation of Administrative Tasks

AI helps to automate administrative tasks in educational institutions by reducing workload for educators and facilitators. AI automates the process of attendance (tracking learners using facial recognition), creates class schedules, resources, formative assessments like quiz, assignments and simple projects and grading the students' performance. Additionally, AI chatbots help students to solve their queries about assignments, deadlines, and policies.

4.2.4. Data-Driven Insights and Analytics

AI handles huge amounts of student data to track the students' performance. It consists of two analytics: Predictive analytics used to predict how many students complete the course or not by analyzing the past and current data. Learning analytics is used to track how much time was spent to solve the tasks and completion level of each student. Based on these analytics, AI can provide resources and tutoring support to improve the performance of the learners.

4.2.5. Smart Content Creation

AI technologies are used to create interactive content, quizzes, games, and discussions. AI also has interactive simulations, like virtual labs, to do their exercise virtually; it gives more effective learning with practical knowledge [7] Additionally, AI tools provide suggestions to improve the curriculum content based on learners' requirements.

4.2.6. Assistants and Chatbots

The Assistants and chatbots provide continuous support for the student. It enables interactive sessions by allowing students to ask questions about assignments or materials at any time. In Duolingo, the Virtual assistant offers real-time corrections in language learning, making it interactive. It also provides recommendations, suggesting exercises or activities based on individual learners.

4.2.7. Assistive Technology for Accessibility

AI also helps disabled students to enrich their education. Speech recognition and text-to-speech technologies are used to help students with dyslexia and visual disability by converting speech into text or reading out written content loudly. AI translates the learning content into various languages for non-native speakers.

4.2.8. Virtual Reality and Augment Reality (VR/AR) Integration

It plays a vital role in modern education by creating immersive, interactive learning experiences. AI-integrated VR platforms are used to learn concepts in virtual environments, such as museums or the human body. AR is used to create digital content by enabling interaction with 3D models, like historical artifacts, through smartphones or AR glasses. AI-driven VR and AR platforms offer practical experiences, allowing students to explore complex concepts like chemical reactions or physics in virtual spaces during STEM education.

4.2.9. Gamification and Motivation

AI enhances education by including game-based learning elements to make it more engaging. AI offers the difficulty of tasks based on student performance, by providing various challenge levels like easy, moderate, and advanced. It also congratulates students by providing awards like badges or progress percentages. These features help the students to be motivated and engage throughout the curriculum.

4.2.10. Collaboration and Communication Tools

AI uses communication and collaboration in education by connecting students, teachers, and parents in a single framework. For example, Google Classroom and Microsoft Teams help the students to collaborate on projects, share resources, and track progress. AI tools are used to provide parent-teacher communication for updating student progress, behavior, and engagement. Based on the above functions, AI can significantly improve the educational experience for students and educators alike and shape the future of global education.

5. Overview of Cognitive Technologies in Education

Cognitive technologies are advanced systems to replicate the mental processes of humans, like perception, learning, reasoning, decision-making, and so on. It relies heavily on various technologies like AI, machine learning, deep learning, and data analytics. In education, cognitive technologies handle huge amounts of data, recognize patterns, understand human language, and continuously adapt to improve the learning experiences [8] The fundamental goal of cognitive technologies in education is to enhance the quality of learning, automating the administrative process, which reduces the workload of teachers and administrators. Cognitive technologies include the following tools:

- *AI and Machine Learning (AI & ML):* It helps in the core of personalized learning systems. For example, Platforms like Knewton and DreamBox used to provide learning material according to the performance, whereas ML algorithms are used to predict the future performance of a student. It is very helpful for educators to find out the at-risk students earlier.
- *Natural Language Processing (NLP):* It is used to enhance communication, like Socratic and IBM Watson Tutor, which offer real-time and personalized feedback to enrich their knowledge. It also automated essay grading and was used to correct the grammar mistakes in the written content.
- *Computer Vision:* This technology is used to track the involvement of students through facial recognition and emotion analysis throughout

the session. It also uses AR/VR tools to simulate the concept in virtual environments to enrich their knowledge of the particular topic.

- *Cognitive Computing:* The adaptive learning environment is the combination of AI, data analytics, and NLP to create and adjust the content based on the learner's requirements. A virtual assistant, Alexa is used to help students manage their tasks.

6. Applications of Cognitive Technologies in Education

Cognitive technologies are transformed in various aspects of education, like teaching, learning, assessment, administration, and the research process. Some of the applications are listed as follows:

- *Personalized and Adaptive Learning*: AI and ML provide the learning content according to the students' requirements. For instance, BYJU'S and Vedantu are educational platforms to customize learning pathways, giving real-time feedback to understand and assess the concept.
- *Intelligent Tutoring Systems (ITS):* It acts like a personal tutor to provide learning material and give feedback to enhance their knowledge.
- *AI-Powered Assessments:* Cognitive technologies are used to automate grading processes and provide various testing levels, like easy, moderate, and advanced, to test and improve the accuracy and learning adaptability of an individual.
- *Classroom Management and Engagement*: AI is used to track student involvement and also uses AR/VR tools to give the concept in a virtually interactive way in a classroom.
- *Administrative Efficiency*: AI tools are used to automate the process of scheduling, maintenance of learners 'data, resource management, and decision-making through data analytics.

7. Benefits of Cognitive Technologies in Education

The several key benefits of cognitive technologies are as follows:

- *Personalized Learning*: AI platforms create the content according to individual learner requirements. It also allows the learners to learn the concept at their own speed, and they can understand their strength and areas they have to develop will be clear for an individual.
- *Scalability and Accessibility*: Cognitive technologies empower educational services to extend large numbers of students in a variety of locations. It will ensure quality education, especially in remote or neglected regions.
- *Time and Resource Efficiency*: The Automation process helps the educators to save time and also focus on more educational activities like assessments, quizzes, and games.
- *Data-Driven Insights*: Cognitive systems are used to analyze student data, track the learners' progress, predict the future, identify trends, and automate the interventions using past and current data.
- *Enhanced Engagement*: Technologies like AR and VR are used to create learning more interactive, offering practical experiences that increase student involvement compared to traditional methods.

8. Challenges and Ethical Considerations

The important challenges are as follows:

- *Data Privacy and Security*: Cognitive technologies rely on data collection; it ensures student data privacy through cryptography techniques and compliance with regulations like the Data Protection Bill.
- *Bias in AI Algorithms*: AI systems can accidentally bias training data, leading to biased results in assessments. It is used to ensure quality and design.
- *Teacher-Technology Balance*: The technology should enhance education, not replace the teachers. The educators should use the technology for support, not as a substitute. Both teacher and technology should balance equally otherwise, it becomes crucial.

9. Concept of Smart Learning Environment (SLE)

9.1. Definition of Smart Learning Environment

It is an environment to provide various technologies like online tools, ALM (Adaptive Learning Methods), and data-centric methods used for education to improve the learning experience. By combining various types of modern technologies like AI, ML, NLP, big data, cloud computing, and IoT to achieve dynamic, flexible, and interactive learning environments [9].

9.2. Characteristics of SLE

The characteristics of SLE utilize modern technology and teaching strategies to create more learning personalization, interactive, and flexible learning. This environment provides learning material based on students' requirements, instant feedback, and data-driven to improve teaching strategies. It includes various tools such as tablets, videos, virtual reality, and cloud storage to facilitate the content at any time and at any place. It is used to promote collaboration by gathering the various types of students' peers locally and globally, promoting teamwork and varied learning opportunities [10]. They also provide support for individual learners with apps and digital resources to access from various locations, and also useful for those with disabilities or language barriers. SLEs use energy-efficient tools to focus on sustainability by minimizing paper consumption. It also gives importance to privacy and security to ensure safe online environments for learners.

9.3. Functions of SLE

The different platforms and tools used to demonstrate how cognitive computing improves personalized learning across a range of courses and expectations. Table 2 below explains the overall functions of SLE with illustrations.

Table 2. Overall functions of SLE

S. No	Sections	Functions	Descriptions
1	Core	Cognitive Computing	It is the main system that personalizes learning. Ex: Squirrel AI uses AI to adapt lessons and provide personalized recommendations based on student performance.
2	Inner Section	Personalized Learning Path and Adaptive Assessments	Customize lessons and Assessments based on students and pace. Ex: Smart Sparrow offers adaptive learning paths in subjects like biology and engineering.
3	Middle Section	Learning Analytics, Real-Time Feedback, and resources	Track student performance, also gives instant feedback, and suggests helpful resources. Ex: Edmentum provides real-time feedback through assessments and offers personalized learning materials.
4	Outer Section	Engagement Tools, Support for All Learners	Makes learning more interactive and supports learners with different needs. Ex: Kahoot makes learning fun and interactive with quizzes.
5	Overall Support	Teacher Support	Helps teachers by providing useful information and tools for teaching. Ex: Classcraft helps teachers manage classroom behavior and track student progress using gamification.

9.4. Real-Time Feedback (RTF) and Personalized Content Delivery (PCD)

The most important components of modern learning systems are Real-Time Feedback and Personalized Content Delivery. Real-Time Feedback (RTF) gives instant feedback for every action of learners, by identifying mistakes and giving them solutions to solve the problem [11]. For instance, the Fillout platform is used to create quizzes and give an immediate score with correct options. Likewise, Duolingo is used to provide instant feedback, identifying mistakes and giving suggestions. The platform for Gamified systems, including Kahoot! and Quizlet used to track their performance during competitive or collaborative activities, and also to make them involved in their activities. Using these systems helps students and also supports teachers effectively.

Personalized Content Delivery (PCD) customises learning materials to individual learners based on their needs and expectations. The following platforms, like DreamBox Learning, are used to change the difficulty level of content according to each individual progress. Services like Coursera and Udemy provide courses based on a learner's concerns. The Socratic platform is a virtual platform to provide detailed explanations and resources for particular student questions. These platforms are used to keep learners engaged, reduce frustration, and facilitate self-paced learning [12]. The combination of instant feedback and personalized content results in a dynamic and effective learning experience suited to individual requirements.

9.5. Case Studies: Smart Learning Platforms in Practice

Table 7.3 summarizes the various case studies that illustrate how smart learning platforms are transforming education in practice.

10. Flexible Learning Framework

10.1. What are Flexible Frameworks?

Flexible Frameworks is a framework to design an application for various requirements or contexts effectively. These frameworks are widely used in domains like education, business, technology, and policy development to strike a balance between standardization and customization. The characteristics of these frameworks include Adaptability, Modularity, Scalability, and Interoperability [13]. For instance, in the Education domain, the Learning Management System (LMS) is an automated system for publishing materials, conducting formative assessments like quizzes and assignments, conducting group discussions, and also efficiently monitoring student performance.

10.2. Characteristics

In the education domain, The Characteristics of this framework are as follows:

- *Adaptability:* it provides courses as per the requirements of beginners to advanced learners, enabling them to complete at their own speed.

Table 7.3. Case studies in Smart Learning Platforms

Platform	Overview	Implementation	Example	Impact
edX	Provides online university-level courses, Micro Masters programs, and professional certifications.	- Partners with universities like MIT and Harvard. - Courses are designed for self-paced learning. - Professional certifications aligned with industry demands.	Global Learners: Students completing edX's Data Science Micro Masters program gain credits toward a full master's degree at institutions like MIT	- Equips learners with advanced skills for career growth. -Facilities credit transfers to traditional degree programs.
Udemy	Offers a wide range of professional and technical courses by industry experts.	-Tailored recommendations for learners based on skill preferences. - Corporate learning programs provide training for teams. - Self-paced courses with lifetime access.	Companies like Adidas use Udemy to train employees in digital marketing, project management, and leadership skills, improving workforce capabilities.	- Accessible and affordable for professionals worldwide. - Flexible learning schedules cater to working adults.
Future Learn	Online short courses, degree programs, and certifications in partnership with global institutions.	- Focuses on collaborative learning through discussion forums. - Provides micro-credentials recognized in specific industries. - University and employer partnerships for job-relevant skills.	Future Learn partners with Open University to offer fully online degrees, enabling students to balance education with work commitments.	- Over 15 million learners benefit from globally recognized credentials. - Expands access to flexible education for non-traditional students.
LinkedIn Learning	Offers courses to develop professional skills across industries and technologies.	- Integrated with LinkedIn profiles to recommend career-relevant courses. - Tracks skill development for employers and individuals. - Courses taught by industry leaders.	Professionals use LinkedIn Learning to complete certifications in project management, significantly increasing their profile visibility to recruiters.	- Helps learners stay competitive in rapidly changing industries. - Employers use it to upskill teams efficiently.

- *Personalization:* it recommends courses based on learners' preferences and career aspects.
- *Blended Approaches*: It integrates all recorded video lectures, quizzes, and opportunities for peer interaction.
- *Access Anywhere:* The learners can access the learning materials through mobile or desktop devices.
- *Scalability:* It accommodates both individual learners and comprehensive training programs for an organization. Currently, a working professional can also join a course, complete lessons at their speed, and earn certifications while balancing their work environment.

10.3. Integration of Cognitive Computing with Traditional Learning Frameworks

Cognitive computing combines both techniques of traditional learning and AI to enhance personalized learning experiences. For example, the IBM Watson Education system will analyze student performance to recommend exercises created according to their needs. Virtual assistants or chatbots can answer student queries outside of the classroom activity. Tools like automated grading save the teacher's time and offer valuable insights. Predictive analytics includes the Microsoft Azure platform [14] to identify struggling students at the beginning stage and provide help to achieve targets. This method improves the learner's engagement, efficiency, and learning outcomes.

10.4. Frameworks for Data-Driven Decision Making in the Field of Education

The aim is to enhance the process of teaching, learning, and administration by utilizing student and institutional data. The primary components of this framework include:

- *Data Collection:* The Student Information Systems (SIS) is a system to retrieve academic records, attendance, and engagement metrics. Ex: Monitoring course completion status.

- *Data Integration*: The system gathers data from various sources, such as Learning Management Systems (LMS) and surveys, into a single system. *Ex*: integrating classroom performance data with feedback surveys.
- *Analytic Tools*: It utilizes analytics platforms such as Tableau or Microsoft Power BI to identify trends.

Ex: finding subjects with high failure rates.

- *Predictive Tools:* It applies models to predict student outcomes, such as dropout risks.
  Ex: implementing early warning systems (EWS) to identify students who need academic support.
- *Visualization and Reporting tool:* It presents insights through dashboards for faculty and administrators to respond accordingly.
  Ex: conducting enrollment trend analysis for resource planning.
- *Decision Tools:* it executes targeted approaches based on identifications like personalized learning paths.

10.5. Case Studies of Flexible Frameworks in Educational Institutions

Many institutions have effectively implemented a framework for flexible learning through its online and offline. It also incorporates MOOCs (Massive Open Online Courses) [15] and other online resources with traditional classroom learning, engaging students to balance both asynchronous and synchronous learning experiences. Online platforms like NPTEL (National Programme on Technology Enhanced Learning) are utilized to provide recorded lectures, whereas the classroom sessions focus on discussions and practical exercises. During the pandemic period, many institutions were transformed to a full online mode, ensuring that students all over India, and also from rural and remote areas, can access the required resources. This model has allowed institutions to maintain high-quality learning with support for diverse learning requirements. This case study shows how flexible learning frameworks are implemented across different regions and institutions by offering education to the students. By incorporating blended learning, data analytics, and personalized pathways, universities are creating a better environment to explain the students 'needs, ensuring continuity and improving educational outcomes.

11. Cognitive Framework In Education

11.1. Cognitive Load Theories (CLT)

In 1980, John Sweller proposed Cognitive Load Theory (CLT) defines the limitations of human working memory and its impact on learning [16]. It consists of three types of cognitive load: they are intrinsic load refers to the natural difficulty of the material, extraneous load caused by poor instructional design or presentation, and germane the effort needed to process and understand information. By using interactive learning and multimedia tools, educators can make learning easier, helping students to engage deeply with content.

11.2. Constructivism

It is a learning method that highlights the learning activities, interactions, and reflections to create their understanding through experiences. The primary concepts, like active learning, refer to the students linking new information with prior knowledge. Scaffolding is a teaching technique where instructors help their students learn how to solve problems on their own. Problem-Based Learning (PBL) is another strategy to solve their real-world problems by their logical skills. Inquiry-based learning is also a strategy to develop their knowledge based on their investigative experiences.

11.3. Metacognition

Metacognition plays a vital role in problem-solving, self-development, and critical thinking. The fundamental components of metacognition are awareness to identify the strategies to solve particular problems, and regulation is another tool to plan which decides how to learn the topic. Monitoring is used to track the learner's progress and evaluate whether the task is being completed effectively. For example, if the student struggles with any math problem, then they think about the previous experience with the same type of problem and solve it on their own. This process will be called a reflective method. This method will improve their learning and understanding deeply.

11.4. Feedback and Motivation

Feedback and motivation are integrated together in the field of education to build the students' involvement and performance efficiently. The educator's feedback gives essential information about the learners and areas where they have to improve, providing suggestions to achieve their learning goals. Positive feedback results in learners' strength, improves their confidence, and motivates them to reach their goals. For instance, an educator pinpointing their mistakes in an assignment and suggesting how to rectify their mistakes and also it will encourage the learners to focus on developing their skills. The negative feedback describes only the weaknesses of the learners without providing any guidance to enhance. The Self-Determination Theory is a theory to suggests that motivation grows when students feel competent, independent, and connected to others. In addition, Goal-Setting Theory is used to help track the learner's progress toward specific goals, and Expectancy-Value Theory, which influences learners' value of tasks and their success.

11.5. Real-World Examples in Educational Tools

Google Classroom is an application for educators to develop content, conduct formative assessments like assignments and quizzes, interact with the learners through discussion, and provide instant feedback. It also integrates simultaneously with Google Drive, Docs, and other apps to handle classroom activities efficiently. It also acts like a central hub where educators and learners can interact, share, and monitor what will happen. Likewise, Edmodo is another social learning platform to connect students, teachers, and parents in a single platform. It also has a space for students to post their assignments, collaborate, and interact with teachers. These platforms support instant feedback to improve student involvement and learning experiences.

Quizlet is an interactive platform to design flashcards, conduct tests, and play games to engage learners continuously. Seesaw is another platform for students to document and reflect on their learning. For instance, educators use Seesaw tools to create an interactive environment for learners to reflect on their learning through multimedia, sharing knowledge, and receiving feedback from educators. These tools provide solutions for the gap between traditional learning and digital technologies.

12. Implementing Smart Learning and Flexible Frameworks

12.1. The Role of Data in Cognitive Computing

In cognitive computing, Data is an important source to enable the systems to think like human processes, decision making, and improve. The data includes structured and unstructured data to provide personalized and adaptive solutions across domains like education, healthcare, and business. During training, the system handles large amounts of data to identify patterns, trends, and relationships. For instance, IBM Watson analyzes medical data to predict diagnostic data. Sentiment Analysis tools are used to handle unstructured data, such as text and images, to interpret social media feedback. Business analytics platforms are used to identify customer trends to guide strategic planning. The ability to process and analyze the real-time complex data is a transformative role across industries, and more efficient decision-making processes.

12.2. Learning Analytics for Improving Student Performance

To enrich the learning outcome, collect, analyze, and data about learners' behavior will be handled by the Learning analytics. By using AI technology and data science, educators are able to recognize patterns, predict challenges, and implement various strategies to help students succeed.

12.2.1. Usage of Learning Analytics Improves Student Performance

- *Identification of Struggling Students*: Learning analytics is used to find at-risk students based on their academic performance. Predictive models suggest that students by giving warning signs and enabling timely interventions to improve better in their studies.

- *Individual Learning Path*: Learning analytics is used to guide each student according to their performance to focus on their weakness and enhance their learning experience.
- *Instant Feedback:* Analytics tools are used to give immediate feedback to the students' strengths and areas for improvement in their learning process.
- *Curriculum Enhancement*: Data from learning analytics is used to highlight areas of a curriculum where the students find difficulty, and educators will revise the content for better understanding.
- *Fostering Engagement:* Analytics tools are also used to track student involvement with learning materials, assessments, and activities. It also provides insights to encourage the participation of learners.
- *Supporting Adaptive Learning Systems*: Learning analytics combines with adaptive learning methods to modify the content delivery in real time based on student requirements.

12.2.2. Predictive Analytics for Resource Allocation

In higher education, Predictive analytics will focus on past and current data to predict resource requirements and optimize their allocation. It also handles decision-making processes like student services, faculty deployment, classroom usage, and funding allocation. It ensures the efficient use of resources, improves learning outcomes, and enhances the student learning experiences.

12.2.3. Applications in Higher Education

- *Student Enrollment Prediction*: Predictive models are used to analyze the past enrollment trends, demographic data, and application patterns to predict future trends. It helps to allocate teaching staff, classrooms, and dormitories in advance.
- *Classroom and Facility Requirement*: Predictive tools are used to predict the use of lecture halls and other facilities based on the data about enrollment and the pattern schedule.
- *Financial forecasting*: Predictive analytics will assist in framing the budget according to the tuition revenue and operational costs, like faculty hiring or new infrastructure.
- *Retention and Student Success*: Predictive tools are used to identify at-risk students of dropping out or underperforming by analyzing

their performance. Universities can arrange counselors or tutors to support these at-risk students.

- *Resource Allocation in Research*: Predictive analytics will also evaluate funding trends and research outcomes to assign grants and lab resources effectively.

12.2.4. Enhancing Administrative Processes with Cognitive Systems

- *Automating Routine Tasks*: Cognitive systems are used to handle repetitive administrative tasks like data entry, scheduling, and document management. The automation of the above process will reduce human error. Currently, in universities, Chatbots and virtual assistants are used to handle student inquiries like course registration or campus services, and so on.
- *Intelligent Document Management*: AI systems are used to organize, analyze, and retrieve documents efficiently and effectively. Healthcare institutions use AI systems to handle patient records for accessing and providing accurate data.
- *Predictive Analytics for Decision-Making*: Cognitive tools are used to analyze the past and current data to predict future trends and guide strategic decisions.
- *Enhanced Customer and Stakeholder Support*: AI-driven chatbots and helpdesk systems are a system to provide real-time responses for queries and satisfy stakeholders.
- *Risk Management and Compliance*: Cognitive systems are used to analyze the data to identify risks and monitor, and suggest possible actions proactively.

12.3. Ethical Considerations in Data-Driven Decisions

Table 7.4 will summarize the ethical considerations and also provide issues and solutions for the real-world applications.

Table 7.4. Summarize the Ethical considerations and solutions for the real-world applications

Ethical Consideration	Issue	Best Practice	Example
Privacy and Confidentiality	Sensitive data like health or academic records may be mishandled or exposed.	Use encryption, anonymization, and comply with privacy laws like GDPR or HIPAA.	Universities safeguard student performance data and restrict access only to authorized personnel.
Discrimination	Algorithms are trained on data may perpetuate inequalities.	Audit datasets and algorithms regularly for biases to ensure fairness.	Hiring platforms ensuring fair evaluation across all genders and ethnicities.
Transparency and Explainability	Stakeholders may not understand complex algorithmic decisions.	Develop interpretable algorithms and explain decisions in simple terms.	Schools explaining why predictive systems label certain students as "at risk."
Consent and Ownership	Individuals may not know how their data is being used or collected.	Provide clear opt-in/opt-out options for data use.	Health apps clearly stating data usage and offering users control over their information.
Accountability and Oversight	Automated systems might make errors or unethical decisions without clear accountability.	Establish accountability frameworks and involve human oversight for significant decisions.	Credit scoring systems with financial officers reviewing decisions for fairness.
Impact on Autonomy	Automated decisions might override personal choices or control.	Allow users to appeal or override automated decisions.	College admissions involve human reviewers for final approvals.
Data Quality and Misinterpretation	Inaccurate or incomplete data may lead to harmful outcomes.	Validate and clean data to ensure it is accurate, complete, and free from misleading biases.	Analyzing complete attendance data to ensure students aren't unfairly labeled disengaged.
Environmental Concerns	Large-scale data analysis may consume significant computational resources, affecting the environment.	Optimize systems for energy efficiency and prioritize sustainable practices.	Universities are using energy-efficient cloud services for large-scale learning analytics.

Table 7.5. Represents the case studies for ai and cognitive systems in modern classrooms

Institution	Application	Description	Outcome	Impact
Georgia Institute of Technology	AI Teaching Assistant	AI-powered chatbot answered student questions with 97% accuracy.	Managed 10,000 queries per semester, reducing instructor workload.	Improved response time and created a more interactive learning environment.
Ivy Tech Community College	Predictive Analytics for Student Success	Analytics identified at-risk students within the first two weeks of the semester.	Over 3,000 students improved their grades, with 98% achieving a C or higher.	Prevented academic failures and offered timely personalized support.
National Technical Institute for the Deaf (NTID)	AI for Accessibility	Text-to-speech and speech-to-text tools were introduced for hearing-impaired students.	Enhanced access to materials and interaction, resulting in a 95% graduate employment rate.	Ensured inclusivity and accessibility in education.
Gradescope	AI for Grading Efficiency	AI-driven software automated assignment grading and detailed feedback analysis.	Educators saved 70% of grading time, focusing more on teaching.	Streamlined grading processes while enhancing student learning feedback.
Edwin AI	Personalized Language Learning	Adaptive learning using natural language processing for English language education.	Over 800,000 students across multiple countries improved their English proficiency.	Provided affordable, scalable, and personalized education solutions.

13. Case Studies: Real-World Applications of Cognitive Computing in Education

13.1. Case Studies: AI in Student Support Systems

- *Arizona State University (ASU):* Chatbots for Mental Health and Campus Life: ASU's use of "Hey Sunny," an AI-powered chatbot used to assist in managing student mental health. It also engages students in regular conversations about mental health, academic concerns, and general well-being, providing timely support and encouraging positive mental health behaviors.
- *University of Nevada - ChatGPT for Learning to Code*: ChatGPT will provide the instructional materials, help with content understanding, and offer detailed schedules for learning. These examples describe about how AI is being used to support students from mental health to personalized learning.

13.2. Case Studies: Learning Environments: Duolingo, Knewton

Duolingo and Knewton are examples of learning environments with AI advanced technology to enrich the education process. *Duolingo* is a free learning AI platform to engage users in gamification. *Knewton* is another tool to focuses on adaptive learning technology, analyzing student data, and adjusting the course material according to the individual needs. Both platforms are used to explain how the technology used for gamification in adaptive learning can create engaging and personalized educational experiences.

13.3. Challenges and Ethical Considerations

Challenges:

- *Data Privacy and Security*: Collecting and storing the data about students' academic performance and personal information raises concerns about data privacy. Institutions must protect this student data from misuse and breaches.

- *Bias in AI Systems*: AI models introduce bias if they are trained on unbalanced data sets then it leads to bias outcomes, like personalized learning or grading.
- *Access and Equity*: Students from underfunded schools or from lower-income status may not be able to access the advanced technology due to their limited benefits.

Ethical Considerations:

- *Transparency:* The AI-driven educational tools are transparent while making decisions. Students and educators can know about the systems and how they make decisions, particularly in assessments and grading.
- *Autonomy:* The AI technologies are used to reduce the work of educators, not to replace it. The relationships between students and educators should be strong for effective emotional and social learning.
- *Accountability:* When AI systems are used to monitor the learners' performance, it becomes unclear who is responsible if something goes wrong.

Conclusion

Smart Learning Environments and Flexible Frameworks support students by providing personalized, adaptable, and technology-enhanced learning experiences. It promotes involvement and learning outcomes through instant feedback

Recommendations for Educators, Administrators, and Policymakers

For Educators:

- *Embrace Technology*: Integrate tools like LMS, AI-driven feedback, and adaptive learning to meet various requirements, like Knewton uses learning paths for each individual student.

- *Focus on Student-Centered Learning*: Duolingo is used to demonstrate gamified language learning to boost the motivation level.
- *Ongoing Professional Development*: Educators require more training on both technical usage and interpreting learning data.

For Administrators:

- *Invest in Scalable Technologies*: Focus on cloud-based and AI systems to support both traditional and non-traditional learners.
- *Ensure Data Privacy*: Establish strong policies to protect student data, ensuring privacy through encryption and audits.
- *Foster Collaboration*: Promote a collaborative approach to adopting new technologies involving teachers, students, and parents, ensuring smooth transitions.

The Future of Cognitive Computing in Education:

- Collaborative and immersive are the two types of learning environments that cognitive computing will improve efficiently.
- Resources to support cross-border student collaboration involve using AI to recommend resources for students and to build shared spaces for working collaboratively with other students' environments effectively.
- Virtual and Augmented Reality will replace theoretical concepts and focus on experience and representation, such as a virtual journey or experiment.
- Such developments are expected to provide career-related further training and continuing professional development through the platforms, so that the learners are ready to deal with the technological changes at different stages of their careers.

References

[1] Zhu, Z. T., Yu, M. H., &Riezebos, P. (2016). A research framework of smart education. *Smart Learning Environments*.

[2] Iqbal, H. M. N., Parra-Saldivar, R., Zavala-Yoe, R., & Ramirez-Mendoza, R. A. (2020). Smart educational tools and learning management systems: Supportive

framework. *International Journal on Interactive Design and Manufacturing (IJIDeM)*.

[3] Aberšek, B., Flogie, A., & Pesek, I. (2024). *AI and cognitive modelling for education*. Springer International Publishing.

[4] Freigang, S., Schlenker, L., & Köhler, T. (2018). A conceptual framework for designing smart learning environments. *Smart Learning Environments*.

[5] Moon, J., Do, J., Lee, D., & Choi, G. W. (2020). A conceptual framework for teaching computational thinking in personalized OERs. *Smart Learning Environments*.

[6] Demir, K. A. (2021). Smart education framework. *Smart Learning Environments*.

[7] Dessì, D., Fenu, G., Marras, M., & Recupero, D. R. (2018). Bridging learning analytics and cognitive computing for big data classification in micro-learning video collections. *Computers in Human Behavior*.

[8] Cheung, S. K. S., Kwok, L. F., Phusavat, K., & Yang, H. H. (2021). Shaping the future learning environments with smart elements: Challenges and opportunities. *International Journal of Educational Technology in Higher Education*, *18*(16).

[9] Ouf, S., Ellatif, M. A., Salama, S. E., & Helmy, Y. (2016). A proposed paradigm for smart learning environment based on semantic web. *Computers in Human Behavior*.

[10] Al-Hunaiyyan, A., Bimba, A. T., Idris, N., & Al-Sharhan, S. (2017). A cognitive knowledge-based framework for social and metacognitive support in mobile learning. *Interdisciplinary Journal of Information, Knowledge and Management*, *12*.

[11] Adorni, G., Coccoli, M., Stanganelli, L., & Maresca, P. (2009). EifFE-L meets ECLIPSE: An integrated open-source e-learning environment. *Journal of e-Learning and Knowledge Society*, *5*(3).

[12] Coccoli, M., Vercelli, G., & Vivanet, G. (2012). Semantic wiki: A collaborative tool for instructional content design. *Journal of e-Learning and Knowledge Society*, *8*(2).

[13] Ronghuai, H., Wei, Z., Jing, D., Feipeng, S., Huanhuan, W., & Haijun, Z. (2019). Three basic computing problems for intelligent education. *Open Education Research*, *25*(5), 11-22.

[14] Chuanjun, S., Shuangshuang, G., & Zhichao, Z. (2018). Cognitive computing: A new perspective on the evaluation of single academic papers. *Journal of Library Science*, *44*(1), 50-61.

[15] Raymund, S., & Masamichi, S. (1998). Student modeling and machine learning. *International Journal of Artificial Intelligence in Education (IJAIED)*, *9*, 128-158.

[16] Earley, S. (2015). Executive roundtable series: Machine learning and cognitive computing. *IT Professional*, *17*(4), 56-60.

Chapter 8

Innovations, Difficulties, and Ethical Issues in the Prospects of Cognitive Computing in Human Psychology

Yogita Thareja*
and Sakshi Khullar†
Vivekananda Institute of Professional Studies Technical Campus,
Vivekananda School of Information Technology, Delhi, India

Abstract

This research project focuses on developing a web-based application using IoT and machine learning techniques to detect diseases affecting psychology and provide a real-life experience to people suffering from it by offering a better view of pictures. The project contributes to developing better visual prowess for these people by utilizing IoT and machine learning technologies to enhance their contribution to society and earn them the respect they deserve. A backend system, developed using Python and web frameworks, retrieves the data from the database, provides suggestions, and displays the pictures in the application with the colors suggested throughout the analysis. The frontend interface, developed using JavaScript, shows the result of the picture and is used for testing color blindness. The project centers on accurate blindness detection and allowing those with it to see pictures in the colors they can differentiate. Through the integration of computer vision algorithms and machine learning models, the collected data from people is being analyzed, and all necessary recommendations are being made. The

* Corresponding Author's Email: yogita.thareja@vips.edu
† Corresponding Author's Email: sakshi.khullar@vips.edu

In: Building Intelligent Systems for the Future
Editors: Anamika Ahirwar, Neelesh Jain and Sumitha Elayaperumal
ISBN: 979-8-90134-050-9

resulting data is stored in a MongoDB database. The project's applications include detecting color blindness, allowing people with color blindness to see things they could not do earlier, enabling them to obtain a driving license in the best way possible, and promoting citizen engagement and awareness on this matter. The results demonstrate the effectiveness of the AI-enabled system in detecting color blindness and any other disease, and allowing these people to differentiate colors they could not do earlier in a much better way.

Keywords: accurate detection, computer vision algorithms, data analysis, MongoDB database, backend system, python, web frameworks, recommendations, frontend interface, JavaScript, testing, driving license, citizen engagement, awareness, AI-enabled system, visual prowess

1. Introduction

In urban areas, color blindness is a major setback for many people in their pursuit of excellence and in contributing to the welfare of society. Moreover, colorblind individuals often struggle to keep pace with the ever-evolving world. The improper treatment and lack of opportunities for these individuals in society cause an unseemly, divide among the population [1-3].

Additionally, we investigate funding patterns for infrastructure development, encompassing public investment, private investment, and public-private partnerships. We also address present-day challenges encountered by the infrastructure sector and spotlight recent government interventions, including the PM Gati-Shakti Initiative, aimed at achieving integrated multi-modal connectivity. The research concludes by assessing sector-specific performance and government interventions in pivotal domains, such as the energy sector, the Smart City Mission, and industrial evolution. It also traces the progression of industrial policies in India preceding and following the year 1991, highlighting the transformative effects of liberalization, privatization, and globalization [4, 8].

There is a standard software testing model, "ISO/IEC/IEEE 29119" that was published in 2013 [2]. Because software testing has become increasingly important due to its critical role in verifying that the software is reliable, an ongoing series of software testing standards has been created. This series of standards for software testing should be regarded as an important component of software testing practice. The International Conference on Software Engineering held its first "Future of Software Engineering" in 2000[9]. The essential part of research in software testing is Experiment [10]. It includes documentation, design test techniques, and testing vocabulary and concepts. In this paper, we have proposed a 5W+1H pattern in automated testing in the healthcare domain [11-15]. This series of standards for software testing should be regarded as an important component of software testing practice, as shown in Figure 8.1.

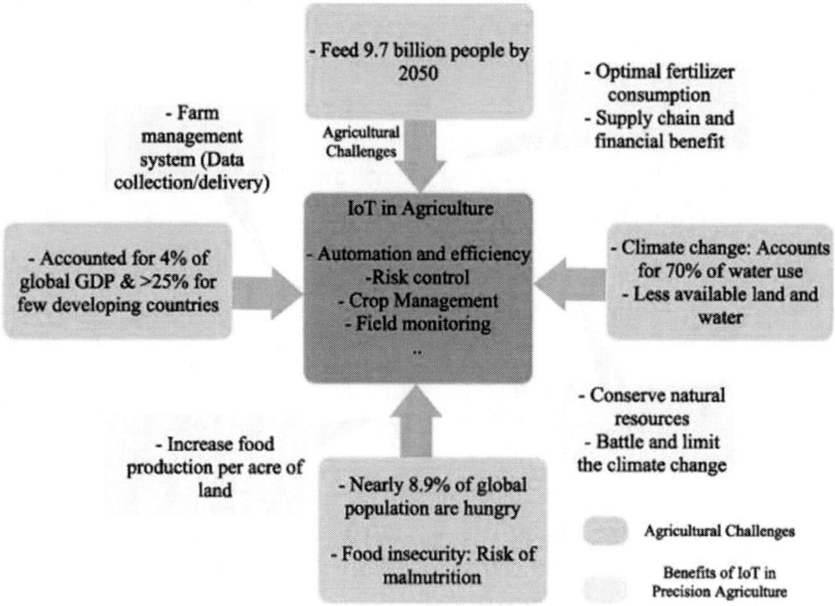

Figure 8.1. Integration of IoT and AI.

2. Literature Review

The idea of making web-based apps that can detect color blindness and change images in real time could be a great solution. There is general agreement that 1 in 12 men (8%) and 1 in 200 women are colorblind (approximately 4.5% of the world population) resulting in more than 350 million colorblind people in the world. India has the highest number of colorblind people in the world, with 70 million being colorblind. This review looks at what researchers have already found in this area and how these tools work.

2.1. Detecting Color Blindness

1. *Online Color Vision Tests*
   Web apps often use various color vision tests helps in finding color blindness. These tests, like the Ishihara test, Farnsworth-Munsell 100 Hue Test, and Cambridge Color Test, use images to point how well a person can see colors. They can be done online, making it easy for people to check their vision.
2. *Diagnostic Algorithms*
   Smart algorithms have been created to spot color blindness through web apps. These algorithms study how people react to images and quickly tell what type of color blindness they have and how severe it is. These algorithms have gotten better over time and give more accurate results [14,18].

2.2. Changing Images for Color Blind Users

1. *Color Correction Filters*
   Web apps often have filters that can change colors in real time. This helps people with color blindness see digital content better. These filters adjust colors, brightness, and how vivid they are to make images easier to understand. Users can even set these filters to match their specific type of color blindness.
2. *Customized Image Adjustment*
   Some web apps let users decide how they want to change images. Users can input their type of color blindness and their preferences. In this way, the app can change an image in a way that's just right for each person.

To summarize, while the previous work represents a valuable step towards assisting individuals with color blindness through image processing, it is essential to address the mentioned drawbacks and limitations to develop more effective and reliable solutions for a wider range of color vision deficiencies and real-world scenarios. Further research and testing are necessary to refine and validate these methods.

Infrastructure as an Economic Driver: Numerous studies affirm the pivotal role of infrastructure in promoting economic development. Development (Regional): Research Design" leads to "Sampling and

Participants," highlighting the connection between the methodology design and participant selection. "Sampling and Participants" connects to both "Data Collection Methods" and "Ethical Considerations" since it involves how data will be collected and the ethical considerations that must be followed [19, 20].

Generation (Employment): Data Collection Methods" links to "Variables and Measures" and "Data Analysis" to show that data collected will be used for variable measurement and subsequent analysis [21, 24].

Table 8.1. Comparison

S.No.	Author(s)	Year	Title	Methodology	Key Findings
1	Smith et al.	2018	Smart Cities and Sustainable Development: A Comprehensive Review	Literature review and case studies	Identified the key elements for building sustainable smart cities, including technology integration, citizen participation, and policy frameworks.
2	Lee and Kim	2020	Sustainable Urban Infrastructure in Smart Cities: A Systematic Review	Systematic literature review	Explored the integration of sustainable infrastructure components in smart city projects and identified

Infrastructure: IT leads to "Sampling and Participants," highlighting the connection between the methodology design and participant selection.

1. Partnerships (both Public-Private): It relies on manual monitoring and decision-making processes, which may be time-consuming and inefficient [12].
2. Analysis (Comparison): Comparative studies on manual monitoring and decision-making processes, which may be time-consuming and inefficient
3. Policy Reforms: Often rely on excessive use of water, fertilizers, and pesticides, leading to wastage and pollution, and the policy for maintaining the stable movement of law

Our writing audit lays out the current information base and sets the stage for our exploration. It highlights the meaning of framework improvement in cultivating financial development and serves as an establishment for our review's discoveries and suggestions as shown in Table 8.1.

3. Research Methodology

The methodology encompasses various stages, including project planning, data collection, system development, testing, and evaluation.

1. *Problem Identification*: The research begins with a clear identification of the problem, which is the need to enhance the online experience for individuals with color vision deficiencies, including detecting color blindness and providing real-time image transformations.
2. *Objective Setting:* The primary objectives are to develop a web-based application for accurate color blindness detection and to provide users with customized image transformations for better color differentiation.
3. *Scope and Limitations*: The integration of IoT and machine learning techniques, data analysis, database management, and front-end and backend system development. limitations include the availability of resources and the need for user engagement.
4. *Node-Oriented Method*: It needs the knowledge of the particular nodes to get all the nodes to be imagined and the "condition" word represents the branching nodes. We have to check the branching conditions carefully to predict True and False. To calculate the approximation level, the nodes need to be grouped. The following characteristics belong to each node group: only one entry node, nodes that belong to one path from entry to the target node. Node group is made according to the rules and doesn't violate the other characteristics.
5. *Path-oriented methods*: It needs certain paths which executes control flow graph. To complete the path coverage, the variations of all the path tests are obtained from the reduced path test belonging to this category. So, the paths that are needed to satisfy the structural test criteria and identified as partial aim.
6. *Node-node oriented methods*: At last, it performs the program on the path that covers the node combinations according to the determined sequence to get the control flow graph between nodes. Many data flow-oriented methods belong to this category [12].
7. *Node-node oriented methods*: At last, it performs the program to the path that covers the node combinations according to the determined

sequence to get the control flow graph between nodes. Many data flow-oriented methods belong to this category [2].

"Research Design" leads to "Sampling and Participants," highlighting the connection between the methodology design and participant selection.

- "Sampling and Participants" connects to both "Data Collection Methods" and "Ethical Considerations" since it involves how data will be collected and the ethical considerations that must be followed.
- "Data Collection Methods" links to "Variables and Measures" and "Data Analysis" toshow that data collected will be used for variable measurement and subsequent analysis.

"Data Analysis" connects to "Variables and Measures" and "Limitations" to indicate that data analysis will be performed to measure variables, and limitations of the study will be considered during the analysis displayed in Figure 8.2.

It needs certain paths for the execution of the control flow graph. To complete the path coverage, variations of path tests are obtained from the reduced path test belonging to this category. So, the paths that are needed to satisfy the structural test criteria and identified as a partial aim.

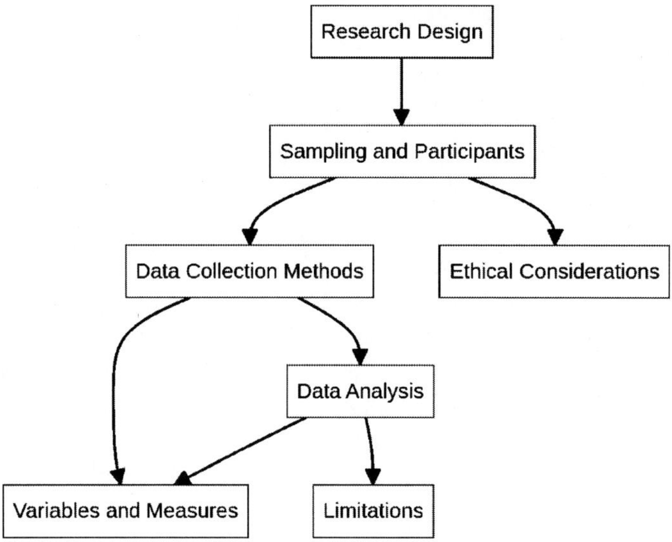

Figure 8.2. Methodology.

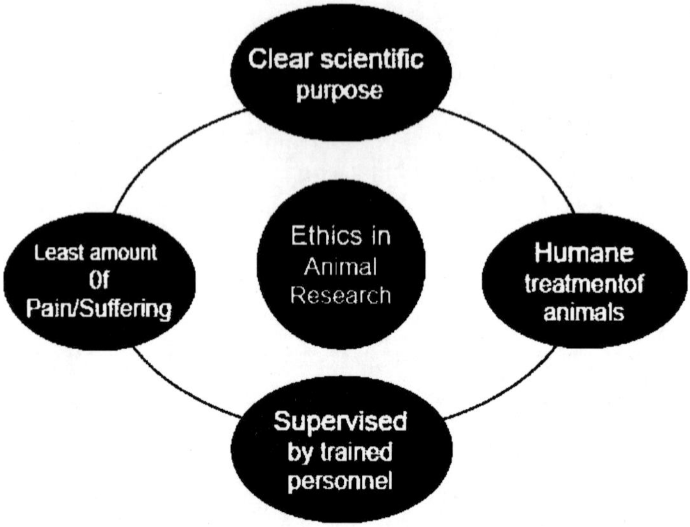

Figure 8.3. Ethics of Animal Psychology.

Process. In the Software Testing Process, 11 steps could be followed to get the solution. Those could be explained as follows:

- *Assess the Development Plan and Status.* Intended to evaluate every aspect of the implemented software solution, all testing is now to be completed with the above functionality [21]. This step has to do with ensuring functionality and presentation of data associated with the software solution. There are varied testing activities in the implementation stage for the efficient execution of the project plan
- *Test Plan Development.* Taking a plan for testing will be going to follow a particular pattern for the process of software testing. The format of planning should be followed as mentioned in the pattern we have taken, but the content of unit modules may vary at the developer's ease and risks of the software [25].
- *Testing the Software Requirements.* The cause of any software failures could be incomplete, inaccurate, or inconsistent. The importance of getting the requirements at the collecting requirement phase time could increase the cost of implementation. In the verification, testers must identify those requirements accurately, completely, and whether they conflict to each other.

- *Testing Software Design.* External design work consists of verifying hardware and software and confirming that the mechanical interface supports desired features. These hardware design issues are best tackled through simulation analysis. Internal design work provides a sense of cohesive design and helps implement the associated hardware features. Information required for internal design.
- *Build Phase Testing.* Characteristics of automation testers, the position of the automation tester is a dynamic one, with no strict physical conditions. Automation tester takes the best solution to get the right functionality from both the developer and the business [26]. When making software, he doesn't need to adhere to a particular methodology, as he can use the solution with relative ease. He takes an active part in the development process is shown in Figure 8.3.

The AMU program requires a certain number of annual quality indicators for each project to provide an independent review of the quality of the AMU efforts [26].

- *Test Software Changes.* Test plan formulation is similar to other phases in software development. When goals are developed and given directions to development teams, the team must deliver this information to development management and obtain approval. This approval creates the infrastructure within which they can implement the system and make necessary changes to the system as they go along.
- *Evaluate Test Effectiveness.* The top of a software testing assignment should be related to the success or failure of the feature development effort [26]. A tester should be empowered to take ownership of tests in a delivery team to make it a true objective assessment. Further, the evaluation should be factored with the rate at which the software is developed, software quality, and impact on business.

3.1. Data Analysis

The development of industries depends upon the development of the power and electricity generation sector, the transport and communication sector, etc. Similarly, the development of the service sector depends upon the efficiency of the human resource, which can be achieved through effective development of soft infrastructure. Thus, if adequate attention is not given to the development of infrastructure, it will work as a hindrance to the economic development of the nation.

Testing becomes a very crucial part of digital transformation because not only does it help to create better products or services, but it helps us to secure our customers' data and protect our consumers [27]. We are in talks with various enterprises to understand their needs better and will be rolling out future testing offerings that would bring together our past capabilities and expertise in functional safety, digital transformation, and add-on testing for applications as varied as IoT, artificial intelligence, and digital materials to enable the customers to move from testing only safety-critical applications to testing safety-critical and other types of application as well. This type of testing becomes a very crucial part of digital transformation because not only does it help to create better products or services, but it helps us to secure our customers' data and protect our consumers [28]. We are in talks with various enterprises to understand their needs better and will be rolling out future testing offerings that would bring together our past capabilities and expertise in functional safety, digital transformation, and add-ons. We can also gather data from medical images, medical records, genomic data, mobile phone data, wearable devices, social media, internet, environmental data, etc. It could gather all the information to predict the disease using past data or big data [29, 30], as shown in Figure 8.4.

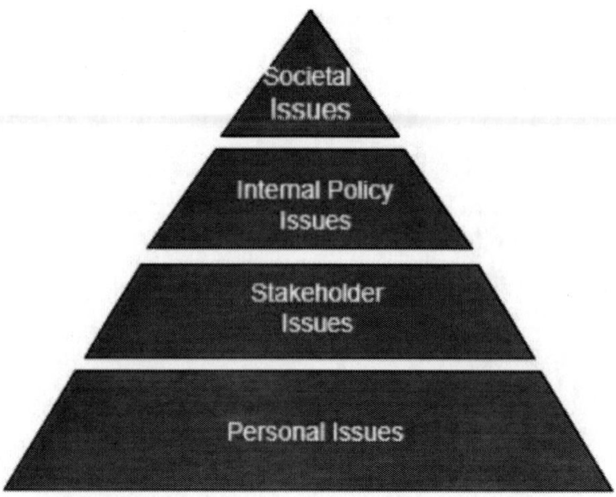

Figure 8.4. Issues of Psychology.

Various enterprises to understand their needs better, and will be rolling out future testing offerings that would bring together our past capabilities and expertise in functional safety, digital transformation, and add-ons, as shown in Table 8.2.

Table 8.2. Conventional versus IoT and AI

Metric	Conventional Agriculture	IoT and AI-Enabled Precision Farming
Water consumption (L)	100,000	60,000
Pesticide usage (kg)	200	100
Crop yield (tons/ha)	4	6
Carbon footprint (kg CO2)	500	300

Removing the fluid from the eyes causes irritation, swelling, and haze. It creates difficulty for the user to drive or walk shown in Figure 8.5 and Table 8.3.

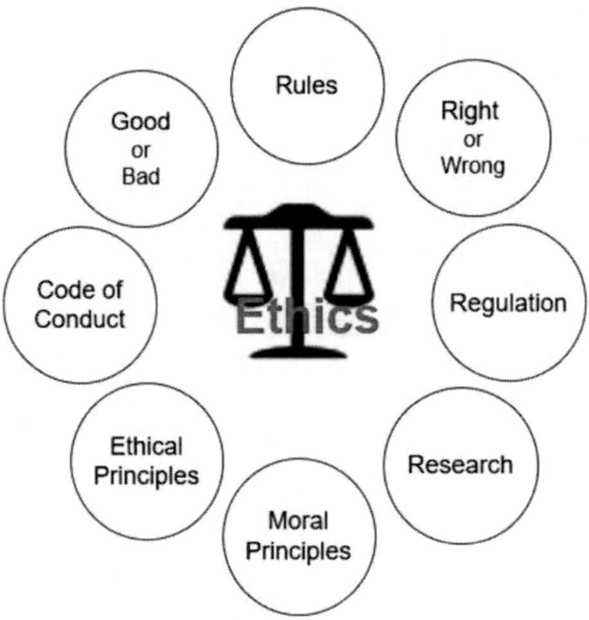

Figure 8.5. Cognitive Computing in Human Psychology.

Table 8.3. Difference

Aspect	Traditional Psychology	IoT and AI-enabled Precision Psychology
Efficiency	Relies on manual monitoring and decision-making processes, which may be time-consuming and inefficient	Utilizes real-time data from IoT sensors for precise resource management and optimized operations, leading to increased efficiency and productivity
Resource Usage	Often relies on excessive use of water, fertilizers, and pesticides, leading to wastage and pollution	Enables precise resource management based on real-time

3.2. Funding of Infrastructure and Various Models

Funding of infrastructure is done through heavy investments. The various models of investment are:

1. *Public Investment Model*: In such a model, the government invests from its resources.
2. *Private Investment Model*: Investment coming through private companies and institutions. Come under private investment; it includes both domestic and foreign investment.
3. *Public-Private Partnership (ppp) Model:* This model aims at implementing the government programmers in partnership with the private sector. Through this model, the private sector gets the chance to design and operate on the public sector programme and projects of the country.

- There are various variants of ppp model.
- The present challenge is the infrastructure sector.
- Poor functioning of the ppp investment models (especially in the power and telecom projects).
- Land and forest clearance issues in terms of delays etc.
- Lack of funds in the balance sheet of the private infrastructure companies.
- Lack of effective planning for the execution of projects.
- Excessive burden on the roadways.
- Obsolete infrastructure.

3.3. Recent Government Interventions: Youth Welfare

3.3.1. PM Initiative for the Welfare of Youth

Lack of effective planning for the execution of projects. Excessive burden on the roadways.

Obsolete infrastructure:

- It comes under Economic infrastructure.
- The Indian energy sector has observed rapid development in recent times.

Private investment and public-private partnerships. We also address present-day challenges encountered by the infrastructure sector and spotlight recent government interventions, including the PM Gati-Shakti Initiative, aimed at achieving integrated multi-modal connectivity shown in Figure 8.6.

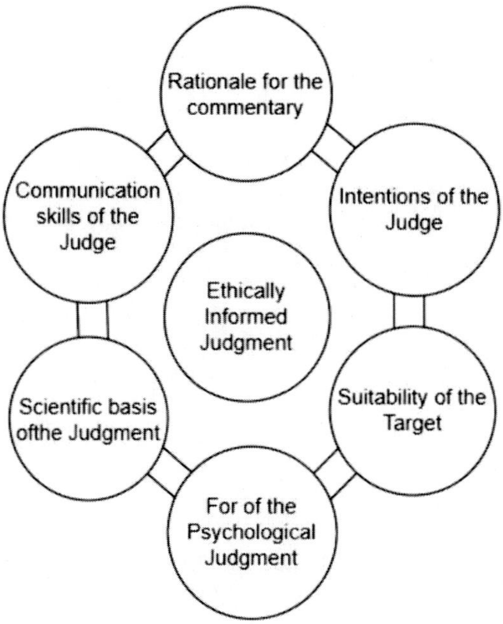

Figure 8.6. Ethically Informed Judgement of Human Psychology.

Conclusion

There are different types of software and various techniques for software testing. Some of these are easier, and some of them are difficult to test. Software testability is a measure in which software is how much supportive in a given context. If the degree of software testability is high, then it is easier to find bugs in the software; otherwise, it would be difficult. We should increase the testability of software such that the cost can be decreased. There are six factors in software testability. These are the following described as Software requirements, Implementation characteristics, Test capability while Built-in, Test cases, Test environment, Software process for testing. It also allows us to maximize the time and effort spent in creating more robust products to serve more customers. For instance, all the testing that happens in a digital manufacturing application can happen in a safety test environment before the application is released in the market. It also gives us more control over the time-to-market. we can understand the testing domain needed in healthcare.

References

[1] Bebber, D. P., Holmes, T., & Gurr, S. J. (2014). The global spread of crop pests and pathogens. *Global Ecology and Biogeography*, 23(12), 1398-1407.

[2] Gubbi, J., Buyya, R., Marusic, S., & Palaniswami, M. (2013). Internet of Things (IoT): A vision, architectural elements, and future directions. *Future Generation Computer Systems*, 29(7), 1645-1660.

[3] Leng, G., Huang, M., Liu, S., & Xing, Y. (2019). Internet of Things (IoT)-based precision agriculture monitoring system for crop disease detection. *Computers and Electronics in Agriculture*, 165, 104961.

[4] Mishra, D., & Prasad, R. V. (2019). Sustainable smart farming using IoT: A review. *Computers and Electronics in Agriculture,* 163, 104859.

[5] Pan, L., Wang, J., & Tian, G. (2019). Precision agriculture technology for crop farming: A review. *Journal of Integrative Agriculture*, 18(2), 291-304.

[6] Shahbandeh, M., Qader, M. H., Qadir, M., & Bahramisharif, A. (2019). IoT and AI based smart agriculture: Towards making the fields talk. *Computers and Electronics in Agriculture,* 165, 104943.

[7] Sharma, R. C., & Bajpai, R. (2018). Precision agriculture with the integration of internet of things (IoT). *Computers and Electronics in Agriculture,* 155, 104-111.

[8] Singh, S., Mishra, D., & Prasad, R. V. (2020). IoT and AI in agriculture: A systematic review. *Computers and Electronics in Agriculture*, 179, 105830.

[9] Srivastava, P. K., Prasad, R. V., & Agrawal, M. (2020). Smart farming: A review on the roles of internet of things and artificial intelligence. *IEEE Internet of Things Journal*, 7(10), 8593-8615.

[10] Wang, J., Guo, L., Wang, X., & Wang, L. (2019). An Internet of Things approach for precision agriculture in greenhouse cultivation. *IEEE Access*, 7, 117953-117963.

[11] Kundu, B. K., & Chakma, B. (2020). Prevalence of color vision defect in the Indian population-results from a pre-employment screening Centre of a tertiary care hospital. *J Contemp Med Res,* 7, I19-23.

[12] Poret, S., Dony, R. D., & Gregori, S. (2009, September). Image processing for color blindness correction. In *2009 IEEE Toronto International Conference Science and Technology for Humanity* (TIC-STH) (pp. 539-544). IEEE.

[13] Fareed, M., Anwar, M. A., & Afzal, M. (2015). Prevalence and gene frequency of color vision impairments among children of six populations from North Indian region. *Genes & Diseases*, 2(2), 211- 218.

[14] Sohaib, O., Lu, H., & Hussain, W. (2017, June). Internet of Things (IoT) in E-commerce: For people with disabilities. In *2017 12th IEEE conference on industrial electronics and applications* (ICIEA) (pp. 419-423). IEEE.

[15] Ochoa, A., & Oliva, D. (2018, November). Smart traffic management to support people with color blindness in a Smart City. In *2018 IEEE Latin American conference on computational intelligence (LA- CCI)* (pp. 1-8). IEEE.

[16] Kynčlová, P., Upadhyaya, S., & Nice, T. (2020). Composite index as a measure on achieving Sustainable Development Goal 9 (SDG-9) industry-related targets: The SDG-9 index. *Applied Energy*, 265, 114755. https://doi.org/10.1016/j.apenergy.2020.114755.

[17] Liu, L., Oza, S., Hogan, D., Chu, Y., Perin, J., Zhu, J., Lawn, J. E., Cousens, S., Mathers, C., & Black, R. E. (2016). Global, regional, and national causes of under-5 mortality in 2000–15: an updated systematic analysis with implications for the Sustainable Development Goals. *The Lancet*, 388(10063), 3027–3035. https://doi.org/10.1016/s0140-6736(16)31593-8.

[18] Nobrega, J. H. C., Rampasso, I. S., Sanchez-Rodrigues, V., Quelhas, O. L. G., Filho, W. L., Serafim, M. P., & Anholon, R. (2021). Logistics 4.0 in Brazil: Critical Analysis and Relationships with SDG 9 Targets. Sustainability, 13(23), 13012. https://doi.org/10.3390/su132313012.

[19] Alkema, L., Chou, D., Hogan, D. R., Zhang, S., Moller, A. B., Gemmill, A., Fat, D. M., Boerma, T., Temmerman, M., Mathers, C., & Say, L. (2016). Global, regional, and national levels and trends in maternal mortality between 1990 and 2015, with scenario-based projections to 2030: a systematic analysis by the UN Maternal Mortality Estimation Inter-Agency Group. *The Lancet,* 387(10017), 462–474. https://doi.org/10.1016/s0140-6736(15)00838-7.

[20] Tomaselli, M. F., Timko, J., Kozak, R., Bull, J. G., Kearney, S. P., Saddler, J. N., Van Dyk, S., Wang, G., & Zhu, X. (2019). SDG 9: Industry, Innovation and Infrastructure – Anticipating the potential impacts on forests and Forest-Based livelihoods. In *Cambridge University Press eBooks* (pp. 279–314). https://doi.org/10.1017/9781108765015.011.

[21] Sinha, A., Sengupta, T., & Saha, T. (2020). Technology policy and environmental quality at crossroads: Designing SDG policies for select Asia Pacific countries. *Technological Forecasting and Social Change, 161*, 120317. https://doi.org/10.1016/j.techfore.2020.120317.

[22] Fullman, N., Barber, R. M., Abajobir, A. A., Abate, K. H., Abbafati, C., Abbas, K., Abd-Allah, F., Abdulkader, R. S., Abdulle, A., Abera, S. F., Aboyans, V., Abu-Raddad, L. J., Abu-Rmeileh, N. M. E., Adedeji, I. A., Adetokunboh, O., Afshin, Agrawal, A., Agrawal, S., Kiadaliri, A. A., . . . Bräuer, M. (2017). Measuring progress and projecting attainment on the basis of past trends of the health-related Sustainable Development Goals in 188 countries: an analysis from the Global Burden of disease study 2016. The lancet *390*(10100), 1423–1459. https://doi.org/10.1016/s0140-6736(17)32336-x.

[23] Küfeoğlu, S. (2022). SDG-9: Industry, Innovation and Infrastructure. In *Sustainable development goals series* (pp. 349–369). https://doi.org/10.1007/978-3-031-07127-0_11.

[24] Ilie, C. M., Brovelli, M. A., & Coetzee, S. (2019). monitoring sdg 9 with global open data and open software – a case study from rural tanzania. *The International Archives of the Photogrammetry, Remote Sensing and Spatial Information Sciences, XLII-2/W13*, 1551–1558. https://doi.org/10.5194/isprs-archives-xlii-2-w13-1551-2019.

[25] Kroll, C., Warchold, A., & Pradhan, P. (2019). Sustainable Development Goals (SDGs): Are we successful in turning trade-offs into synergies? *Palgrave Communications*, *5*(1). https://doi.org/10.1057/s41599-019-0335-5.

[26] Kandaswamy, A., Malar, E., Ahilaa, T. D., & Indrani, R. (2021). Detection of dichromacy and achromatopsia using LabVIEW. *International Journal of Medical Engineering and Informatics,* 13(4), 334-345.

[27] Teixeira, A. R., & Gomes, A. (2020). A study of color using the Mindwave EEG sensor. In *Augmented Cognition. Theoretical and Technological Approaches*: 14th International Conference, AC 2020, Held as Part of the 22nd HCI International Conference, HCII 2020, Copenhagen, Denmark, July 19–24, 2020, Proceedings, Part I 22 (pp. 176-188). Springer International Publishing.

[28] Gunis, J., Šnajder, Ľ., Misianikova, A., Kotlárová, D., Brinzikova, K., & Leskova, A. (2024, May). Programming STEAM Applications in Informatics Education and Their Use in Biology Education. In *2024, 47th MIPRO ICT and Electronics Convention* (MIPRO) (pp. 583-588). IEEE.

[29] Sharif, R., Azam, M., Hashmi, M. U., & Naseem, C. (2024). The Usability of Mobile Devices for Individuals with Vision Impairments and Color Blindness, as well as Image Correctness. *Journal of Computing & Biomedical Informatics*, 7(01), 666-677.

[30] Olson, G. M., & Olson, J. S. (2003). Human-computer interaction: Psychological aspects of the human use of computing. *Annual review of psychology*, 54(1), 491-516.

Chapter 9

Big Data and Cognitive Computing: Scalability and Efficiency Issues

Lovkesh Singh Vermani[1,*], PhD
Anamika Ahirwar[2,†], PhD
and T. Velmurugan[3,‡], PhD
[1]School of Computer Application, JECRC University, Jaipur, India
[2]Department of Computer Science and Engineering
Compucom Institute of Technology and Management, Jaipur, Rajasthan, India
[3]PG and Research Department of Computer Science, D. G. Vaishnav College, Arumbakkam, Chennai, India

Abstract

Technological development has focused on the domain of artificial intelligence (AI) and data analytics; however, the associated increasing amount of massive data has introduced a host of challenges of scale and efficiency. The contemporary digital space offers information on scales too extensive and too complex and dynamic to process using the conventional data-processing frameworks. To address these deficiencies, industries have resorted to AI, machine learning, and cognitive computing procedures that are capable of replicating the thought patterns of human beings that enables systems to reason, learn and make decisions based on vast volumes of information. Combining big data and mimicking human cognition (AI) is altering sectors such as healthcare,

* Corresponding Author's Email: Lsvermani@gmail.com
† Corresponding Author's Email: aanamika77@gmail.com
‡ Corresponding Author's Email: velmurugan_dgvc@yahoo.co.in

In: Building Intelligent Systems for the Future
Editors: Anamika Ahirwar, Neelesh Jain and Sumitha Elayaperumal
ISBN: 979-8-90134-050-9

finance, logistics, and manufacturing by enhancing the accuracy of prediction, automation, and operational intelligence.
However, these technologies have barriers that have been set. The computation of the cognitive models is intensive and the efficiency of the training and inference decreases as the volumes of the data are increased. The high environmental and cost implications of the high energy use also add to the concerns of the large-scale data centres and distributed systems. To overcome these restrictions, modern research is dedicated to distributed and hybrid cloud systems that offer the opportunity to process data in parallel and scale up in case of need. The optimization protocols are model pruning, quantization, and federated learning, which operate by reducing the number of computations, and edge computing is processing information in a location closer to the source of information to reduce the loss of time. A combination of all these improves performance, responsiveness and sustainability in the mental systems.
Integrating big data with artificial intelligence simulation of human cognition has groundbreaking prospects for smart and data-oriented decisions. The further developments in distributed computing, optimizing algorithms and achieving green infrastructure will be the basis of the proposed future developments in cases where future generations will be able to develop scalable and energy-efficient cognitive architectures. The innovations will be one of the components of the entire potential of cognitive technologies in a more information-oriented world.

Keywords: artificial intelligence (AI), big data, distributed cognitive models, cognitive systems, simulation

1. Introduction to Big Data and Process of AI Human Thought Simulation

1.1. Introduction to Big Data

Massive information pertinent to diverse large data sets of unstructured or structured information, or semi-structured information, is on the rise with time. These datasets are so massive and large in size that these cannot be handled, processed, or analyzed by ordinary data management systems. The studies analyzing the overlap between machine learning and big data also identify the necessity of sophisticated data structures that are capable of guaranteeing scalability and adaptability in real-time settings [1].

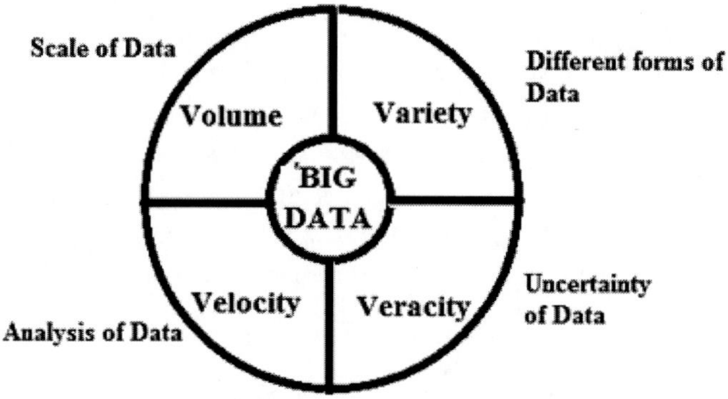

Figure 9.1. Introduction to Big Data.

This figure provides an overview of the concept of Big Data, illustrating data sources, storage, and analytical flow across different systems. As shown in Figure 9.1, Big Data represents the exponential growth of structured and unstructured datasets that require scalable computing models.

1.2. AI Human Thought Simulation and AI Along with Modern Technology

The human thought simulation with AI is a component of Artificial Intelligence, which is typically trying to replicate the way human beings think. It entails machine intelligence that is capable of learning, reasoning and comprehending language just like the human mind [2].

1.3. Relation Between Big Data, AI, and AI Human Thought Simulation

Figure 9.2 depicts the interrelationship between Big Data analytics, AI, and human thought simulation. It demonstrates how AI leverages Big Data to enable reasoning, learning, and decision-making processes similar to human cognition.

Big data, artificial intelligence, and AI human thought simulation are connected in such a manner that the organizations have much wider access for deeper decision-making with advanced analyses of data on more efficiently run operations:

- *Big data:* These refer to large datasets that can be studied to come up with insights.
- *AI:* applies human thought simulation AI to learn on large data to aid in decision-making.
- *AI simulation of human thoughts:* The process of observing, reasoning, evaluating, and decision-making to process huge volumes of data. The hybrid of AI and human thought modeling to process big data to derive insights is a novel research field that will develop with time. [3].

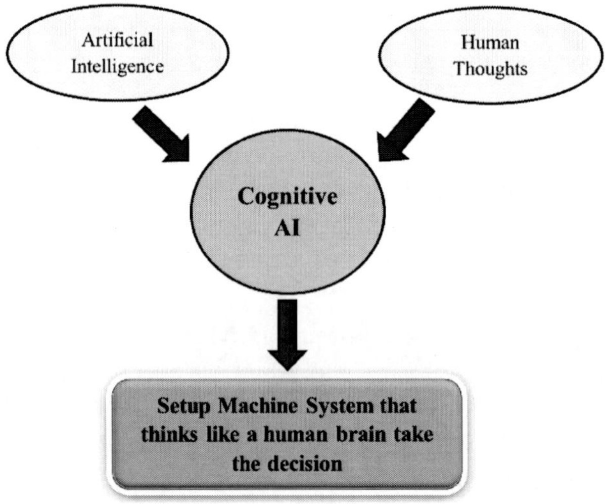

Figure 9.2. Relation between Big data, AI, and AI human thought simulation.

2. The Exceptions or Challenges of Cognitive Systems and Big Data

The trend is on the use of cloud computing and big data to support cognitive systems as opposed to intelligent decisions and automation. Such systems are facilitated by cognitive computing architectures, which are important in facilitating intelligent data processing and contextual reasoning [4]. However, there are also the problems of scalability of these systems, inconsistency of the data and inefficiency of the processing [5]. Massive data sets may have errors, redundancy, partial records and inaccuracies. This kind of data may result in poor decisions. In order to deal with this issue, data may be processed with automated cleansing programs, and data quality metrics may be set.

2.1. Scaling and Efficiency Issues in Big Data

- *Data Volume*: The amount of data can be in the order of terabytes hence it requires sufficient infrastructure and computation model.
- *Data Variety:* The data are being presented by a number of varying sources, and various meanings are presented in various forms.
- *Data Velocity:* There are situations when data is generated in real time (i.e., the sensor of the machine would be recording the readings after every couple of milliseconds).
- *Data Quality:* Inaccuracy or outdated or otherwise poor-quality records were an impediment to insights.
- *Data Sharing:* There is still some structural complexity in the data sharing, between organizations.

2.2. Limitations of Data Processing in the Traditional Way for Big Data

The traditional-type data processing methodology is incompatible with the range of complexities and expectations that the Big Data processing is associated with. There are several restrictions as follows.

- *Scalability:* The old systems are facing challenges with huge volume of data. Scaling up also may involve costly equipment, making it a long and less efficient process than relying on alternative systems that have a distributed nature.
- *Performance:* The velocity and diversity of data have overwhelmed the traditional systems, lowering the rate and precision. It is because a high latency response implies that there is a slim probability of real-time analyses or decision-making taking place [6, 7].
- *Complexity*: The conventional systems have been customized in the case of datasets which have to be standardized and structured. They do not stand a chance of effectively processing a heterogeneous and diversified or complex data sets that are the main features of Big Data.

- *Functionality:* Unlike Big Data systems, prospective measuring systems, like machine learning techniques and natural processing or language, this system does not have any automatic systems with the computation power to have applied systems in AI-supported applications model [6, 7].

Interoperability Traditional data is highly inept at integrating in other systems in terms of Big Data technologies (Hadoop, Spark). Any compatibility problems eventually have a positive relationship with reduced innovation and improvement of systems upgrades [8].

- *Flexibility:* When it comes to unstructured data, data management systems, which include online content, images, and sensors, are clogging the normal tools. As an example of the structured requirement of traditional tools, they will typically be rigid models and may require pre-processing of data to have datasets.
- *Manual Effort:* Data cleaning, preparation and analysis require a lot of manual effort that significantly prolongs the time spent working on data cleaning, preparation and analysis. This also leads to the possibility of human error, wastage of time and effort that is not efficient.
- *Flexibility:* Old systems have not been made to analyze real-time or dynamically changing data. The situation in which the data landscape is fast or there is a new source of data are time intensive, labour intensive and rather difficult to adapt the traditional systems to work.

2.3. Bottlenecks in Distributed Data Processing Environments

Bottlenecks in Distributed Data Processing with situations wherein a system's overall performance is considerably restrained or restricted with the aid of a specific element or aid. In essence, a bottleneck represents a factor inside the device in which the flow of facts or methods is restricted, main to a slowdown in normal performance.

In Figure 9.3, the significant points of limitation in the concept of distributed data processing architectures are identified. As seen in Figure 9.3, performance bottlenecks may be as a result of a limited bandwidth, a lack of balance in the distribution of data or the contention of resources in the system.

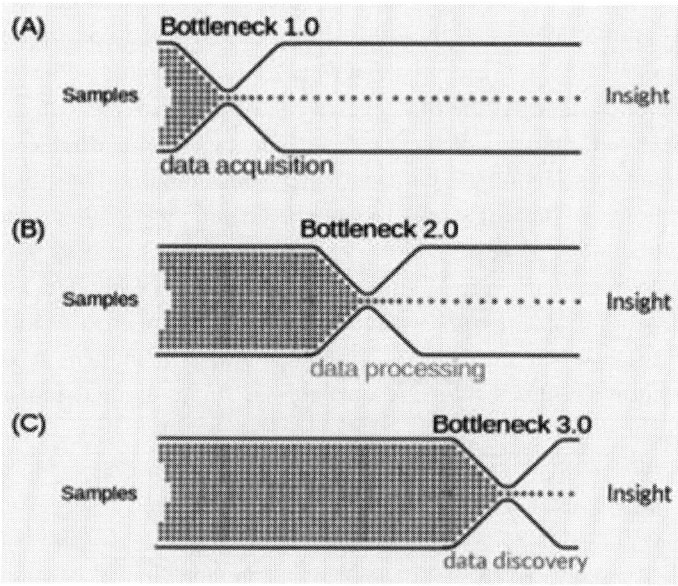

Figure 9.3. Bottlenecks in Distributed Data Processing Environments.

A bottleneck, in a communications context, is a factor within the company in which the flow of information is impaired or stopped totally. Effectively, a bottleneck results whilst there is insufficient statistics coping with ability to cope with the current quantity of site visitors [7].

3. Big Data and Its Scalability

3.1. Scalability in Big Data System

Scalability in big data is the possibility of a device to handle big volume of information effectively without compromising with the overall performance. It is very important in organizations that require saving, systematizing and analyzing vast amounts of information like those in the e-commerce, social media, and finance fields.

3.2. Challenges of Big Data in Cognitive Systems

Certainly, four challenges occur in the Cognitive system of big data:

- *Security:* The greatest threat to society from large-scale data lies in cognitive attacks. Cyber attackers are far more likely to attack AI models that store sensitive data and try to breach each dataset.
- *Data Quality:* At the first level, we have to ensure the data is correct, relevant, and complete. There are biases in data, whether through manual selection or humans using some device. Due to the vast amount of data, it's easy to have inaccurate, incomplete, erroneous, and duplicated data.
- *Integration of Data:* While various techniques of big data allow and fill large gaps of work with integrated data, there are also integration issues. When needing to compile multiple document types from multiple sources into one data format for traditional tools, this is difficult.
- *Data S*torage: The storage of big data will be a much more challenging and costly task. The economic numbers show companies have spent huge amounts of money on computing and infrastructure to try to handle the enormous amounts of data being created due to its rapidly increasing volumes, its increasing velocity, the number of sources, its complexity and the increasing and ongoing handling fees.

3.3. Data Consistency and Overhead in Distributed Cognitive Models

Data consistency is the requirement to provide data that is of the same quality and quantity across a data storage. Simply put, in reality, it is the case that if the remove operation in any situation is given, it should return the same data. This does so by ensuring the integrity of the data in a system. This main point is quite essential to Distributed Cognitive Models, especially in cases where they are becoming more complex and remote. The presence of consistency of data in the system is not maintained many data anomalies may occur, which may cause problems with application logic, mis-analysis, and the loss of trust in the system.

Figure 9.4 presents how distributed cognitive systems maintain data consistency and balance computational load. The visual demonstrates the role of load balancers and synchronization mechanisms in ensuring reliability across nodes.

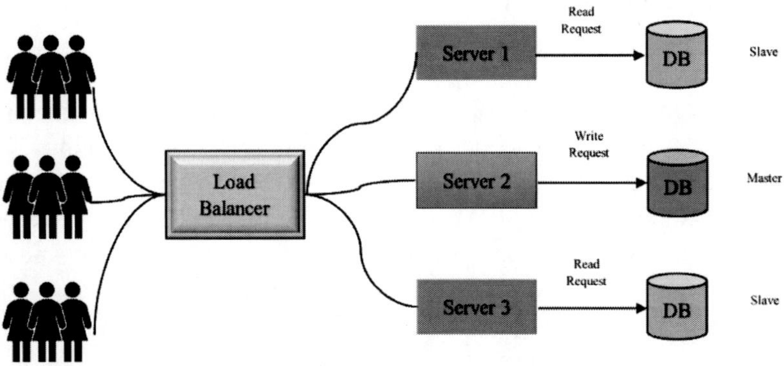

Figure 9.4. Data Consistency and Load Balancer in Distributed Cognitive Models.

4. Efficiency of Big Data Scale in AI Human Thought Simulation

4.1. Role of Deep Learning in Cognitive Models

Although the deep learning models are founded on the connection models, more recently, developments have been undertaken with future prospects in mind, even in its applied interests. Lastly, the deep-learning module is then applicable to cognitive purposes. It will be viewed as one of the forms of biological processes in which the anatomy structure may be employed with a functionality other than the chosen one. One will argue that it is high time to take scientific cognition seriously by way of deep learning. And we attempt to give the reasons of why this is so. To begin with, establish a way of developing a Project based on deep research in learning, with continuity and difference. Then, think of what good deep learning is. There are various cognitive disciplines that a model can prove helpful. The areas studied specifically that are accomplished. There is one such question, such as why are depth diffraction models omitted? Slow, context-dependent, and static and are near an activation pattern within the visual system of the brain.

The use of machine learning and natural language processing to address complex big data issues is evidenced by AI-driven cognitive computing systems, including IBM Watson, which can be applied to various areas, in particular, life sciences [9]. These learning systems also exploit cross-domain recommendation systems that combine massive data and AI human thought simulation to enhance personalization and flexibility [10].

4.2. Trade-Offs Between Accuracy and Efficiency in Cognitive Systems

The four major characteristics of a goal-driven system define a fundamentally functional business, which include efficiency, robustness, and flexibility. The question of efficiency versus accuracy trade-off can have a lot of effects beyond the computing field. It has come up with policies on how to strike a balance amid various uncertain conditions. We believe that, as the study of such positives and negatives is useful in the process of governance in other fields, then there is a need to discuss such issues when managing computer systems. The distributed machine-learning systems are also based on these trade-offs, and the question of accountability and fairness arises because balancing between computational efficiency and model accuracy is at stake [11].

Understanding the policy implications in this area is extremely urgent. Given the high stakes and safety importance of such systems involving autonomous vehicles, 1) describe how trade barriers for these systems are emerging, 2) highlight the gaps between risk assessment standards of the country's business available and these systems are suitable to assess what is needed, and 3). We call for specific actions for accountability for risks. The trade-off between efficiency and accuracy is an accidental happened in the real world. We need to promote more equitable and transparent governance that is consistent with public values.

4.3. Impact of High-Performance Infrastructure on Energy Consumption

The next-generation data center systems should be able to incorporate interlocked networks, storage and servers that can accommodate massive data applications using energy-efficient solutions. It is important to optimize passive and active cooling measures to ensure sustainability of the modern high-performance data centers [12].

These machines are used to process and store big volumes of data and they have to consume substantial electrical power. The amount of power used by servers is directly proportional to their workload, and the high-performance computing tasks can raise the power consumption significantly. The potential data center architectures, which combine networking, storage, and computing solutions via software-defined and cloud-based solutions, allow to enhance scalability and energy efficiency [13].

It should be able to support big data applications in an energy-efficient manner. In this chapter, we aim to explore various aspects of possible data centers for big data analytics. First, data center architecture, including computer and network technology, and data centers for cloud services are presented, and then some existing cloud data center platforms are introduced, including the concept of big data cloud computing and tools for big data analysis [8, 14].

5. Strategies for Enhancing Scale and Efficiency

5.1. Distributed Processing Frameworks

Hadoop, Apache, and Kubernetes are distributed processing frameworks and are foundational in Big Data analytics and AI human thought simulation. Table 9.1 summarizes the main features, advantages, and Big Data applications of Hadoop, Apache Spark, and Kubernetes, emphasizing their roles in distributed and AI-enhanced environments.

5.2. Hybrid Cloud Solutions for Scalability and Performance

The hybrid cloud solutions would assist in the scaling of the big data and performance because the resources can be scaled according to the demand and the integration of both the public and the private clouds [14].

- *Scaling resources*: Organizations are able to scale computing resources to an up or down as per the demand. As an illustration, they are allowed to utilize the public cloud when peak season comes and the private cloud as a part of everyday functions.
- *Facilitating growth*: Scalability enables businesses to scale to accommodate growth and performance at low costs.
- *Supporting workloads:* Mixed clouds can also be used to support workloads of an organization.

Table 9.1. Comparative overview of distributed processing frameworks

Hadoop: The foundation for big data processing:	Apache Spark: Speed and in-memory Computing on Big data.	Kubernetes: Kubernetes is an open-source framework for automating the deployment, scaling, and management of containerized applications.
• Hadoop is useful for the distributed storage and processing of large datasets. • It is an open source.	Spark accelerates Hadoop and takes advantage of in-memory computing capability to overcome Hadoop's pitfalls.	
Key Features:	Key Features:	Key Features:
• Hadoop's distributed file system is scalable and fault-tolerant for storing data.	• RDD- Resilient Distributed Dataset: • Fault-tolerant group of objects to process.	• Scalability: Dynamically adjusts resources based on workload. • Fault Tolerance: Automatically redeployed failed components. • Compatibility: Supports various data and AI/ML tools.
For parallel computation across clusters. Processing vast datasets in batches. Horizontal scalability to accommodate growing needs for data.	Real-time: through a component called Spark Streaming of Big data	Big data Apps: Hosting distributed databases like Cassandra or MongoDB.
It has interfaces with tools like Apache Hive and Pig for SQL-like structured data querying	MLib: Library of algorithms that can be used in big data for machine learning computation	Managing clusters as containerized workloads - Spark or Hadoop. AI human thought simulation Applications: Deploying AI models to production with efficient scaling.
	GraphX: an open-source graph-processing computer program	

- *Virtualization services*: Cloud providers have the capability of adding/removing computing resources in the form of virtual server instances.
- *Developing flexible IT infrastructures*: Virtualization decouples computing resources with physical hardware allowing flexible, scalable and cost-effective IT infrastructures.

The other advantages of hybrid cloud computing are: security, cost, control, and speed. In order to succeed with a hybrid cloud solution, you can: Make it visible, Secure cloud integration, consistent security policies, and protection tools both on-premises and in the cloud are used [14].

5.3. Differentiating Hot Storage vs. Cold Storage for Data Management

- *Hard Storage*: This is meant to hold data that are in high frequency and quick access. Hard disk storage can be utilized in absolute applications like editing, rendering and effect application. The hard disk storage has low latency and a high access speed. Hot storage can be of greater initial and maintenance expense.
- *Cold storage:* This is created to be used on long term data stored and is accessed very infrequently. Cold storage may be applied with long-term archives, back-ups, or historical data storage. Cold storage is more reasonable compared to hot and the access fees are high.

Other factors that are worth taking into consideration, when defining the use of hot storage or cold storage are:

- *Cost:* Cold storage tends to be the one that is cheaper than hot.
- *Speed of retrieval:* The cold storage will be able to take longer than the hot.
- *Data significance:* The level of importance of data to business and the frequency of access to data by business.
- *Prioritization of data:* Hot data should be prioritized, and cold data should be automated, which may contribute to the success of business in the future.

6. Optimization Techniques for Cognitive Models

6.1. Model Pruning and Quantization

Model pruning is an artificial neural network method of eliminating irrelevant parameters. This will enhance the efficiency without a radical impact on the performance, and this will be fair in balancing between the model accuracy and the reduction in size.

This is conforming to be used in a limited environment or real time application [15]. Quantification assists in eliminating the weights and model activations precision. In most cases, the 32-bit floating point values are truncated to 8 bit in order to eliminate extraneous weights or combinations of the model. We can do that in the course of customization or post-model training. These optimization strategies are necessary to make big data-based cognitive computing systems more efficient, especially when it comes to tasks such as social media analytics [16].

6.2. Federated Learning to Reduce Computational Demand

The network is made more aware by using federation learning and inference learning. Federated learning is a method of ML where the algorithms are trained by a number of decentralized machines or holding servers where cloudless samples of local data are not shared. We are able to have better and generalized models.

This is the significance behind federated learning.

- *Privacy:* This is opposed to the usual procedures whereby the data must be transmitted to a central server to either train or optimize a model.
- *Date Security:* Encrypted models are sent to the central server. This ensures that there is data security. Also, secure clustering techniques have been invented including secure clustering theory that only enables you to decode the results of the clustering.
- *Availability of heterogenous data*: Federated learning enables us to gain access to data that is distributed across devices/ locations and organizational boundaries.

6.3. Benefits of Edge Computing in Reducing Latency

It is a computing paradigm whereby data processing is done near the source other than central data centers. It is implementing servers and storage products nearer to places where data is being generated. By so doing, the edge computing will ensure that data does not have to travel far to be processed and therefore accelerates the processing. This is particularly needed in applications when there is need to process real time data. The advantage is that this proximity is useful to IoT gadgets, autonomous vehicles, and smart cities as it allows quicker decision-making.

The edge computing minimizes the latency since the processing of data occurs nearer to the source. It is because the distance data to be covered will be minimized. This approach is useful in the latency reduction due to several important mechanisms. Decentralizing the computing resources, edge computing allocates the computing resources to various places. In this manner, data can be processed on closer proximity to the point of creation, which increases speed and decreases latency.

7. Energy-Efficient Solutions and Sustainability

7.1. The Environmental Impact of Big data and Cognitive Systems

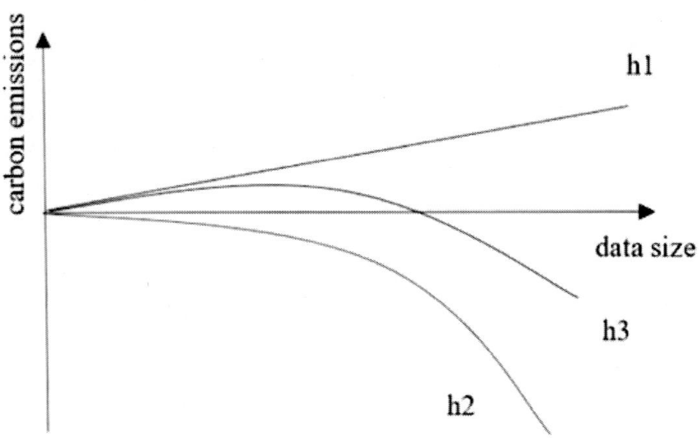

Figure 9.5. Mechanism Analysis Showing Reduction in Urban Carbon Emissions Through Big Data.

In general, the area of big data has decreased the amount of carbon emissions considerably. The analysis of the mechanisms demonstrates that big data decreases urban carbon emissions due to the stimulated green innovation. Make the energy infrastructure more efficient, alleviate problems with investment inequalities, and improve environmental protection awareness.

Figure 9.5 illustrates how Big Data analytics contributes to the reduction of urban carbon emissions through energy optimization, predictive maintenance, and sustainable resource allocation.

7.2. Hardware Accelerators and Algorithmic Improvements

Since hardware accelerators are hardware that is dedicated to a particular job, their resources can be right-sized with data precision that is dedicated to the precise needs of the algorithm, as opposed to processors that provide resources in 8, 16, 32 or 64 bits.

7.3. Eco-Conscious Computing Solutions for Sustainable Technology

With the concept of big data, a few green computing choices are available, such as:

- *Green data centers:* These data centers use renewable energy sources and make use of modern technologies to meet the data need and reduce environmental degradation.
- *Green cloud computing:* Any organization whose cloud data centers are being run on renewable sources as the main fuel source will be virtually free of greenhouse gases.
- *Green Big data analytics*: It should have energy-efficient cooling systems, modular data centre designs and will monitor and maintain systems on a regular basis.
- *Green data management*: that includes data deduplication, data compression and effective indexing methodology.
- *Sustainable IT procurement*: This is in source of goods and services that would have a minimum environmental or social impact.
- *Selecting a green web host*: A green web host will help your firm to be environmentally friendly.

- *Address the environmental impact of technology*: This is through a decrease in the usage of energy and electronic waste.

8. Future Directions and Applications

8.1. Potential for Big Data and AI Human Thought Simulation in Key Sectors

The integration of big data and cognitive processing leads to a new prototype that enables the most complex advancements in information and communications technology (ICT) in every sector. The combination of massive data analytics and AI simulation of human thought is changing the world of industry and business as it allows to conduct data-driven marketing, predictive analysis, and personal decision-making [17].

This integration is also being realized in industrial contexts through cognitive IoT and big data–assisted intelligent equipment design [18].

8.2. Scaling Smart Power Grids and Other Information-Centric Industries

A smart grid is an electrical system with a data layer that allows two-way communication between a middle controller and locally available operators to respond digitally to the current state of physical components or rapid changes in energy demand.

Such interconnected systems reflect the broader concept of cognitive IoT frameworks for smart cities and sustainable urban operations [19].

A smart grid is defined as an electrical grid that intelligently integrates the functions of all users connected to the grid. It includes consumers & generators, and those who do both. To deliver a sustainable, economical, and safe power supply smart grid of the future is a grid that uses digital technologies to improve reliability, safety, and efficiency of the electrical system through the exchange of data. The AI's data analytics has also been used successfully in cognitive communication system in heterogeneous wireless networks that allow the data exchange between the complex infrastructures to be more intelligent, adaptive, and efficient [20].

Therefore, the bilateral operation of small distribution grids to connect small generators also need to be controlled—in the face of the challenge of increasingly complex control and protection strategies in the 3 kW to 10 kW range, traditional electromechanical grids should thrive with the help of digital data and telecommunications networks Innovations to address the billions of dollars in costs from downtime and power quality disruptions every year.

8.3. Breaking Barriers for Global Adoption of Cognitive Systems

Cognitive systems, AI, machine learning, natural language processing, and data analytics have begun transforming all the segments of the field, enhancing smarter decision-making, automating more effectively, and creating novel experiences. Nevertheless, these few impediments notwithstanding, there are in favor of the adoption of this system. The cons needed a multi-faceted analysis, and they included a combination of technological boosts, regulations and adoptability.

Among the Key Barriers, some are discussed here:

- *Infrastructure deficiency*: Infrastructure to support cognitive systems is not available in many areas. Their scalability is limited due to limited access to high-speed internet, cloud platforms and high-performance computing capabilities.
- *Privacy and Security of Data*: Cognitive systems are best implemented on small masses of data, yet the strict data aegis laws and the escalating cyber threat are causing organizations to be reluctant to embrace such technologies.
- *Skilled worker:* Cognitive system adoption requires a workforce with high proficiency in AI, data analytics, and other associated disciplines. The adoption is greatly hindered by the lack of talent.
- *Ethical and Cultural Concerns*: There is the problem of ethical concerns, such as algorithm bias and the effects of automation on society. Also, culture is usually resistant to embracing new, unknown technologies, which acts as a setback. The AI human thought simulation is already transforming the education sphere and the learning processes and pedagogical patterns, providing new possibilities to increase cognitive involvement and individualized learning [21-23]. Another application of cognitive computing in

adaptive and data-driven learning systems is also involved in enhancing learning engagement and personalization [24].

- *Interoperability Problems*: Cognitive systems should be integrated into the already existing technologies. Platform and device incompatibilities cause delays during implementation.

9. Conclusion

9.1. Key Challenges and Solutions for Adoption of Cognitive Systems

Primary Challenges:

- *Infrastructure Constraint*: Low access to the high-speed internet and computer resources.
- *Data Privacy and Security Problems*: Legal and growing cyber threats restrict the use of data.
- *Cost*: Cost of implementation and cost of maintenance is too costly to many organizations.
- *Skills Gap*: The number of people possessing the AI, analytics, and cognitive systems necessary to manpower such systems is insufficient.
- *Ethics and Culture:* There is a problem of Algorithmic bias, and opposition to automation in society.
- *Interoperability Problems*: Inability to integrate the current technologies seamlessly is due to the absence of compatibility with the current technology.

Strategies for Solutions:

- *Develop infrastructure*: Invest in cloud computing, edge technologies and digital network connectivity.
- *Secure systems:* To enhance security, use advanced methods - e.g., federated learning and encryption - to safeguard data.
- *Reduce costs through partnerships:* Form alliances to subsidize the acquisition of enabling technology and access to the SMEs and the developing regions.

- *Upskill core workforce:* Increase the opportunities to use learning paths ways as an avenue to education and reskill core workforce to overcome the shortage of talent.
- *Develop ethical systems in AI:* Develop established ethical systems of responsible use of technology across the globe.
- *Improve interoperability:* Encourage open standards / API based ecosystems to improve interoperability.
- *Cooperation strategies:* Policy Harmonization: Align the rules as compared to communicating the deployment of technology across the borders.
- *Public-Private Partnerships:* The joint ventures would share resources and capabilities and also create innovation opportunities.
- *Awareness Campaigns:* Train the stakeholders (public, private, workforces, etc.) on capabilities, principles, and safe use to instill confidence by leveraging the advantages of the cognitive technologies.

By strategically developing approaches to these obstacles using collaborative and ethical principles in mind, cognitive systems can be developed exponentially globally.

9.2. Path Forward for Organizations in Leveraging Big Data and AI Human Thought Simulation

Next perspective of organizations, as it applies big data and AI to simulate human thought, organizations are also taking a model where both big data and AI are incorporated in the operations of organizations to enable them remain competitive, as well as establish an environment of innovation. At the time of employing this strategy, the management of the organization takes into consideration the following points.

- However, this is supposed to be directed towards the enhancement of the user experience, streamlining operations, and organizational creativity. The difficulties should be predetermined in the organization.
- Install the expandable cloud computing and the high-performance computing to store and process high data volumes. Supply cleansing,

integration and validation to be trustworthy. Implement the use of tools capable of working with live information and enhance decision-making.

- Established the partnership between the IT, data science and business departments in order to reconcile the technical potential to the strategy. Obtain industry gurus in the description of data insights.
- This new AI, generative AI, deep learning, recommendation systems: discover them. Enhanced, improved decision-making cognitive AI model [1].
- Sensitive data are encrypted, access to sensitive data is monitored, and AI-based systems of anomaly detection. Make use of the law in data protection including GDPR, CCPA and ethical AI standards. Keep customers by leveraging their information, and is open with artificial intelligence.
- Ask everyone to find and apply the data knowledge in decision making. Make sure that the activities of the different departments within an organization will lead to the goal.
- The employees are being also trained in such areas as data analytics, artificial intelligence, and simulation of human thinking and the policies of certifications and workshops of the new big data instruments and strategies.
- Create cognitive AI projects that are valuable and worthy; expand successful projects into other fields of the organization. Better outcomes should be accomplished through strategic testing.
- A customer service experience can be provided with the help of cognitive systems, as well as individual data insights. The predictive analytics will then be projected to predict the customer demand and the automation of the services will then meet the demand.

A successful combination of big data and cognitive AI computing provides an advantage when it comes to the innovation of new things. The processes here are the ever-advancing decision-making processes. Big data assists us in providing various patterns, trends, but on the other hand, the cognitive AI computing entails human intelligence that will give predictions and solutions to overcome obstacles.

These kinds of effective methods are invented and implemented today in all industries including in the school education field. And in case of any form of risk arises, then this is solved day by day by establishing the necessary solution. Firstly, we need to train the interested employees and illustrate the large and intricate systems to prosper in the future. The unification of employee capabilities and information as well as AI-related solutions provide us with the novel ways of doing things, which are consistent with futuristic goals.

References

[1] Dritsas, E., & Trigka, M. (2025). Exploring the intersection of machine learning and big data: A survey. *Machine Learning and Knowledge Extraction*, 7, 13. https://doi.org/10.3390/make7010013.

[2] Duan, Y., Edwards, J. S., & Dwivedi, Y. K. (2019). Artificial intelligence for decision-making in the era of Big Data: Evolution, challenges, and research agenda. *International Journal of Information Management*, 48, 63–71. https://doi.org/10.1016/j.ijinfomgt.2019.01.021.

[3] Gupta, S., Kar, A. K., Baabdullah, A., & Al-Khowaiter, W. A. (2018). *Big data with cognitive computing: A review for the future. International Journal of Information Management*, 42, 78–89. https://doi.org/10.1016/j.ijinfomgt.2018.06.005.

[4] Chen, M., Herrera, F., & Hwang, K. (2018). Cognitive computing: Architecture, technologies, and intelligent applications. *IEEE Access, 6*, 19774-19783.

[5] Zhang, Y., & Abbas, H. (2019). *Cognitive Internet of Things assisted by cloud computing and big data. Future Generation Computer Systems*, *90*, 477–488.

[6] Surur, F. M. (2025). *Unlocking the power of machine learning in big data. Data Science and Management*, *7*, 100150. https://doi.org/10.1016/j.dsm.2025.02.004.

[7] Zhang, Y., Huang, T., & Bompard, E. F. (2018). *Big data analytics in smart grids: A review. Energy Informatics, 1*(8). https://doi.org/10.1186/s42162-018-0007-5.

[8] Hashem, I. A. T., Yaqoob, I., Anuar, N. B., Mokhtar, S., Gani, A., & Khan, S. U. (2015). *The rise of "big data" on cloud computing: Review and open research issues. Information Systems, 47,* 98–115. https://doi.org/10.1016/j.is.2014.07.006.

[9] Chen, Y., Argentinis, J. E., & Weber, G. (2016). *IBM Watson: How cognitive computing can be applied to big data challenges in life sciences research. Clinical Therapeutics, 38*(4), 688–701. https://doi.org/10.1016/j.clinthera.2015.12.001.

[10] Zhang, Y., Ma, X., Wan, S., Abbas, H., & Guizani, M. (2018). *CrossRec: Cross-domain recommendations based on social big data and cognitive computing. Mobile Networks and Applications*, 23(6), 1610–1623. https://doi.org/10.1007/s11036-018-1112-1.

[11] Cooper, F., Levy, K., & De Sa, C. (2021). Accuracy-efficiency trade-offs and accountability in distributed ML systems. *Equity and Access in Algorithms, Mechanisms, and Optimization (EAAMO '21)*. ACM. https://doi.org/10.1145/3465416.3483289.

[12] Cai, S., Zhang, L., Chen, H., & Wang, J. (2024). *Towards energy-efficient data centers: A comprehensive review of passive and active cooling strategies. Energy*

and Built Environment, 5(3), 231–248. https://doi.org/10.1016/j.enbenv.2024.04.021.

[13] Zhang, M., Lin, W., & Zhang, Y. (2023). *Energy-efficient data center architectures: A review of networking, storage, and computing integration. IEEE Access, 11,* 45121–45138. https://doi.org/10.1109/ACCESS.2023.3268219.

[14] Botta, A., De Donato, W., Persico, V., & Pescapé, A. (2016). *Integration of cloud computing and Internet of Things: A survey. Future Generation Computer Systems, 56,* 684–700. https://doi.org/10.1016/j.future.2015.09.021.

[15] B. Jacob et al., "Quantization and Training of Neural Networks for Efficient Integer-Arithmetic-Only Inference," *2018 IEEE/CVF Conference on Computer Vision and Pattern Recognition*, Salt Lake City, UT, USA, 2018, pp. 2704-2713, https://doi.org/10.1109/CVPR.2018.00286.

[16] Sangaiah, A. K., Goli, A., Tirkolaee, E. B., Ranjbar-Bourani, M., Pandey, H. M., & Zhang, W. (2020). *Big data-driven cognitive computing system for optimization of social media analytics. IEEE Access, 8,* 82215–82226. https://doi.org/10.1109/ACCESS.2020.2991394.

[17] Lytras, M., Visvizi, A., Zhang, X., & Aljohani, N. R. (2020). *Cognitive computing, Big Data analytics and data-driven industrial marketing. Industrial Marketing Management*, 90, 663–666. https://doi.org/10.1016/j.indmarman.2020.03.024.

[18] Wan, J., Li, J., Hua, Q., Celesti, A., & Wang, Z. (2020). *Intelligent equipment design assisted by cognitive Internet of Things and industrial big data. Neural Computing and Applications*, 32(9), 4463–4472. https://doi.org/10.1007/s00521-019-04146-0.

[19] Park, J. H., Salim, M. M., Jo, J. H., Sicato, J. C. S., Rathore, S., & Park, J. H. (2019). CIoT-Net: A scalable cognitive IoT-based smart city network architecture. *Human-Centric Computing and Information Sciences, 9*(1), 1-20.

[20] Lin, K., Li, C., Tian, D., Ghoneim, A., Hossain, M. S., & Amin, S. U. (2019). *Artificial-intelligence-based data analytics for cognitive communication in heterogeneous wireless networks. IEEE Wireless Communications*, 26(3), 83-89.

[21] Lytras, M., Visvizi, A., Damiani, E., & Mathkour, H. (2019). *The cognitive computing turn in education: Prospects and applications. Computers in Human Behavior*, 92, 446–449. https://doi.org/10.1016/j.chb.2018.11.040.

[22] Wang, S., Wang, F., Zhu, Z., Wang, J., Tran, T., & Du, Z. (2024). *Artificial intelligence in education: A systematic literature review*. Expert Systems with Applications, 252, 124167. https://doi.org/10.1016/j.eswa.2024.124167.

[23] Gerlich, M. (2025). *AI Tools in Society: Impacts on Cognitive Offloading and the Future of Critical Thinking*. Societies, 15(1), Article 6. https://doi.org/10.3390/societies15010006.

[24] Coccoli, M., Maresca, P., & Stanganelli, L. (2017). The role of big data and cognitive computing in the learning process. *Journal of Visual Languages & Computing, 38*, 97-103.

Chapter 10

Harnessing Deep Learning and Cognitive Computing to Revolutionize Medical Image Diagnostics

Hafsa Ihteshamuddin Ahmed[1,*]
T. Monika Singh[1,†]
C. Kishor Kumar Reddy[1,‡]
and Srinath Doss[2,#]
[1]Department of Computer Science and Engineering,
Stanley College of Engineering and Technology for Women, India
[2]Faculty of Engineering and Technology, Botho University, Botswana

Abstract

This chapter discusses the transforming role of deep learning in cognitive computing within medical analysis. Technological advances in health care have led to the use of more sophisticated techniques of deep learning to progress the sensitivity and effectiveness of medical diagnostic analysis. The chapter begins with a general overview of medical imaging, cognitive computing, DL, and its affinity to health care; it then discusses deep learning fundamentals, covering neural networks and their architectures and core methodologies, including CNN, transfer learning, and GANs, about different kinds of medical imaging modes such as CT scans. This chapter also details the RNN 's application in data analysis

[*] Corresponding Author's Email: hafsa@stanley.edu.in
[†]Corresponding Author's Email: thakursingh.monika@gmail.com
[‡] Corresponding Author's Email: ckishorkumar@stanley.edu.in
[#] Corresponding Author's Email: srinath.doss@bothouniversity.ac.bw

In: Building Intelligent Systems for the Future
Editors: Anamika Ahirwar, Neelesh Jain and Sumitha Elayaperumal
ISBN: 979-8-90134-050-9

and attention mechanisms to enhance interpretability in models. It continues on the rationale about the necessity of multi-modal learning, in which the system tries to integrate multiple data sources for enhanced precision in diagnostics. The chapter continues to address issues like scarcity of data, ethical issues, and limitations of the existing models. It ultimately concludes with future work in deep learning and cognitive computing in terms of collaboration between different disciplines that leads to high improvements in patient results.

Keywords: cognitive computing, deep learning, CNN, RNN, multimodal learning, transfer learning, GAN (Generative Adversarial Networks), CT scans

1. Introduction

Medical imaging technologies have transformed the healthcare characteristics [1]. Starting from the early use of X-rays, giving a very elementary view of internal structures, medical imaging has progressed incredibly from the advent of advanced modes such as Magnetic Resonance Imaging (MRI), Computed Tomography (CT), and Positron Emission Tomography (PET), shown in Figures [10.1-10.3]. These technologies have improved the visualization to unprecedented levels, helping in early detection and illness management. This development has made medical imaging an important area of modern medicine, performing multi-functions including those within radiology, oncology, surgery, etc., based on their application or subject of investigation [2].

Therefore, the complexity of images and medical data has increased proportionally with the increase in technological advancement of imaging mechanisms. The high-resolution detail pictures that can be obtained in modern imaging techniques provide so much more than detailed structural information, including many features related to physiology or functions. For instance, some soft tissue contrast for certain MRI images, on the other hand, shows anatomic views of bodies while scanning CTs, so their use in complex evaluation goes hand in hand. These complexities provide a lot in terms of opportunities but simultaneously present greater challenges for healthcare practitioners to decipher vast amounts of data toward decision-making in clinical settings [3].

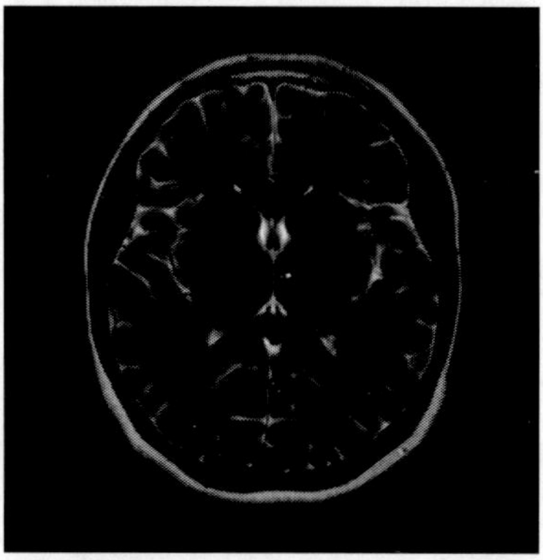

Figure 10.1. Magnetic Resonance Image of Human Brain (*Brain MRI Images for Brain Tumor Detection*, n.d.).

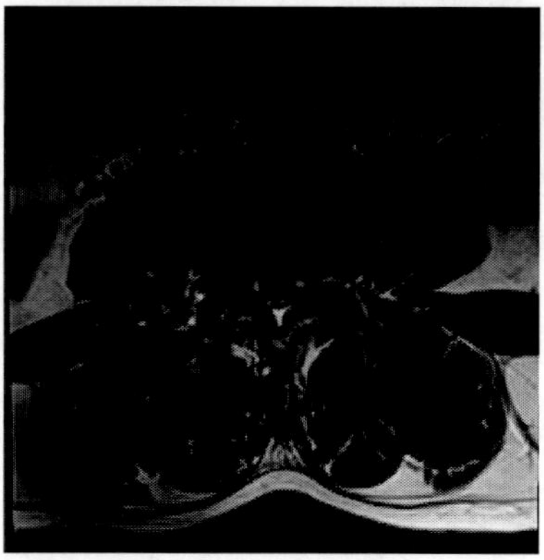

Figure 10.2. Computed Tomography scan of Human Spine (*RSNA Lumbar, Spine Analysis*, n.d.).

The huge volume of data collected in medical images makes the need for relevant, sophisticated analytical tools to guide practitioners in the extraction of insightful material. Traditional forms of medical image analysis, commonly done as manual interpretation, increasingly leave healthcare professionals bereft with modern medical images. The process of image interpretation would require more automated and semi-automated solutions to enhance efficiency and increase accuracy. Advanced analytical techniques, particularly cognitive computing and deep learning-based approaches, have very well promised to solve all the future challenges related to the process of image interpretation.

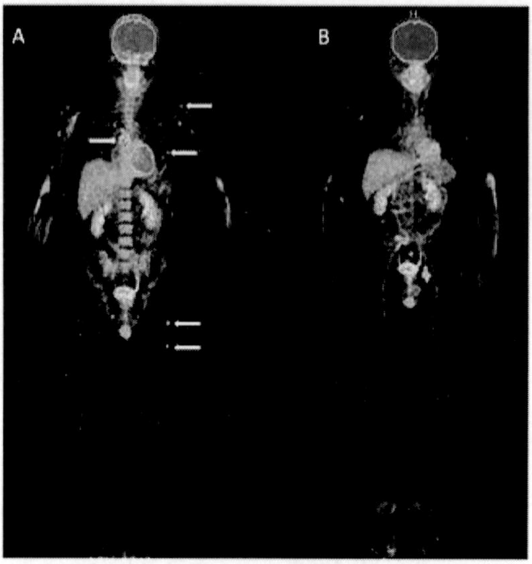

Figure 10.3. Positron Emission Tomography of Human Body (Sachpekidis et al., 2019).

Cognitive computing is a revolutionary approach in simulating the processes of human thinking within an enhanced computerized model that involves several advanced technologies developed to boost human decision-making by being able to give smart systems the capability to analyze huge quantities of information and detect patterns to generate insights [4]. Cognitive computing hopes to integrate data analytics in aiding humans to improve their abilities to make decisions, thus leading to its critical use within sensitive fields like healthcare, wherein one medical professional diagnosis the future well-being of a patient.

The core of cognitive computing lies in the amalgamation of the latest methodologies, such as AI, ML, and data analytics at work. AI & ML empower systems with a foundation of intelligent and independent supervisory capabilities. Data analytics is the concept of extracting crucial, intensive information from the raw data available. It provides the necessary tools and methods to extract useful patterns, trends, correlations, outliers, and anomalies. This capability is very useful in healthcare because it requires the synthesis of huge amounts of patient data, imaging data, and clinical research to inform the decision regarding treatment. With these technologies, efficiency and accuracy can be improved through better decision-making processes and positive outcomes.

Deep learning technology has become a raging trend recently, extending assistance to Medicare in making accurate diagnoses and future disease predictions. In doing this, Deep learning technology implements neural networks trained to function similar to a human brain.

Such algorithms automatically learn hierarchical features from raw data, useful to spot patterns with surprisingly impressive accuracy [5]. In the area of medical imaging, the extraction of relevant features from complicated images becomes extremely vital to draw appropriate inferences at times about the disease conditions or accurate planning of further treatments. Deep learning is very effective for medical image analysis since feature extraction does not require much human intervention. Most conventional methods of image analysis often rely on handcrafted features, which may be slow and may not cover every detail. On the contrary, deep learning has the ability to learn features from large datasets automatically. This automation reduces the load of healthcare practitioners and also improves the consistency and dependability of the interpretation of images. DL models have outperformed traditional or conventional approaches in tasks of image segmentation, classification, and detecting anomalies in the human body.

Deep learning methods can be integrated into a cognitive computing system, which empowers healthcare professionals with advanced analytics capabilities that can improve their decision-making processes. Potentially, deep learning may help a clinician with algorithms that can sift through enormous amounts of imaging data and yield insights that may be applied to improve patient care. Some of these may include a cognitive computing system especially tailored for deep learning capabilities, such as an ability to make analyses of medical images, especially in less time and even with minimal probabilities of human factor inconsistencies. Cognitive computing provides contextual information coupled with suggestions from data by imaging so that clinicians can use that as a tool to get better at decision-making.

The incorporation of deep learning into cognitive computing further enhances the efficiency of medical image analysis overall and thus saves the precious time of healthcare professionals for patients and not data processing. The learning and adaptability process is very pertinent in the fast-evolving area of medical imaging, wherein new techniques and technologies will keep surfacing. Drawing on the power of deep learning within cognitive computing frames, healthcare systems can sustain innovation and improve quality of care for patients.

Deep learning can enable the cognitive computing system to aid health professionals in various ways. For instance, medical images may be analyzed automatically by it and thereby save the amount of time required for interpretation of these images along with the error committed by human beings. Cognitive computing can thus provide contextual information along with recommendations for further decision-making on the part of clinicians based on the analysis of imaging data. This incorporation of deep learning into cognitive computing does improve the overall efficiency of image analysis from the medical aspect, so that physicians can attend to patients rather than fiddle with data processing. Table 10.1 provides an overview of DL approaches in the analysis of images.

Continuous learning & improvement can be achieved through combining deep learning and cognitive computing. Cognitive systems can update algorithms and models based on practical outcomes resulting from new groups of imaging data, and eventually result in better accuracy and reliability as time goes on. This learning and adaptation cycle plays a crucial role in medical imaging, as it needs to be well-informed of new techniques and emerging technologies. Utilizing deep learning in cognitive computing enables health systems to stay innovative, which improves the quality of care offered to patients.

Table 10.1. Applications of DL approaches in Medical Image Analysis

Reference	Application	Description	Technology Used
[6]	Tumor Detection	Identifying and localizing tumors in MRI, CT, and PET scans.	Convolutional Neural Networks (CNNs)
[7]	Image Segmentation	Segmenting anatomical structures or lesions from medical images.	U-Net
[8]	Disease Classification	Classifying diseases based on X-rays, MRIs, or CT scans.	Dense-Net
[9]	Histopathological Analysis	Analyzing histopathological slides for cancer detection.	Transfer Learning
[10]	Anomaly Detection	Detecting anomalies in scans for early intervention.	Deep Learning Techniques

The rest of the chapter is structured as below: Section 2 discusses base areas of cognitive computing; section 3 bases a comprehensive knowledge of deep learning technology. Section 4 then moves to diversified deep learning strategies employed for classification, segmentation, and prediction, respectively. Section 6 highlights challenges & limitations in deep learning and cognitive computing for medical image analysis. Section 7 delivers the upcoming enhancements. Section 8 completes the chapter.

2. Understanding Cognitive Computing

Cognitive computing is a group of advanced technologies that resemble human thought processes in the computerized model. There are many AI techniques that may be used in developing systems that can understand and learn, as well as converse with people, almost in a human-like manner. Major elements of cognitive computing are NLP, ML, computer vision, and reasoning capabilities, depicted in Figure 10.4. All these elements combined look at the huge volumes of unstructured data, trace trends, and make insights that make decision-making processes better. This ability to imitate the human mind provides cognitive computing systems with context-sensitive responses, and they continue to transform based on information that eventually reaches them; they turn out to be of utmost value in health care, finance, and customer care.

This feature of cognitive computing is, therefore, closely related to artificial intelligence, used for the attainment of goals in the application of AI techniques. Artificial intelligence, though encompassing a wide array of technologies aimed at designing intelligent systems, targets more narrowly the simulation of human-like understanding and reasoning. Thus, it may be asserted that AI constitutes a foundation on which cognitive computing builds models for processing and learning from data. However, cognitive computing takes these elements a step further than the others because it aims to include perception, reasoning, and emotional intelligence about human cognition in systems that communicate with users more intuitively and meaningfully.

The most basic difference between cognitive computing and the conventional computing paradigms lies in the approach taken toward processing data. Conventional computing systems depend on predetermined algorithms and rules for tasks and require explicit programming for every specific application. They work well with structured data and executing well-defined instructions, but are poor with unstructured data, like text, images, and audio. Such systems, therefore, can handle structured and unstructured data, learn from experiences, and adapt their responses according to new information. With such flexibility, cognitive systems can present insights and solutions that traditional systems are not always able to produce.

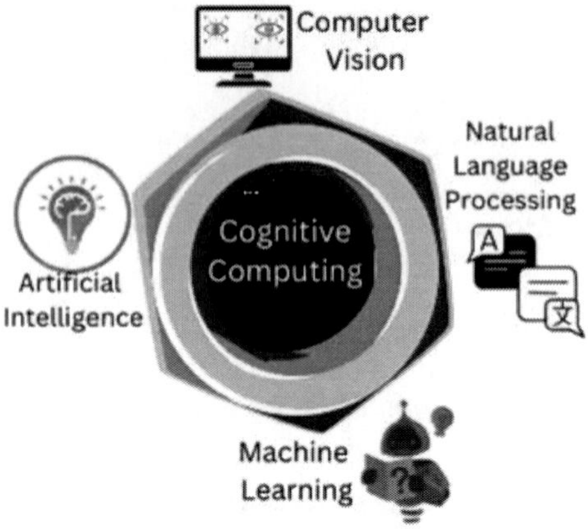

Figure 10.4. Components of Cognitive Computing.

Medical imaging leads to a huge volume of data that is otherwise complex and too confusing to be interpreted. Through a transformational role played by a cognitive computing system, health care professionals would be empowered. For example, by integrating deep learning algorithms into cognitive computing frameworks, the systems can automatically identify medical image abnormalities, such as a tumor or lesion that would further enhance diagnostic accuracy and efficiency. This synergy, therefore, not only makes an early detection but also helps personalize the treatment plan according to the specific needs of a patient.

Cognitive computing is the most recent frontier in artificial intelligence and represents a more human-like, intuitive approach toward data analytics and decision-making. A cognitive computing system, incorporating the most crucial constituent elements of NLP, ML, and the ability to reason, can complement many applications, such as medical image analysis. Indeed, such integration of cognitive computing would play a crucial role as the healthcare industry continues to evolve in the future, so more accurate and timely diagnoses as well as improved patient outcomes and streamlined workflows are observed.

3. Understanding DL Fundamentals

Data analysis and AI have been greatly influenced by deep learning (DL). This is a subsection of machine learning, which processes large amounts of data using neural networks having more than one layer that can mimic the human ability to learn by experience, improve over time, and therefore perform better than before. Deep learning is of incredibly high importance in data analysis since it can automate highly complex tasks. Inferences drawn from huge datasets and resulting insights and patterns serve as a vital tool for businesses and researchers who are seeking to leverage data for decision-making and innovation.

A group of neurons makes a neural network, and it contains different types of neurons. Every neuron within the network receives its input data, sends it through some form of activation function, and then proceeds to send that output on to another layer.

Each neuron within the network will receive input data, send it through some sort of activation function, and pass the output on to the next layer. This enables neural networks to learn hierarchical representations of the data where simpler features are captured by the lower layers and complex patterns by the higher layers. The neural network architecture is flexible; the resulting architectures in the context of image-related tasks or for recurrent neural networks on sequential data enhance the model performance, resulting in accurate outcomes.

An activation function is an important part of a neural network. It eliminates linearity from a model such that relationships within data, complex enough not to be expressible via linear transformations, may be learned by the network. The most common activation functions are sigmoid, which maps input values into the range of 0 & 1, and the rectified linear unit, which simply gives the input data if it exceeds zero and will output zero otherwise. Moreover, the SoftMax output layer is often used in a multi-class problem where a network can give the probability value for each class.

The most important role of the loss functions in training a DL system is to define the calculation of change between the model's resulting and expected values. It guides the adjustments of parameters to lower that difference. Loss functions generally used are MSE and cross-entropy functions. A model is optimized by minimizing the loss value through an iterative approach called backpropagation with updates in its weights and biases to enhance its predicted outputs. Optimization is something at the heart of how one trains deep learning; it directly determines if it is accurate and effective.

Optimization techniques are imperative to enhance the training procedures of a DL model. Among all these, the popular gradient descent optimization algorithm belongs to the family of methods that modifies the model parameters based on the negative loss gradient. Variants such as SGD and Adam have been implemented to accelerate convergence speed or enhance stability. These optimization techniques should help deep learning models better learn from the data, which means training less on the computer. That means having more robust models that, from practitioners' viewpoints, could perform complex tasks. There is no significance of big data for training deep learning models. Deep learning algorithms best capture complex patterns and relationships when given a large number of diverse data points. Large datasets ensure the model has a big enough variety of examples to generalize to unseen data, a requirement for high performance in many real-world applications.

Advances in computing power that accompanied the growth of big data have only increased the popularity of deep learning. It's now finally possible for researchers and practitioners to train deep learning models on datasets that are massively large but unmanageable by previous computational power. It has created breakthroughs in several different fields, from health to finance and self-governed systems. The applications for deep learning models, mainly in the healthcare sector to analyze complex data for good decision-making and the use of processing datasets, opened new avenues in research and innovation for actionable insights about the data by the organization.

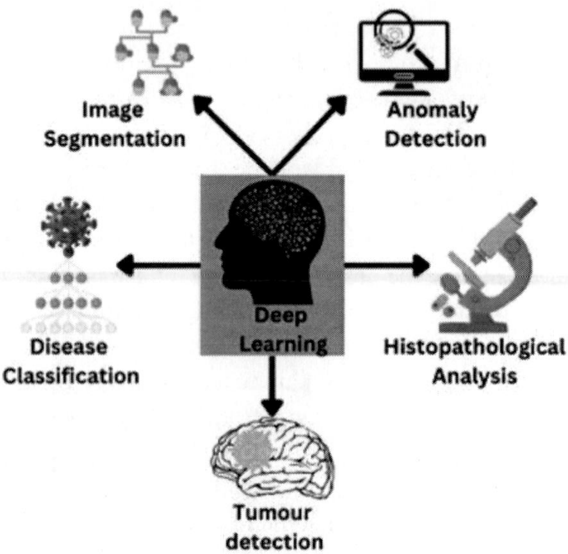

Figure 10.5. Various real-time applications of deep learning.

Deep learning is a paradigm shift in data analysis where the underlying patterns and insights from a huge amount of information can be uncovered with the use of neural networks. Based on its foundational concepts, such as neural network architecture, activation functions, loss functions, and optimization techniques, deep learning has become the backbone of modern artificial intelligence. As the demand for data-driven solutions keeps rising, it becomes pretty much indispensable to master the basic lessons of deep learning to unloosen this horizon of innovation across many fields, along with its promise of this sort of development. Naturally, with ongoing research on novel architectures, new strategies for optimization, and hundreds of other applications further ingraining the capacity to address complex data, surely improved versions of deep learning are going to be found. Various real-time applications of Deep Learning are depicted in Figure 10.5.

4. Key Deep Learning Approaches in Medical Image Analysis

Deep learning techniques have transformed how analysis techniques have evolved into methods delivering not only greater accuracy concerning the diagnosis of conditions but also regarding patient recovery outcomes. The key deep learning techniques include CNN, GANs, RNNs, attention mechanisms, Multi-modal learning, transfer learning, and explainable AI. Their capabilities are different, providing features of various applications into a set of functionalities that enable analyses with medical images, thus equipping medical professionals with better insight into making the appropriate health decisions [11].

4.1. Convolutional Neural Networks (CNN)

CNN is a dedicated category of networks for processing structured grids of image data. They include convolutional pooling and fully connected layers in their architecture, shown in Figure 10.6. This network automatically learns spatial hierarchies of features through the application of multiple filters to images provided as input, followed by the classification of images as the output of the network [12]. Convolutional layers capture detailed edges as well as textures from image data; pooling layers, in turn, decrease dimensions while preserving important information along with increasing the computational efficiency.

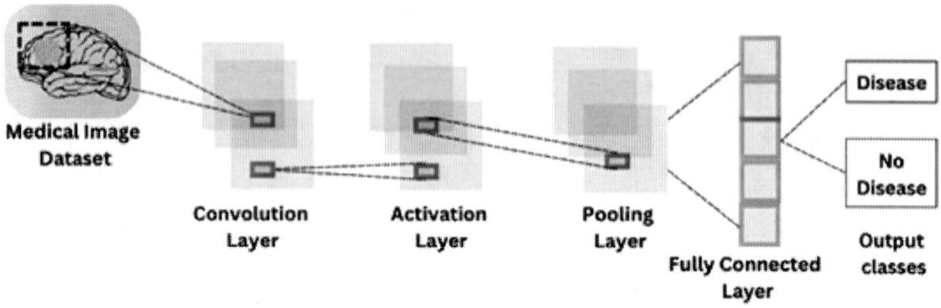

Figure 10.6. CNN architecture.

CNNs are popularly used in classification, segmentation, and detection in medical images. For instance, in medical images, CNN could classify images that determine whether a tumor was benign or malignant. In segmentation tasks, the CNN can delineate detailed structures on images, such as organs or lesions, to allow for a better localization for treatment purposes. Furthermore, CNNs are used in detection tasks. They detect the existence of abnormalities in medical scans, such as tumors in a mammogram or nodules in chest X-rays. Thousands of case studies have proven CNNs' usefulness in medical images and the ability of CNNs to match the performance of expert radiologists [13].

4.2. Generative Adversarial Networks (GANs)

GANs are the other innovation in deep learning, which includes two networks: a generator and a discriminator. A generator produces synthesized pictures, and a discriminator compares the synthesized images against real images according to the feedback given in changing the output from the generator. Figure 10.7 depicts a detailed GAN Architecture. Thus, this adversarial process goes on until the images produced by the generator have the same characteristics as those of real images. Because the synthetic image created by the GAN may be comparable to a realistic one, such GANs have lately been introduced into medical imaging. Moreover, GANs might prove useful whenever labeled data cannot be gained.

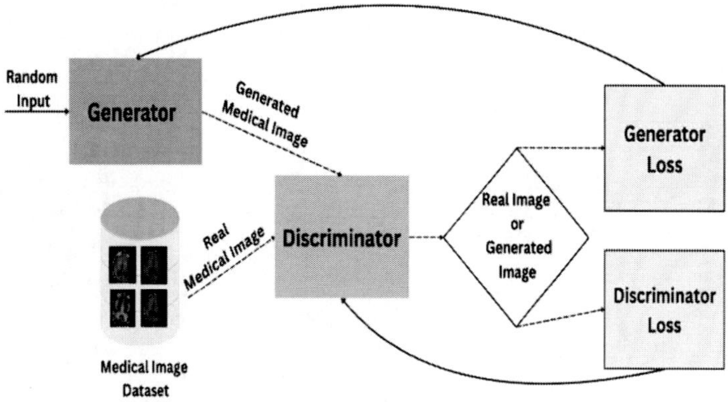

Figure 10.7. Generative Adversarial Network (GAN) architecture.

The applications of GANs in medical analysis involve data augmentation through synthetic image generation that visually closely approaches the real one, dramatically enlarging, thereby eliminating one of the problems faced: a lack of sufficient datasets for training purposes [14]. This is particularly helpful for rare diseases, as getting enough labeled data is challenging. Besides this, GANs can be used to improve existing images and enhance the outcomes of the DL models. The change GANs brought along in the training datasets is immense, as it helped create more robust models that will generalize better on unseen data [15].

4.3. Recurrent Neural Networks

They are another specialized class of networks, designed for processing serial information, and so were particularly appropriate for use in applications such as processing time-series medical data. RNNs are inherently different from feedforward networks, as connections in this network loop back on themselves, allowing these networks to remember previous states, as shown in Figure 10.8. With the ability of RNNs to follow temporal dependencies, they also become highly suitable for usage in cases where disease monitoring over multiple images or over time from a patient has to be followed.

RNNs in medical image analysis work with time-series data to track changes in tumor sizes by following a series of MRI scans or monitor how degenerative diseases progress. Through this, RNNs can give insights about the evolution of conditions for health professionals to intervene when the condition is at an advanced stage. This, however, is highly appreciated in personalized medicine, where following the trajectory of a patient's condition can help improve the outcome of treatment [16].

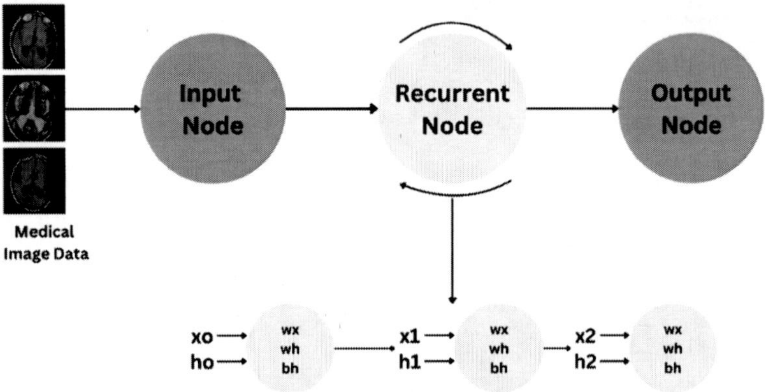

Figure 10.8. Recurrent Neural Network (RNN) architecture.

4.4. Transfer Learning (TL)

A highly influential DL concept, Transfer Learning, is useful on tasks, particularly when minimal amounts of data are available. It follows that acquiring large sets of labeled data in medical image analysis is practically difficult since much time and human expertise are needed for acquiring labeled data. It's thus possible to make use of pre-trained models from huge datasets for refining them with much smaller medical datasets in hand, leading to considerably better performances on those smaller medical datasets [17]. Figure 10.9 depicts a transfer learning model's architecture.

This technology helps cut down on computational resources and time that could otherwise be spent in the process of training deep learning models, so that researchers could come close to achieving a good score using fewer data sets. Several healthcare applications, including various forms of classifying different skin lesions, identifying diabetic retinopathy through analysis of retinal images, and pneumonia from chest X-rays, have utilized the capabilities of transfer learning and have proven successful. These examples demonstrate how transfer learning fills the gap between an apparently very small set of medical data and a rich demand for models with guaranteed robustness and high accuracy in practice [18].

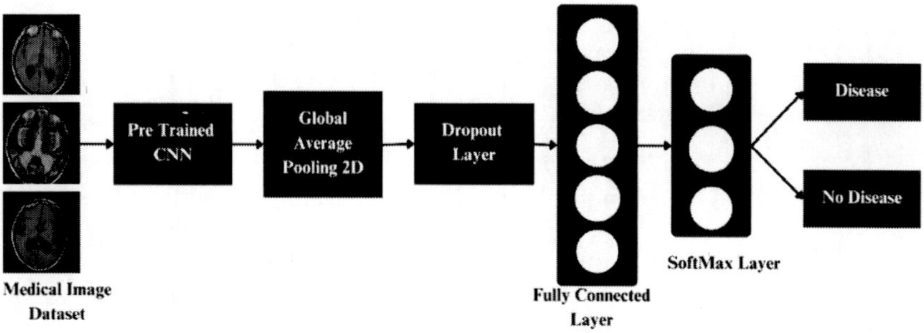

Figure 10.9. Transfer learning architecture.

4.5. Attention Mechanisms

Attention mechanisms in medical image analysis are very important to be used for deep learning models. Models are allowed to focus on areas of interest within radiographs, such as identifying tumors or lesions in MRI scans. It generally enhances the correctness of diagnoses and segmentation tasks. This selective focus imitates human cognitive processes; hence, models can highlight the relevant features and context for tasks as complex as disease detection and classification. Attention mechanisms revolutionize the way medical images are processed, such that more efficient and effective analyses are done [19]. Table 10.2 highlights the key components of an attention mechanism model.

4.6. Multimodal Learning

Multimodal learning is an advanced learning approach that allows the models to learn data coming from multiple modalities, including text, audio, and images, with the intent of improving the interpretation of the data. In terms of image analysis, this approach harnesses the relative strengths of different data types towards a performance that supports the use of visual data featuring textual descriptions or metadata. Multimodal learning is effective for image analysis because it allows richer feature representations and contextual understanding explained in Figure 10.10.

Table 10.2. Components of an attention mechanism

Component	Description	Function
Input Sequences (Query, Key, Value)	Query (Q): current state or token.	These vectors get passed through the attention mechanism.
	Key (K): Represents input data to be attended to.	
	Value (V): Contains the actual information to be passed based on attention.	
Query and Key	Calculate the dot product between the query (Q) and each key (K).	This step is to calculate attention scores, which denote the relevance of every key to a query.
Scaling	Scale the dot product of Q	Scaling stabilizes the gradients and prevents high values during SoftMax because SoftMax tends to allow very high values to overtake during training.
SoftMax Activation	Apply SoftMax to the scaled attention scores.	Converts the attention scores into a probability distribution in such a manner that the weights add up to 1.
Weighted Sum	Compute a weighted sum of the values (V).	This produces a context vector, highlighting the most important input areas.
Multi-Head Attention (Optional)	Perform multiple attention operations in parallel	It enables simultaneous attention to various inputs. Aspects. For example, syntax and semantics capture a wide range of relations.
	Concatenate the results and apply a linear transformation.	
Residual Connection	Add the input of the layer to the attention output.	Gradient flow is better at preventing vanishing gradients and enabling deeper networks
Layer Normalization	Apply layer normalization after the residual connection.	Normalization of Output, stabilization of learning, thereby improving overall training
Feedforward Neural Network (FFN)	The output is passed into an FFN.	This introduces further processing to enhance the information coming from the attention mechanism.

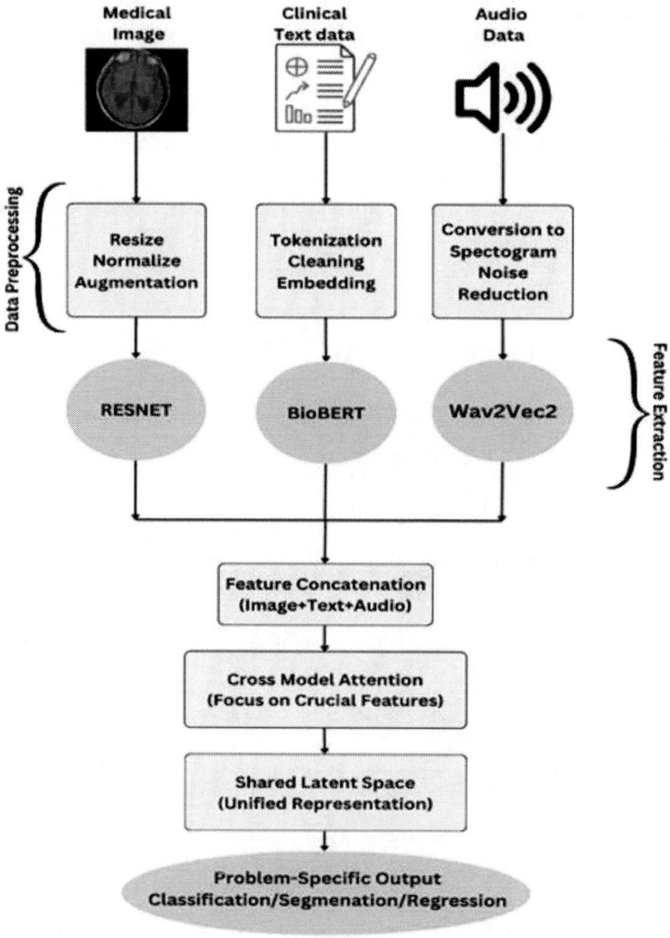

Figure 10.10. Multimodal learning architecture.

With the integration of data from different sources, the performance of Medicare models' robustness toward noise and variability in data can improve, not only enhancing model performance but also allowing for a more delicate interpretation of images since the context provided by other modalities can delineate ambiguities in visual data. Despite these problems that are associated with data alignment, complexity, and interpretability, multimodal learning continues to evolve as a promising approach for advancing image analysis techniques.

It becomes more and more significant to learn medical analysis through the multi-modal approach since the data is drawn from several sources.

Therefore, by utilizing multi-modal learning methods, one can gain a more critical look into the status of the disease development in a patient. For example, matching the imaging data with clinical notes and laboratory test reports will help in increasing the accuracy of diagnosis and the design process of the treatment. It is the challenge of bringing together and fusing different types of data in a single representative form that captures complexity in understanding medical conditions, and potentially better patient outcomes and personalized medicine [20].

4.7. Explainable AI Explainable AI (XAI)

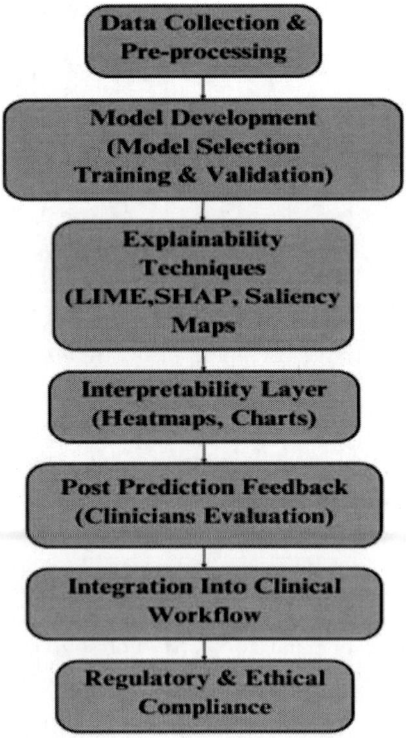

Figure 10.11. Explainable AI (XAI) architecture.

Explainable AI, where the clinical acceptability of AI models critically depends on their understanding of the decision-making. Increasing complexity in DL models normally leads to opaque outputs, therefore raising questions about reliability in a high-stakes domain like healthcare. Techniques in XAI seek to provide insights on how models are interpreting the medical images and arriving at their conclusions [21]. Other techniques include the use of saliency maps, feature attribution, and model-agnostic explanations highlighted in Figure 10.11. Such methods aid clinicians in their understanding of the rationale behind the AI-based diagnosis to eventually allow for improved human-AI collaboration [22].

5. Deep-Learning and Cognitive Computing Applications

- *Disease Classification:* Deep learning models identify diseases from medical images, such as pneumonia, through the chest X-ray and others
- *Segmentation of Organs:* Cognitive computing techniques are used to separate the organs in the imaging studies for surgical planning and treatment.
- *Analysis of Lesions:* Deep learning algorithms isolate and examine lesions to derive the characteristics that help evaluate the formulation of the treatment plan.
- *Fracture Detection:* Automatic identification of fractures in X-ray images, enhancing high-speed and accuracy in diagnosis
- *Diabetic retinopathy*: Deep learning on retinal images is used for screening diabetic retinopathy.
- *Patient outcome predictive analytics*: The cognitive computing analyzes the imaging data as well as the history of the patient to anticipate health problems and outcomes.
- *Radiomics for Personalized Medicine:* Feature extraction from imaging data, along with its correlations to clinical outcomes, is the future towards personalization of treatment strategies.
- *Automated Reporting Systems:* The cognitive computing scans images for the generation of real-time reports. This increases the productivity of radiology.
- *Clinical Decision Support Systems:* In clinical care and support in radiological decisions, cognitive computing uses models of deep learning in real time.

- *Telemedicine by Remote Image Analysis:* Cognitive computing enables remote image analysis; hence, there is greater access to health care.
- *Real-time Monitoring in Intensive Care:* Images analysed quickly give real-time feedback to manage patients in an ICU.
- *Clinical decision support systems:* cognitive computing would be used to evaluate imaging data from clinical trials for identifying patient cohorts and evaluating the efficacy of treatment.
- *Integration of imaging and genomic data:* Combining imaging features with genomic data, thereby better understanding diseases and adapting individual treatments.
- *Natural Language Processing for Radiology Reports:* This is a use of cognitive computing that leverages the power of NLP for interpreting and producing radiology reports from image data.

6. Challenges and Limitations

Deep learning has been realized in medical applications, despite various challenges and limitations surrounding deep learning approaches to cognitive computing for medical image analysis. Some of the major challenges and limitations are as follows:

- *Availability and Quality of Data*
  This one, amongst many common problems, is the reduced accessibility of data, and with a lack of data variety, that leads to overfitting by the model and worse generalizations to unseen data.
- *Data Availability and Quality*
  One of the common problems when dealing with medical images is limited availability of data and lack of data variety, resulting in model overfitting and worse generalizations to unseen data.
- *Interpretability and Explainability*
  DL models, especially CNNs, are typically "black boxes," hence it is difficult to elucidate why the model has decided on something. Lack of interpretability could be a great limitation for clinical adoption, as clinicians have to trust and understand what the model predicts to make better decisions.

- *Generalization to Unseen Data*
When exposed to a domain shift, models learned on specific datasets are unable to generalize well to diverse populations or imaging modalities. It sometimes introduces bias in terms of diagnosis and treatment because the training data may not characterize the entire miscellany of the patient population.
- *Computational Resources*
Training DL models are memory-intensive and not readily feasible in healthcare settings. Since the cost of the resource itself for GPUs and cloud computing is very steep, it can be utterly unaffordable for most of the smaller institutions or even for developing countries, thereby giving rise to a large inequality in its adoption over healthcare technologies.
- *Regulatory and Ethical Concerns*
Ethical considerations in implementing deep learning into clinical practice include patient privacy, data security, and bias in algorithms. Regulatory frameworks to evaluate and approve AI-based medical devices are still in development, which slows down the deployment of deep learning solutions in healthcare.
- *Integration with Clinical Workflows*
The biggest challenge is the integration of deep learning-cognitive systems with the existing clinical workflows. It requires collaboration between data scientists, clinicians, and IT professionals. A significant limitation associated with these new technologies is the fear of change, besides the training requirement of healthcare professionals in using them.
- *Performance Measures*
With DL models in the medical image analysis domain, standard performance metrics such as accuracy do not reflect well on clinical relevance. In many cases, sensitivity, specificity, and area under the ROC curve are more appropriate measures, but they cannot be optimized simultaneously.
- *Data Imbalance*
Class imbalance would be a common issue in most medical datasets, as they have the majority of the most common conditions but underrepresent the minority conditions. There is a possibility with many models to be biased on the majority class as opposed to the minority.

7. Future Directions and Innovations

The next big future for deep learning in cognitive computing of medical images is to bring about significant improvements in several key areas. First among them would be the application of transfer learning and pre-trained models, which may enable improving generalization ability without the necessity of requiring huge amounts of labeled data. Applying federated learning can empower several institutes to learn their models without decentralizing data in terms of anonymity, while eliminating the possibility of regulatory challenges.

Reliability for explainable AI can be established by building trust and pushing deep learning models into clinical workflow. Advanced methods of interpretation assist the clinicians in their decision-making. It becomes imperative in the execution of Medicare with the aid of XAI. Multimodal learning, where imaging or genomics or electronic health record data come together, provides an integrated view of patient health and thus increases chances of diagnostic accuracy along with meaningful treatment plans.

Real-time analysis with cognitive computing will be further developed, as automated annotation techniques and deep learning will be incorporated into the clinical decision support systems to streamline clinical workflows, enabling better decision-making in crucial situations. The transfer learning frameworks would also be adapted to model changes with the new data and the altered practices of the future to keep them accurate and up to date. The acceptable use of deep learning technologies in health care conveyance can be standardized by collaborating with the regulatory bodies to guide them on its effective and safe deployment.

Conclusion

DL, for the analysis of medical images within the scope of cognitive computing, thus marks an example shift in the entire healthcare diagnostics arena. The methodologies developed in deep learning, such as CNNs, transfer learning, and GAN, further improved sensitivity and efficiency with regard to diagnostics in various image sense modalities like X-rays, MRIs, and CT scans. This would further stress multi-modal learning, and it will then be possible to integrate diversified data sources to gain more accurate diagnostic precision as well as more personalized treatment plans. Thus, this approach would enhance the accuracy of the medical assessment while bringing in more knowledge concerning the patient's health status.

Looking forward, deep learning of cognitive computing is in for great strides since its future is poised to address some of the pressing problems of the present. Transfer learning and federated learning techniques would ease the development of robust models without the laborious preparation of tens of thousands of labeled datasets, hence streamlining the procedure while keeping patient privacy intact. Additionally, explainable AI will also be important in enabling clinicians and patients to learn about deep learning models, which, though effective, should be developed with interpretability and reliability in clinical settings, thus aiding in informed decision-making and higher-quality outcomes for patients.

All such healthcare providers, regulatory agencies, and those who have developed the technologies will be required to cooperate to establish harmonized practices when using these deep learning technologies in delivery systems. As acceptable practice guidelines are created to securely deploy such high-end technology safely and effectively, the ethics-related issues of all stakeholders will be minimized, while in the end, the overall reliability of AI-driven diagnostics increases. Increased use of real-time analysis and auto-annotation techniques, along with the inclusion of deep learning in clinical workflows, would make it easier for clinicians to streamline processes and provide timely, data-driven decisions. The Medical image analysis has immense potential for cognitive computing in the far future as we step into this new era of precision medicine directed towards enhanced patient care and outcomes.

References

[1] "Medical Imaging | FDA." Accessed: Nov. 08, 2024. [Online]. Available: https://www.fda.gov/radiation-emitting-products/radiation-emitting-products-and-procedures/medical-imaging.

[2] S. Hussain et al., "Modern Diagnostic Imaging Technique Applications and Risk Factors in the Medical Field: A Review," *Biomed Res. Int.*, vol. 2022, p. 5164970, 2022, doi: 10.1155/2022/5164970.

[3] D. Rangarajan, A. Rangarajan, C. Kishor Kumar Reddy, and S. Doss, "Exploring the Next-Gen Transformations in Healthcare Through the Impact of AI and IoT," *https://services.igi-global.com/resolvedoi/resolve.aspx?doi=10.4018/979-8-3693-8990-4.ch004*, pp. 73–98, Jan. 1AD, doi: 10.4018/979-8-3693-8990-4.CH004.

[4] H. N. Fakhouri, S. Alawadi, F. M. Awaysheh, F. Alkhabbas, and J. Zraqou, "A cognitive deep learning approach for medical image processing," *Sci. Reports 2024 141*, vol. 14, no. 1, pp. 1–17, Feb. 2024, doi: 10.1038/s41598-024-55061-1.

[5] C. K. K. Reddy et al., "A fine-tuned vision transformer based enhanced multi-class brain tumor classification using MRI scan imagery," *Front. Oncol.*, vol. 14, p. 1400341, Jul. 2024, doi: 10.3389/FONC.2024.1400341/BIBTEX.

[6] K. Kawauchi et al., "A convolutional neural network-based system to classify patients using FDG PET/CT examinations," *BMC Cancer*, vol. 20, no. 1, p. 227, Mar. 2020, doi: 10.1186/S12885-020-6694-X.

[7] W. Weng and X. Zhu, "U-Net: Convolutional Networks for Biomedical Image Segmentation," *IEEE Access*, vol. 9, pp. 16591–16603, May 2015, doi: 10.1109/ACCESS.2021.3053408.

[8] A. Choudhary, S. Ahlawat, S. Urooj, N. Pathak, A. Lay-Ekuakille, and N. Sharma, "A Deep Learning-Based Framework for Retinal Disease Classification," *Healthcare*, vol. 11, no. 2, p. 212, Jan. 2023, doi: 10.3390/HEALTHCARE 11020212.

[9] Y. Zheng et al., "Application of transfer learning and ensemble learning in image-level classification for breast histopathology," *Intell. Med.*, vol. 3, no. 2, pp. 115–128, May 2023, doi: 10.1016/J.IMED.2022.05.004.

[10] H. Ahn and I. Yeo, "Deep-Learning-Based Approach to Anomaly Detection Techniques for Large Acoustic Data in Machine Operation," *Sensors 2021, Vol. 21, Page 5446*, vol. 21, no. 16, p. 5446, Aug. 2021, doi: 10.3390/S21165446.

[11] M. Li, Y. Jiang, Y. Zhang, and H. Zhu, "Medical image analysis using deep learning algorithms," *Front. Public Heal.*, vol. 11, p. 1273253, Nov. 2023, doi: 10.3389/FPUBH.2023.1273253/BIBTEX.

[12] C. K. K. Reddy, S. R. Pullannagari, S. Doss, and P. R. Anisha, "Dactylology Prediction Using Convolution Neural Networks," *https://services.igi-global.com/resolvedoi/resolve.aspx?doi=10.4018/979-8-3693-1638-2.ch004*, pp. 61–72, Jan. 1AD, doi: 10.4018/979-8-3693-1638-2.CH004.

[13] S. S. Kshatri and D. Singh, "Convolutional Neural Network in Medical Image Analysis: A Review," *Arch. Comput. Methods Eng. 2023 304*, vol. 30, no. 4, pp. 2793–2810, Mar. 2023, doi: 10.1007/S11831-023-09898-W.

[14] P. Abhinaya and C. Kishor Kumar Reddy, "Utilization of Generative AI in Medical Imaging to Improve Evaluation and Therapy," *https://services.igi-global.com/resolvedoi/resolve.aspx?doi=10.4018/979-8-3693-8990-4.ch007*, pp. 159–176, Jan. 1AD, doi: 10.4018/979-8-3693-8990-4.CH007.

[15] W. Ahmad, H. Ali, Z. Shah, and S. Azmat, "A new generative adversarial network for medical images super resolution," *Sci. Reports 2022 121*, vol. 12, no. 1, pp. 1–20, Jun. 2022, doi: 10.1038/s41598-022-13658-4.

[16] M. Puttagunta and S. Ravi, "Medical image analysis based on deep learning approach," *Multimed. Tools Appl. 2021 8016*, vol. 80, no. 16, pp. 24365–24398, Apr. 2021, doi: 10.1007/S11042-021-10707-4.

[17] K. K. Reddy C, A. Rangarajan, D. Rangarajan, M. Shuaib, F. Jeribi, and S. Alam, "A Transfer Learning Approach: Early Prediction of Alzheimer's Disease on US

Healthy Aging Dataset," *Math. 2024, Vol. 12, Page 2204*, vol. 12, no. 14, p. 2204, Jul. 2024, doi: 10.3390/MATH12142204.

[18] H. E. Kim, A. Cosa-Linan, N. Santhanam, M. Jannesari, M. E. Maros, and T. Ganslandt, "Transfer learning for medical image classification: a literature review," *BMC Med. Imaging 2022 221*, vol. 22, no. 1, pp. 1–13, Apr. 2022, doi: 10.1186/S12880-022-00793-7.

[19] D. Soydaner, "Attention Mechanism in Neural Networks: Where it Comes and Where it Goes," *Neural Comput. Appl.*, vol. 34, no. 16, pp. 13371–13385, Apr. 2022, doi: 10.1007/s00521-022-07366-3.

[20] J. N. Acosta, G. J. Falcone, P. Rajpurkar, and E. J. Topol, "Multimodal biomedical AI," *Nat. Med. 2022 289*, vol. 28, no. 9, pp. 1773–1784, Sep. 2022, doi: 10.1038/s41591-022-01981-2.

[21] S. Fatima, C. Kishor Kumar Reddy, A. Sunerah, and S. Doss, "Innovations in Education: Integrating Explainable AI Into Educational Intelligence," *https://services.igi-global.com/resolvedoi/resolve.aspx?doi=10.4018/979-8-3693-8151-9.ch002*, pp. 19–52, Jan. 1AD, doi: 10.4018/979-8-3693-8151-9.CH002.

[22] B. H. M. van der Velden, H. J. Kuijf, K. G. A. Gilhuijs, and M. A. Viergever, "Explainable artificial intelligence (XAI) in deep learning-based medical image analysis," *Med. Image Anal.*, vol. 79, p. 102470, Jul. 2022, doi: 10.1016/J.MEDIA.2022.102470.

Conclusion

All the chapters in this volume demonstrate how cognitive computing is transforming the frontiers of artificial intelligence and redefining the concept of human–machine collaboration. Moving from theoretical foundations to practical applications, the discussions show how cognitive systems learn, adapt, and make decisions in ways that bring technology closer to human reasoning.

This book illustrates that cognitive computing is not limited to a single field but spans healthcare, finance, education, and data-driven decision-making. The contributors integrate insights from neuroscience, machine learning, and computational theory to highlight a shared framework for developing intelligent systems that think and act with greater contextual awareness and precision.

While the potential of cognitive computing is immense, the chapters also draw attention to the accompanying challenges—ethical considerations, data scalability, interpretability, and the need for transparent algorithms. Addressing these issues will be essential for ensuring that cognitive technologies evolve in a responsible and inclusive manner.

Ultimately, this collection serves as both a guide and a call to action for researchers, developers, and policymakers. It encourages continued exploration into how cognitive systems can enhance human capabilities, strengthen decision-making, and contribute to a smarter and more adaptive technological future.

About the Editors

Anamika Ahirwar, PhD, is a Professor in the Department of Computer Science & Engineering at Compucom Institute of Technology & Management, Jaipur, Rajasthan, India. With over 21+ years of academic and research experience, she earned her PhD. in Computer Applications from Rajiv Gandhi Technical University, Bhopal, where her doctoral research focused on data mining schemes for medical imaging. Her areas of expertise include medical imaging, data science, machine learning, sentiment analysis, and celestial sound. Dr. Ahirwar is a prolific researcher with more than 80 publications in SCI-indexed journals, Scopus, as well as in international and national journals and conference proceedings. She has authored and edited several books with reputed international publishers such as Wiley, CRC Press, IGI Global, Cambridge Scholars, and Nova Science. She is the recipient of several awards, including the I2OR National Eminent Researcher Award, the Academic Influencer Award, and the Faculty Excellence Award. Dr. Ahirwar holds five published patents and has supervised numerous postgraduate and doctoral research scholars in computer science. As a reviewer and editorial board member for various reputed journals and conferences, she plays an active role in promoting research in emerging technologies. She is a life member of esteemed technical bodies such as IAENG and I2OR and has contributed significantly as a session chair, expert speaker, and convener at numerous international academic forums.

Dr. Neelesh Jain, PhD, is a distinguished academician and administrator with over two decades of experience in education, research, and institutional leadership. He is a Professor and Head of the Department of Computer Science and Engineering at the Prestige Institute of Management and Research, Bhopal. He holds a Chanakya Post-Doctoral Fellowship from iHub Anubhuti-IIITD Foundation Delhi, a PhD. in Computer Science from Dr. Harisingh Gour Central University, and advanced degrees in VLSI Design, Electrical Engineering, and Computer Applications.

Dr. Jain has published extensively in Scopus-indexed journals and international conferences on cutting-edge topics such as Artificial Intelligence, Big Data, Blockchain, and Cybersecurity. He has authored multiple books, holds patents in IoT and stress detection devices, and has supervised several PhD. and MPhil. scholars. An active contributor to professional development, he has participated in and organized numerous FDPs and workshops. His dedication to academic excellence and impactful contributions to education and research make him a highly respected figure in his field.

Dr. Sumitha Elayaperumal, MSc, PhD, currently works at the JSS Academy of Higher Education and Research as Assistant Professor, Mysore, Karnataka. She has more than 10 years of teaching and Research (Junior and Senior Research Fellow, at Christian Medical College (Department of Hematology), She has a specialization in Molecular diagnosis of Coagulation platelet, thrombotic, and Oncology disorders. She served as a Post Doctoral Fellow at the Vellore Institute of Technology at the Centre for Bioseparation Technology (CBST) funded by BIRAC. She worked as a Molecular Biologist at the Meenakshi Mission Hospital and Research Centre. She has authored several book chapters and journal Publications. She has 3 international patents filed, 12 international publications, and authored more than 30 book chapters.

Index

A

accurate detection, 206
adaptive, 12, 19, 21, 38, 40, 41, 43, 46, 47, 48, 56, 59, 70, 72, 74, 75, 82, 98, 105, 109, 116, 117, 118, 121, 148, 155, 167, 168, 172, 175, 177, 185, 187, 188, 195, 196, 199, 200, 201, 237, 239, 271
AI-enabled system, 206
architecture(s), 11, 13, 14, 17, 23, 25, 26, 35, 39, 40, 47, 48, 49, 50, 51, 62, 77, 79, 82, 83, 92, 93, 95, 107, 111, 112, 124, 125, 126, 127, 133, 138, 144, 165, 167, 224, 226, 230, 231, 242, 243, 245, 253, 255, 256, 257, 258, 259, 261, 262
artificial neural networks (ANN), 16, 25, 107, 111, 116, 117, 126
automatic image, xv, 81, 96
awareness, 20, 39, 41, 65, 124, 155, 156, 193, 206, 236, 240, 271

B

backend system, 205, 206, 210
big data, 35, 42, 49, 77, 78, 79, 101, 154, 173, 187, 203, 214, 221, 222, 223, 224, 225, 226, 227, 228, 229, 231, 232, 234, 235, 236, 237, 240, 241, 242, 243, 254, 274
brain atrophy measurement, 82, 95

C

CANs, 129
chatbot, 120, 148, 199, 200
citizen engagement, 206
cognitive architectures, 17, 23, 24, 38, 47, 48, 50, 95, 108, 222
cognitive load theories (CLT), 193
cognitive systems, 37, 39, 40, 42, 43, 45, 46, 47, 49, 50, 51, 54, 55, 56, 57, 58, 59, 60, 61, 62, 63, 64, 65, 66, 68, 69, 70, 71, 72, 73, 74, 75, 76, 83, 95, 110, 115, 116, 121, 123, 148, 149, 154, 155, 159, 165, 166, 167, 170, 171, 177, 179, 186, 197, 199, 222, 224, 227,228, 230, 235, 238, 239, 240, 241, 250, 251, 265, 271
color blindness, 205, 206, 207, 208, 210, 219, 220
computer vision algorithms, 205, 206
constructivism, 193
convolutional neural networks (CNN), 11, 12, 25, 36, 54, 82, 83, 91, 92, 93, 101, 102, 103, 108, 112, 125, 126, 129, 134, 137, 139, 144, 145, 245, 246, 250, 255, 256
CT scans, 57, 97, 245, 246, 250, 266
cyber security, 148

D

data analysis, 14, 25, 27, 30, 51, 52, 58, 167, 198, 206, 209, 210, 211, 213, 231, 245, 253, 255
data analytics, 148, 164, 171, 180, 184, 185, 192, 221, 231, 236, 237, 238, 241, 242, 243, 248, 252
data privacy, xv, 38, 56, 69, 77, 98, 122, 172, 186, 200, 202, 239

data-driven, 20, 52, 55, 56, 75, 83, 95, 144, 157, 177, 178, 182, 186, 187, 191, 197, 237, 239, 243, 255, 267, 271
decision-making, xv, 2, 3, 4, 6, 9, 10, 14, 15, 16, 17, 20, 23, 25, 27, 28, 30, 32, 37, 38, 39, 41, 42, 43, 46, 47, 48, 51, 53, 54, 55, 56, 65, 67, 68, 71, 72, 73, 76, 77, 78, 83, 94, 99, 105, 109, 114, 115, 120, 121, 122, 124, 129, 144, 147, 148, 149, 150, 151, 152, 153, 154, 157, 159, 160, 161, 162, 163, 164, 165, 166, 167, 168, 171, 172, 173, 174, 175, 180, 184, 185, 195, 196, 197, 209, 216, 223, 224, 225, 235, 237, 238, 241, 242, 246, 248, 249, 250, 251, 252, 253, 254, 262, 266, 267, 271
deep learning (DL), xv, xvi, 2, 5, 6, 9, 16, 22, 25, 29, 30, 38, 41, 42, 45, 49, 50, 54, 61, 77, 81, 82, 83, 87, 92, 93, 96, 97, 98, 100, 101, 102, 103, 105, 106, 108, 110, 111, 112, 113, 114, 117, 122, 123, 125, 126, 127, 131, 144, 145, 155, 172, 173, 174, 184, 229, 241, 245, 246, 247, 249, 250, 252, 253, 254, 255, 256, 257, 258, 259, 262, 263, 264, 265, 266, 267, 268, 269
discriminator, 22, 112, 129, 131, 135, 136, 137, 138, 256
disease(s), 2, 3, 42, 57, 72, 78, 81, 82, 83, 84, 85, 87, 95, 96, 98, 99, 100, 102, 154, 159, 205, 214, 218, 219, 220, 249, 250, 257, 259, 262, 263, 264, 268
distributed cognitive models, 222, 228, 229
driving license, 206

E

Edge AI, 170, 171, 172
education, xiii, xv, 1, 2, 4, 6, 7, 8, 9, 10, 11, 13, 14, 15, 19, 22, 24, 31, 32, 37, 43, 51, 56, 59, 65, 68, 70, 71, 72, 74, 76, 78, 79, 103, 126, 170, 177, 178, 179, 180, 181, 182, 183, 184, 185, 186, 187, 189, 190, 191, 192, 193, 194, 195, 196, 199, 200, 202, 203, 220, 238, 240, 241, 243, 269, 271, 274, 275
educational institution(s), 38, 59, 182, 192
efficiency, 9, 16, 50, 52, 58, 60, 61, 62, 67, 71, 87, 109, 152, 167, 172, 180, 185, 186, 191, 198, 199, 213, 216, 221, 222, 225, 229, 230, 231, 234, 237, 242, 247, 248, 249, 250, 252, 256, 266
electroencephalography (EEG), 2, 3, 10, 17, 23, 25, 36, 104, 220
energy-efficient, 187, 198, 222, 230, 231, 235, 236, 242, 243
environment(s), xv, 2, 6, 9, 16, 20, 24, 30, 34, 35, 41, 47, 48, 49, 50, 54, 55, 56, 59, 62, 64, 66, 67, 68, 70, 76, 108, 115, 116, 120, 130, 147, 148, 150, 155, 156, 157, 159, 160, 161, 163, 167, 168, 170, 171, 172, 173, 174, 175, 177, 179, 180, 181, 183, 185, 187, 191, 193, 195, 198, 199, 200, 202, 203, 218, 226, 227, 231, 234, 240, 243
error, 14, 18, 27, 57, 64, 71, 72, 108, 113, 119, 129, 131, 139, 140, 141, 142, 144, 150, 157, 158, 197, 198, 224, 226, 250
ethical considerations, xv, xvi, 6, 13, 17, 21, 24, 26, 27, 32, 38, 43, 61, 64, 77, 79, 186, 197, 198, 200, 201, 209, 211, 265, 271
evolution, xv, 29, 37, 42, 64, 77, 96, 169, 206, 242, 257

F

feature extraction, 118, 129, 132, 143, 144, 249, 263
financial applications, 129
frontend interface, 205, 206
functional magnetic resonance imaging (FMRI), 3

G

generative adversarial networks (GAN), 22, 30, 98, 102, 112, 135, 137, 140, 144, 246, 256, 257, 266
generator(s), 22, 112, 129, 131, 135, 136, 137, 138, 142, 237, 238, 256

global, 3, 26, 27, 31, 32, 36, 77, 78, 79, 80, 86, 103, 125, 149, 150, 171, 172, 174, 184, 190, 218, 219, 220, 238, 267, 268, 269, 273
government interventions, 206, 217

H

Hebbian learning, 105, 106, 108, 115, 116, 117, 118, 124, 126, 127
human psychology, xv, 205, 215, 217
hyperparameter tuning, 139, 145

I

image analysis, 71, 72, 73, 80, 89, 94, 95, 100, 101, 247, 249, 250, 251, 252, 255, 257, 258, 259, 261, 264, 265, 267, 268, 269
image segmentation, 82, 83, 85, 86, 87, 88, 89, 91, 92, 95, 96, 97, 100, 101, 102, 103, 127, 249, 250, 268
innovation(s), xv, xvi, 4, 8, 10, 14, 15, 17, 19, 21, 24, 25, 27, 29, 31, 32, 38, 42, 43, 56, 61, 71, 77, 100, 106, 169, 172, 174, 175, 205, 219, 220, 222, 226, 236, 238, 240, 241, 249, 253, 254, 255, 256, 266, 269
internet of things (IoT), xv, 30, 32, 36, 49, 66, 67, 68, 77, 79, 80, 148, 172, 175, 187, 205, 207, 210, 214, 215, 216, 218, 219, 235, 237, 242, 243, 267, 274

J

JavaScript, 205, 206

L

lesion detection, 81, 88, 91, 92, 93, 94, 95
lesion(s), 81, 82, 84, 85, 86, 87, 88, 91, 92, 93, 94, 95, 96, 99, 100, 101, 103, 250, 252, 256, 258, 259, 263

M

machine learning (ML), xv, 2, 5, 6, 9, 11, 12, 13, 16, 17, 25, 31, 32, 33, 34, 35, 36, 37, 38, 39, 40, 41, 42, 43, 45, 48, 49, 50, 51, 54, 57, 58, 59, 60, 65, 69, 70, 71, 76, 81, 83, 86, 91, 92, 93, 94, 97, 99, 101, 103, 109, 119, 123, 126, 145, 147, 148, 152, 153, 154,155, 157, 158, 159, 163, 164, 166, 168, 169, 171, 172, 173, 174, 175, 177, 178, 180, 184, 185, 187, 203, 205, 210, 221, 222, 226, 229, 232, 234, 238, 242, 248, 251, 252, 271, 273
magnetic resonance imaging (MRI), 79, 81, 82, 85, 87, 88, 92, 93, 97, 99, 100, 101, 102, 103, 104, 246, 247, 250, 257, 259, 268
mean absolute, 129, 131, 140, 141, 142, 144
mean squared, 113, 140, 141
medical imaging, xiii, xv, 54, 65, 71, 72, 81, 82, 83, 84, 89, 90, 94, 96, 97, 100, 101, 102, 103, 245, 246, 249, 250, 252, 256, 267, 268, 273
metacognition, 193
MongoDB database, 206
motivation, 109, 183, 194, 202
multimodal learning, 65, 246, 259, 261, 266
multiple sclerosis (MS), xv, 64, 81, 82, 84, 85, 86, 87, 88, 89, 91, 92, 93, 94, 95, 96, 100, 101, 103

N

natural language processing, 9, 11, 12, 13, 14, 16, 17, 18, 20, 23, 29, 32, 35, 37, 38, 41, 43, 44, 50, 58, 64, 75, 76, 83, 94, 110, 114, 120, 124, 126, 148, 166, 168, 171, 177, 178, 184, 199, 229, 238, 264
neural mechanisms, 10, 105, 106
neural network(s), 6, 8, 9, 11, 13, 14, 16, 20, 22, 24, 25, 29, 32, 35, 36, 38, 39, 40, 41, 42, 45, 47, 48, 49, 50, 51, 54, 80, 105, 106, 107, 110, 111, 112, 113, 114,

117, 119, 124, 125, 126, 129, 131, 132, 134, 137, 138, 139, 143, 144, 145, 157, 234, 243, 245, 249, 253, 255, 258, 260, 268, 269
neuroscience, xv, 1, 3, 4, 7, 8, 9, 10, 11, 13, 14, 15, 25, 26, 27, 31, 33, 34, 42, 103, 105, 106, 108, 110, 116, 125, 127, 180, 271

P

pattern(s), 2, 6, 9, 12, 14, 15, 16, 17, 23, 25, 31, 36, 38, 39, 43, 45, 47, 48, 50, 51, 52, 53, 54, 55, 57, 60, 62, 66, 71, 73, 74, 79, 83, 92, 100, 105, 110, 111, 114, 116, 117, 118, 119, 121, 122, 124, 126, 131, 134, 148, 150, 152, 154, 155, 157, 162, 163, 166, 169, 171, 172, 179, 180, 184, 195, 196, 206, 207, 212, 221, 229, 238, 241, 243, 248, 249, 253, 254, 255
personalized content delivery (PCD), 188
philosophy, 1, 3, 7, 8, 9, 10, 33, 125
psychology, xiii, 1, 2, 3, 7, 8, 9, 11, 13, 14, 17, 18, 25, 42, 125, 205, 212, 214, 216, 220
python, 50, 205, 206

Q

quantum computing, 30, 32, 66, 67, 68, 77, 170, 171, 172

R

real-time feedback (RTF), 185, 188, 264
real-world, xiii, 20, 51, 64, 77, 115, 160, 165, 178, 193, 194, 197, 198, 200, 208, 254
recommendations, 39, 40, 41, 45, 54, 58, 60, 121, 122, 166, 180, 183, 188, 190, 201, 205, 206, 242, 250
recurrent neural network (RNN), 22, 54, 112, 120, 144, 245, 246, 253, 257, 258
ResNet, 82
risk assessment, xv, 41, 56, 58, 59, 72, 74, 129, 144, 167, 172, 230
robotic(s), 11, 12, 13, 18, 19, 20, 24, 45, 49, 54, 67, 68, 105, 117, 148, 169, 175
root mean square, 129, 131, 140, 141, 142, 144
R-square (R2), 129, 131, 140, 142, 144

S

scalability, 37, 50, 54, 56, 61, 62, 63, 64, 66, 67, 72, 77, 110, 114, 122, 167, 172, 186, 189, 191, 221, 222, 224, 225, 227, 231, 232, 238, 271
SegNet, 82, 92
simulation, 126, 127, 134, 154, 158, 213, 222, 223, 224, 229, 231, 232, 237, 238, 240, 241, 251
smart learning, xv, 59, 177, 178, 179, 187, 189, 190, 195, 201, 202, 203
smart learning environment (SLE), 59, 177, 187, 188, 201, 202, 203
stock prediction, 129
stock price, 52, 130, 131, 132, 133, 134, 137, 139, 140, 144, 145
sustainability, 102, 175, 187, 219, 222, 230, 235

T

testing, 82, 140, 185, 205, 206, 208, 210, 212, 213, 214, 215, 218, 241
transfer learning, 78, 82, 92, 101, 113, 245, 246, 250, 255, 258, 259, 266, 267, 268, 269
treatment(s), 2, 4, 8, 15, 17, 18, 21, 24, 26, 28, 39, 56, 57, 72, 73, 74, 82, 85, 94, 95, 96, 99, 121, 206, 248, 249, 252, 256, 258, 262, 263, 264, 265, 266

U

U-Net, 82, 92, 93, 102, 250, 268

V

visual prowess, 205, 206

W

web frameworks, 205, 206
welfare of youth, 217